BANNED!

Popular Cultural Studies

Series editors: Justin O'Connor and Derek Wynne.
Series sub-editor: Maggy Taylor.

The editors are, respectively, Director and Research Director of the Manchester Institute for Popular Culture where this series is based. The Manchester Institute for Popular Culture, at The Manchester Metropolitan University, England, was set up in order to promote theoretical and empirical research in the area of contemporary popular culture, both within the academy and in conjunction with local, national and international agencies. The Institute is a postgraduate research centre engaged in comparative research projects around aspects of consumption and regulation of popular culture in the city. The Institute also runs a number of postgraduate research programmes, with a particular emphasis on ethnographic work. The series intends to reflect all aspects of the Institute's activities including its relationship with interested academics throughout the world. Current theoretical debates within the field of popular culture will be explored within an empirical context. Much of the research is undertaken by young researchers actively involved in their chosen fields of study, allowing an awareness of the issues and an attentiveness to actual developments often lacking in standard academic writings on the subject. The series will also reflect the working methods of the Institute, emphasising a collective research effort and the regular presentation of work-in-progress to the Institute's research seminars. The series hopes, therefore, both to push forward the debates around the regulation and consumption of popular culture, urban regeneration and postmodern social theory whilst introducing an ethnographic and contextual basis for such debates.

Banned!

Censorship of popular music in Britain: 1967–92

Martin Cloonan

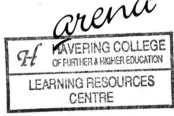

Published by
Arena
Ashgate Publishing Limited
Gower House
Croft Road
Aldershot
Hants GU11 3HR
England

Ashgate Publishing Company
Old Post Road
Brookfield
Vermont 05036
USA

British Library Cataloguing in Publication Data

Cloonan, Martin
    Banned!: Censorship of Popular Music in
    Britain: 1967–92. – (Popular Cultural Studies;
    No.9)
    I. Title II. Series
    306.484

Library of Congress Catalog Card Number: 95-81149

ISBN 1 85742 299 6 (Hardback)
ISBN 1 85742 300 3 (Paperback)

Printed and bound by Athenaeum Press, Ltd.,
Gateshead, Tyne & Wear.

Contents

Acknowledgements

This book began life as a Ph.D. thesis and there are numerous people who have been kind enough to help me through both the thesis and the book. I would like to thank, and acknowledge the help of, the following: David Buckley, Sara Cohen, Neil Gavin, David Horn, Lynn Hancock, Karen Lury, Ron Moy, Keith Negus, Steve Redhead, Philip Tagg and Liz Wake.

All those listed under the interviews section are thanked for their time and accessibility.

I would also like to thank my parents, Liz and Dixie, for letting me do my own thing for so long and helping me to keep solvent.

Very special thanks for support and encouragement are due to Lucy Hunter, whose patience and insights are responsible for this ever being finished.

List of abbreviations

AOR: Adult Orientated Rock
BBFC: British Board of Film Classification (British Board of Film Censors from 1912 until 1985)
BBC: British Broadcasting Corporation
BPI: British Phonographic Industry
BSC: Broadcasting Standards Council
CAP: Campaign Against Pornography
CFG: Conservative Family Group
CSA: Community Standards Association
DPP: Director of Public Prosecutions
DTI: Department of Trade and Industry
FWS: Festival Welfare Services
FYC: Family and Youth Concern
GLC: Greater London Council
GWF: Great Western Festivals
IBA: Independent Broadcasting Authority
ICA: Institute of Contemporary Arts
ILR: Independent Local Radio
IOC: Index On Censorship
ITC: Independent Television Commission
ITV: Independent Television
MM: Melody Maker
MOR: Middle of the road
MRA: Moral Rearmament Army
MU: Musician's Union
NCCL: National Council for Civil Liberties (Liberty)

NCROPA: National Campaign for the Reform of The Obscene
   Publications Acts
NFU: National Farmers' Union
NME: New Musical Express
NOTW: News of The World
NUPE: National Union of Public Employees
NVALA: National Viewers and Listeners Association
PFF: People's Free Festivals
PPL: Phonographic Performance Limited
RAH: Royal Albert Hall
RAR: Rock Against Racism
RIAA: Record Industry Association of America
RM: Record Mirror

To me Nan

Introduction

The object of this book is to reveal a hidden part of the history of popular music in Britain - that of the various attempts that have been made to prevent, via censorship, its dissemination(1). This is the story of how a particular society reacted to a cultural phenomenon and how that phenomenon has antagonized elements (and often powerful ones) within it. It is a story of cultural struggle.

It is noticeable that books on pop usually only fleetingly mention censorship and books on censorship rarely mention pop(2), but examples of censorship are scattered throughout pop's history and here many examples are brought together for the first time. Along with providing important historical documentation, my aim is to give insights into the **way** in which pop is censored and into those seeking to censor it.

This history needs to be written if the impact of arguably **the** most important mass culture of the last forty years in Britain is to be fully comprehended. It also redresses the balance and concentrates not on the songs and gigs that got played and heard, but upon those that **did not**.

The history is one which quickly calls upon the reader to take sides - to back the censors or the censored. This being the case, it is as well to make my own position immediately clear. It is the apparently contradictory one of being a socialist who defends the often puerile and offensive products of a major, multi-national, capitalist industry. This can be justified simply by stressing the importance of those products to their consumers. This need not entail indifference to pop's alleged effects, but it does entail a commitment to pop's message - however unpleasant that message may be. I am undecided as to whether Adorno's thesis that popular music serves only false

1

needs is correct (Adorno 1990), but I do know that the pleasure pop gives is genuine enough.

I deal later with the notion of the pop audience as a totally malleable one, but it is worth noting here that it is a notion I reject. The pop audience is **not** passive, but active(3). Thus defending a right to consume becomes the defence of genuine pleasure, not the defence of a false taste catered for by a cynical industry. Pop is worth defending because its pleasures contrast so markedly to the routine of life under capitalism. Pop is not revolutionary, but the pleasures it gives under the existing system of exploitation are worth cherishing and defending. This may be a romantic view of pop, but without such romance there can be neither worthwhile pop, nor worthwhile life.

Moreover, it is also the case that the pop which has been most seriously censored, both in Britain - for example with Crass (see below) - and in America - for example with the Dead Kennedys (Denselow 1989, pp.269-71) - has often been the product not of vast multinationals, but of small independent companies promoting counter-hegemonic views on a shoestring budget. It would be too simplistic to say that "political" groups are more likely to be censored, but empirical evidence suggests this to be the case. Such bands may, of course, tend to be more "provocative" than other bands but they also tend to form a disproportionate percentage of those who suffer censorship (see below).

The case for defending pop becomes still more valid when its main opponents are considered. Whilst the left is not immune from calls to censor rock (see below) and Wells is wrong to classify all censors as 'conservative' (Wells 1990a, p.19), it is generally the case that those who would censor rock are also those who would keep women in the kitchen, censor **all** media to fit in with their religious convictions and adhere to a classical aesthetic which sees all mass culture as, at best, intrinsically worthless and, at worst, positively harmful. The chapters on religious censors and pressure groups illustrate this.

I do not develop a "grand theory" about the censorship of pop in Britain because it has been so sporadic and uncoordinated that it defies neat categorization. Rather, I shall illustrate some common features and show their links to censorship within other media, as well as showing how the censorship of pop takes the general debate on censorship into unchartered waters.

The basic format is that of a critical history of the censorship of popular music in Britain in the years from 1967 to 1992, falling into five parts. The first part, contextualization, gives some background details. In Chapter 1 I examine the history of censorship in Britain and Chapter 2 outlines the philosophic and historical characteristics of censorship, finishing with consideration of the particular problems that surround the censoring of pop.

Parts Two to Four consist of a number of case studies. Part Two (Chapters 3 to 5) considers the industry and the law. Chapter 3 looks at pop in its recorded (and visual) form, beginning at the point of production with the censorial role of record companies. Chapter 4 moves pop on to the market and examines retailers' censorial policies over the years, while Chapter 5 considers attempts to impose the ultimate sanction - that of declaring musical products to be illegal.

A bridge between recorded music and live music is provided by broadcasting, which forms Part Three. Chapter 6 deals with radio censorship and Chapter 7 with television and video censorship.

Live music is dealt with in the two chapters which form Part Four. Chapter 8 deals with indoor gigs, whilst outdoor concerts, festivals and raves are dealt with in Chapter 9.

The material thus far deals with the outcome of censorship and those who censor as part of their jobs, whereas the fifth part deals with those who campaign to censor pop. These campaigners can be divided into two camps - permanent, or at least regular, campaigners and those whose censorial activity is more intermittent. In the first category fall the various moralist pressure groups who have the mass media in their sights. Chapter 10 deals with these groups, focussing in particular on Mary Whitehouse's National Viewers and Listeners Association (NVALA). Chapter 11 details another group of "permanent" campaigners against pop - the various anti-rock clerics and churches.

The more intermittent censors I look at are the press and MPs, in Chapters 12 and 13 respectively. The press can pick up on issues within pop and create censorship via a feeling that "something must be done" about pop's latest pop outrage, whilst MPs are in the corridors of power and their roles both as individuals and as part of governments who help to mould the legal framework within which pop operates will be considered. I also look at censorship by the left in this chapter. I conclude by bringing the various strands together and making some tentative suggestions about future prospects.

Before this some notes of caution are necessary. The first concerns source material. With one or two exceptions, such as The Sex Pistols and the breaking up of the Windsor festival in 1974, censorship of pop attracts little attention in the "quality" press. The researcher is thus practically forced to use the established weekly music press as his or her main resource. I used the *Melody Maker* (*MM*) as my main source of material from 1967 to 1974 and the *New Musical Express* (*NME*) from 1975 to 1992. The validity of such sources has often been questioned[4], but unfortunately they are the only regular source for such a history. I have also used anecdotal evidence in places. Whenever possible I have tried to authenticate cases of censorship by getting more than one source, but this has not always been possible. Readers will thus have to decide in any particular case the plausibility of the evidence offered here.

Matters are further clouded by the fact that artists' publicists often plant stories in the music press about their charges being censored in order to court a rebellious image[5]. Artists may also set out to provoke a deliberate censorial backlash in order to court that image. Such "scams"[6] are part and parcel of pop's daily process and are at least a reminder that limits are in place.

Another factor to be borne in mind is the need to retain a sense of perspective. Once released most recorded pop passes by unimpeded by any censor. Similarly, each week hundreds of gigs take place with no censorial problems. But this simply makes those records and events that **do** get censored all the more interesting. Moreover, censorship of books is even less frequent than that of pop - yet is both more written about and more reviled by British intellectuals. That it has taken this long to produce a work on the censorship of pop in Britain reflects not a lack of censorship, but a lack of attention. This in turn reflects the elitism with which popular music studies have to contend.

As Britain obviously does not exist in isolation censorship elsewhere (particularly in the United States) often has implications for it. I will allude to such cases as and when necessary and shall argue that such cases have become increasingly important to the British climate.

Why 1967?

The most important reason for starting in 1967 is that it is a landmark year for pop. In record terms this centres on the release of The Beatles' *Sergeant Pepper* on 1 July. This album begins pop's slow

4

climb out of a cultural ghetto. Whilst some classical music critics, such as Mann (1963), had been praising The Beatles' work for some time, it is *Pepper* which sees many critics seriously examine pop as a musical form for the first time (see Fowler 1972, p.17).

1967 also sees pop embroiled in controversy. It saw the closing down of the pirate radio stations on 15 August, an act seen by many as a highly censorial (Hewison 1986, p.130) and the launching of the BBC's first avowedly pop station - Radio 1 (referred to as "1" hereafter) - on 30 September. Henceforth 1's censorial policy effectively became the official banning policy of British pop. Lack of plays on 1 could "kill" a single and debate raged throughout the next twenty-five years over what it would and would not play (see below for 1's playlist).

1967 was the "summer of love", with "swinging London" at its height. Links between London's swinging and pop's tempo have been well documented[7], but 1967 was also the start of something of a backlash against the permissiveness which appeared to have pop at its core. It saw police moves against the Underground, the publication of Mary Whitehouse's first book and the Private Places of Entertainments Act, which gave local authorities more power to control night clubs in their areas (see Redhead 1991).

Pop hit the headlines in a number of ways. *M M*'s first front page in 1967 was headlined: "Don't Knock The Pop" (*M M* 7/1/67). Containing comments such as: 'War has been declared on pop' (ibid), this was a plea for pop to be given more access to the media. At this time the only regular television show for pop was BBC 1's Top of The Pops (*TOTP*), while radio pop consisted of limited amounts of the BBC's Light Programme, Radio Luxembourg at night and the doomed pirate stations. By its 14 October edition *M M* was complaining about the closing of many London "beat" clubs, the arrests of various Rolling Stones on drugs charges and the arrest of Mama Cass on a bogus theft charge. The following week its main writer, Chris Welch (1967), wrote an article which pleaded "Stop Picking On Pop". Retrospectively this can be viewed as mid-60s paranoia, but that pop was seen as a legitimate target for some censors seems evident enough.

Such targeting was often sharpened by the links between pop and recreational drug usage. For Hall et al (1978, p.239) 1967 was 'the year of the great English (moral) "panic" about drug use' and it saw the popular press implicating pop as a danger to society via its association with drugs. The *News of The World* (*NOTW*) ran a five week expose of drugs in the pop world and was implicated in the police raid on Rolling Stone Keith Richards' Sussex home, Redlands, on 12 February (see below). In the resultant court case, for possession of various drugs, Mick Jagger and Keith Richards were briefly imprisoned before the case was effectively dismissed in the Court of Appeal.

Pop festivals, which later saw many censorial battles, also began to proliferate in 1967. Highlights here included the Technicolour Dream at London's Alexander Palace in April and the three day Festival of The Flower Children at Woburn Abbey in August. Abroad June's Monterey festival raised the events to global importance. The year also saw the closure of one of London's leading clubs, UFO, after various problems following a *NOTW* "orgy" story (*M M* 28/10/67).

Although the *Times* editor William Rees Mogg's "Who Breaks A Butterfly on A Wheel" editorial in defence of Jagger and Richards on 1 July showed that some establishment figures were tolerant of pop's excesses, only two months later the paper used drug imagery to tell its readers that: "The world of pop has its own freakish laws of economy and success" (Jassell 1967). In October Prime Minister Harold Wilson sued The Move for using an unflattering image of him in an advertisement (Denselow 1989, p.100) and *M M* commented that, as far as pop was concerned: 'The love year of 1967 has brought more hate, violence and intolerance than any other' (*M M* 26/8/67). So 1967 is an ideal place to start an examination of censorship in pop. It sees pop under suspicion and its stars in conflict with the law.

Why 1992?

This history runs thematically rather than chronologically to avoid problems concerning continual cross-referencing and reader memory. But its chronological end is 1992, for a number of reasons.

First, 1992 sees the twenty-fifth anniversary of Radio 1 and so a quarter of a century of its censorial, and other, policy can be documented. It also saw much debate over the future of the BBC and the possibility of pop once more becoming marginalized within it (see National Heritage Department 1992 and BBC 1992). The year also saw attempts to establish a fifth television station in Britain refused, plans being laid for Britain's first national commercial pop station and the death of Radio Luxembourg (see *The Independent* 27/12/92 and *The Guardian* 31/12/92).

The General Election of 1992 meant that a new parliament sat for the first time and this entailed the usual round of Private Members' Bills going into a ballot, raising the possibility of attempts to strengthen censorship laws. The year also saw attacks on "new age travellers", part of pop's community, by Prime Minister John Major at the Conservative Party Conference (see *Conservative Newsline* November 1992, p.11). In the USA Albert Gore, whose wife Tipper was a leading member of the censorial Parents Music Resource Center (PMRC)(8), was elected Vice President and within weeks of his taking office rapper Ice T was dropped by his label, Warner Brothers, in a censorship dispute.

Of course there are numerous differences between Britain and its pop scene in 1967 and in 1992. The country had witnessed further economic decline and an unprecedented period of Conservative rule. Talk of permissiveness was replaced by that of responsibility, especially in the wake of AIDS. In pop dance dominated where once The Beatles and The Rolling Stones had. The industry had centralized and appeared more concerned with expanding into computer games than in investing in new talent. If 1967 saw the beginning of rock as art, 1992 saw rock as nostalgia, with cover versions and songs linked to films vying with dance for chart domination.

But the similarities are also striking. Both years saw moral panics over drug usage. In 1967 this took the form of concern over stars' drug habits influencing their fans, by 1992 the use of ecstasy by ravers meant that fans themselves were the catalyst for concern. LSD vied with ecstasy as the fashionable drug and *The Independent* (25/5/92) was able to headline with: 'Sixties hippie drug makes a comeback'.

Inevitably then, elements of 1967's culture were carried forward into 1992. By ending with that year I am able to study a period which is long enough ago to give tangible conclusions, but close enough to warrant analogies. In order to further contextualize my evidence I shall now look in more depth at Britain's censorial heritage and methodology.

Notes

1. The main work thus far is Martin and Segrave's *Anti-Rock*. This is useful for cataloguing cases of censorship, but flawed in attributing censorial actions to generational malice. The truth is somewhat more complicated than this. For other examples see the work of Wells in *NME* referred to in the bibliography. For the situation in America, see S. Jones 1991 and McDonald 1988 and Denselow 1989, Chapter 10.

2. For example, Frith 1983 and Street 1986 contain a few passing notes on censorship, whilst O'Higgins 1972 mentions pop only on page 133. The last government committee on obscenity did not see fit to address the issue of pop. See Committee on Obscenity and Film Censorship (The Williams Report) 1979.

3. For examples of audience autonomy see groups who failed in Chapple and Garofolo 1977 and Stratton 1983, p.300.

4. For example Dave Haslam (Redhead 1990, p.37) accused *NME* of doing pop a disservice via its factual inaccuracies and Terry Christian, in *NME* 22/2/92, noted its inaccuracies.

5. One example of such a planted story was Sex Pistols' manager Malcolm McLaren's false claim that A&M artists were involved in a campaign to sack the Sex Pistols in March 1977. See Savage 1991, p.339.

6. "Scams" are attempts to promote publicity either by planting false press stories or staging gratuitous stunts. See A. Hart 1991, pp.208-9.

7. For example, in a BBC 2 programme on the *Oz* trial on 9/11/91 Richard Neville, its former editor, claimed that the whole "Swinging London" scene was entirely due to The Beatles and The Rolling Stones.

8. For PMRC see Cosgrove 1985 and 1986, Denselow 1989, pp.265-9 and Wells, 1986, 1990a and 1991. Tipper Gore subsequently left the PMRC, see *NME* 27/3/93.

Part One
Contextualisation

1 A concise history of British censorship

Like any nation state, Britain has its own history of censorship and this has included music. This chapter outlines some of the major censorial actions and debates that have taken place in Britain, with particular emphasis on the changing censorial climate during the years between 1967 and 1992.

British censorship and control of popular recreations took a somewhat haphazard and local form until well into the nineteenth century. Ever since then, the British state has generally seen fit to leave censorial and regulative duties to a series of local mediators, such as councils, the police and "quangos" such as the British Board of Film Classification(1). The importance of local censors has continued down the years but, as I shall show, the central state has increasingly intervened in recent years.

The first notable instance of musical censorship came in the 1410s when Henry V issued an edict that: 'No ditties shall be made or sung by minstrels or others' (Hillman 1968, p.15). This was cancelled in 1422. In 1533, during the upheavals of the Reformation, a Royal Proclamation suppressed 'ballads and rimes and other lewd treatises in the English tongue', whilst a 1543 edict banned all printed ballads for worry that they might 'subtilly and craftily instruct the kings' people and especially the youth of the realm' (ibid). This ban was lifted by Edward VI, reinstituted by Mary, and finally lifted by Elizabeth I (ibid). But it is important here to note the concern with effect on children, a concentration on lyrics rather than music and the link between censorship and contemporary events - features which, as I shall show, have also characterized various attempts to censor pop.

In 1551 theatre censorship was introduced, blasphemy became an offence in 1617 (*New Statesman* 1991, p.9) and swearing was banned six years later (Hughes 1991, p.195). In 1642 Prynne's *Histriomatrix* successfully called for the closing of playhouses because of lewd plays (St. John-Stevas 1965, p.15). 1644 saw the publication of John Milton's *Areopagitica* - the first major anti-censorship treatise of the English language. Here Milton called for 'the liberty to know, to utter and to argue freely according to conscience above all liberties' (Eccleshall 1986, p.69). Locke's 1666 *Letter on Toleration* was a milestone in calling for religious toleration.

But, under Puritan influence, obscenity law was tightened. In 1663 Sir Charles Sedley was prosecuted for blaspheming, stripping and urinating in the street - an event which eventually gave birth to charges of obscenity and conspiracy to corrupt public morals (Newburn 1992, p.72). At the end of the century ballads were again censored for being too lewd (St. John-Stevas 1965, pp.9/10).

Obscenity became a crime in 1727 when an erotic book, *Venus In The Cloister*, was held to contravene common law by weakening the bonds of 'civil society, virtue and morality' (Robertson 1991, p.18). In 1737 the Lord Chamberlain was given the task of censoring plays. This power was confirmed by the Theatres Act of 1843 and lasted until the Theatres Act of 1968 abolished the post (Petley 1991b).

In 1824 and 1838 came Vagrancy Acts which forbade the display of obscene material. The 1847 Town Clauses Act forbade the dissemination of profane or indecent literature and 'the singing of obscene songs' or using obscene language in such a way as to annoy other members of the public (O'Higgins 1972, p.301). Britain's first Obscene Publications Act arrived in 1857 and gave the authorities the power to destroy, but not prosecute, "suspicious" books (Newburn 1992, p.72). 1859 saw the publication of Mill's *On Liberty*, the definitive statement of the liberal position that the only reason to stop the words and actions of people is if they caused harm to others.

Chief Justice Cockburn's judgement in the R v Hicklin case of 1868 defined "obscenity" in British law for the next 91 years. It determined the test of obscenity to be 'whether the tendency of the matter charged as obscenity is to deprave and corrupt those whose minds are open to such immoral influences, and into whose hands a publication of this sort may fall' (Robertson 1991, p.180). The Customs Consolidation Act of 1876 allowed Customs to seize obscene articles.

12

1911 saw an Official Secrets Act, which was supplemented in 1933. In 1912 D Notices were introduced, and were subsequently used to silence the press. This year also saw the setting up of the British Board of Film Censors (BBFC). It recommended certificates for films, but local authorities could then choose whether or not to accept them - another instance of how censorship in Britain often varies locally. The BBFC became statutory with regard to videos in 1985, when the last word of its title became "Classification".

During the first world war songs were carefully vetted in music halls[2]. In 1915 D. H. Lawrence's *The Rainbow* was prosecuted under the 1868 provisions, as was Radclyffe Hall's *The Well of Loneliness* in 1928. Copies of both were destroyed. During the Second World War morale was kept up by making sure only the right sort of music was played on the BBC. Forces' networks ensured nothing that might make soldiers homesick was broadcast and Wagner was effectively banned (Abraham 1983, p.3). The works of Marxist composer Dr. Alan Bush were banned for a time in 1941 (O'Higgins 1972, pp.132/3).

In the 1950s censorial concern often focused on materialism and worries over the Americanization of British culture (Chambers 1986, p.23 and pp.38-40), particularly after the introduction of commercial television in 1954. A moral panic around American comics saw the 1955 Children and Young Persons Harmful Publications Act, which outlawed the printing or dissemination of certain books and magazines likely to fall into the hands of young people (Barker 1984a).

By the end of the decade it was clear that Parliament was keen to protect literature, whilst at the same time clamping down on pornography. The Obscene Publications Act of 1959 defined obscenity as that which would be likely to deprave and corrupt those who came into contact with it (see below). Like much legislation in the moral arena it came via a Private Members' Bill, here introduced by Roy Jenkins. It is still in force in 1995.

The Act's first test was the unsuccessful attempt to prosecute D. H. Lawrence's *Lady Chatterley's Lover* in 1961. This was cleared under the Act's "public good" defence, which allows expert witnesses to attest to the relevant work's social worth. At the same time Frederick Snow was jailed for publishing a *Ladies' Directory* of prostitutes (Newburn 1992, pp.88-90), so the law seemed to be doing its job of preserving "art", whilst punishing "filth".

13

The rest of the 1960s saw a certain amount of liberalization, but the decade was by no means the free for all that its detractors claim it to be. Censorial moves continued. Control was relaxed, not abolished. In 1964 the Obscene Publications Act was extended (ibid, p.95) and in 1965 the BBC banned a television dramatization of a nuclear bombing, *The War Game*, from British screens. 1965 also saw the Race Relations Act which, whatever its aims, lessened the scope of free expression. In 1967 *MM* reported a backlash on the Underground (*MM* 7/1/67 and 21/10/67), while 1968 brought the Theatres Act alluded to earlier, and the prosecution, and fining of, a Brighton avant-garde bookshop for selling obscene prose and poetry (Neville 1971, p.63). An Arts Council report of 1969 which urged liberalization of obscenity laws was ignored (see The Obscenity Report 1971, pp.219-250 and Newburn 1992, p.101).

The 1970s saw a string of obscenity cases in which Underground magazines seemed to be disproportionately targeted. In November 1970 *IT*, a keen promoter of pop festivals, was found guilty, and fined, for conspiring to corrupt public morals and to outrage public decency by publishing advertisements soliciting males for homosexual acts (Newburn 1991, pp.115-118).

The longest and most famous case here was the prosecution of *Oz* magazine in 1971 (see Palmer 1971 and de Jongh 1991b). Its editors were eventually found guilty under the 1959 Act and jailed, but freed when the Appeal Court noted a misdirection in the original trial. The trial concerned the magazine's "Schoolkids" edition and much was made of alleged attempts to corrupt youth, despite the fact that the issue was written by the "schoolkids" themselves, rather than being an attempt by adults to corrupt them. Brian Leary, prosecuting, had noted darkly that the magazine's philosophy was that of: 'dope, **rock 'n' roll** and fucking in the street' (de Jongh 1991b. Emphasis mine). One of the editors accused the prosecution of believing that 'rock 'n' roll is a coded plea for fucking in the streets' (Palmer 1971, p.224). As I argue below, whatever pop is, it is not simply music (see below) and the prosecutions of *IT* and *Oz* can be seen as an attempt to silence pop **culture**, if not pop **music**.

At the same time as the *Oz* trial the *Little Red Schoolbook* was found guilty under the 1959 Act and its publisher fined. Various appeals, including one to the European Court of Human Rights, failed. Once again opponents picked up on the fact that the book was aimed at children, although Newburn (1992, p.130) suggests that this was a smokescreen to hide those opponents' objections to its political content. September 1972 saw the publication of the Longford Commission's Report on pornography which was much debated but ignored by legislators (see ibid, pp.103-114). But attempts to censor continued. In 1973 an unsuccessful attempt was made to prosecute the *Nasty Tales* magazine, although it folded soon after as a result of legal costs.

The 1976 acquittal of *Inside Linda Lovelace* seemed to have put an end to prosecutions of literary works for which **any** merit could be shown, but in 1977 *Gay News* was found guilty of, and fined for, blasphemous libel in publishing James Kirkup's *The Love That Dares To Speak Its Name* poem (see Lemon 1992). This case re-established the crime of blasphemy which had been thought of as something of a dead letter and a man was later fined for sending the poem through the post (*IOC* Vol.7, No.1 January 1978, p68). The Law Lords rejected *Gay News*'s appeal.

1977 also saw Home Secretary Merlyn Rees exclude Danish film maker Jens Jorgen Thorsen from the country on the grounds that 'his presence in the country is not conducive to the public good' (*IOC* Vol.6, No.3 May/June 1977, p.67) because he planned to make a film about Christ's sex life(3). Film came under the auspices of the Obscene Publications Act in this year. In 1978 the plays *Scum* and *Willie* were banned by the BBC and an IBA ban was placed on an Amnesty International programme about the mistreatment of prisoners in Northern Ireland.

But an entire new era of censorship opened up with the election of a Conservative Government in 1979. Pop was by no means exempt from this and it may be no coincidence that the first attempts to prosecute pop under the Obscene Publications Act began in this period (see below).

In 1979 the BBC banned film of an IRA roadblock under the terms of the 1974 Prevention of Terrorism Act and the the Williams Report on Obscenity and Film Censorship was published. It recommended liberalization of the obscenity laws but, having been commissioned by a Labour Government, its advice - based on what a "reasonable" person might find offensive - was ignored by the new Conservative administration which effectively shelved it.

Television suffered in the new censorial climate. In 1981 the BBC banned an Open University programme on the arms race and the *Index on Censorship* (*IOC*) reported that Britons were becoming more accommodating to censorship (Greer 1981, p.31). The 1982 Falklands War saw various forms of censorship and control of information and in March 1983 the Theatre Directors Guild of Britain formed to protect entertainment industry workers' rights and to 'fight against artistic, commercial and political censorship and interference' (IOC Vol.12, No.4 August 1983, p.40).

The era's moral panic concerned "video nasties". In November 1983 Luton South MP Graham Bright introduced a Private Members Bill - the Video Recordings Bill - which sought to set up an official body for licensing videos and fines for the dissemination of unclassified videos. This Bill received government support of a type not normally associated with a Private Members Bill and became law in 1985 (see Robertson 1991, pp.216-226). Inverting traditional liberal attitudes to censorship, it made censorship in the home (a private place) stricter than that in a cinema (a public place) as the BBFC often made further cuts to films which were being transferred on to video which was easier for children to access. Changes to broadcasting law, which I deal with below, also occurred at this time.

In 1984 censorial attention turned to drug related literature which magistrates were increasingly willing to see as coming under the ambit of the Obscene Publications Act (IOC Vol.13 No.4 August 1984 p.39). Raids on shops selling such literature followed. London's Gay's The Word bookshop also encountered a number of police raids. An unsuccessful attempt to prosecute it for importing obscene material was made which cost the shop heavily both in defending itself and having stock impounded for nearly two years.

1985 saw the setting up of the censorially motivated PMRC in America and the British government returned to the censorial fore in 1986 with its ultimately doomed attempt to keep former spy Peter Wright's memoirs, Spycatcher, out of the country. In 1987 a BBC film on the Zircon missile project was banned from its Secret Society series. A raid by Special Branch on the BBC's Glasgow offices in connection with this precipitated an unprecedented strike by BBC journalists over government interference in editorial freedom. In December a Channel 4 reconstruction of the Birmingham pub bombings of 1973 was banned and the Government successfully applied for an injunction against a Radio 4 series, My Country Right Or Wrong, which included interviews with former security service staff (IOC Vol.17, No.2 February 1988, pp.34-35). Tory MP Gerald Howarth made a failed attempt to extend the 1959 Act and pop seemed to suffer a surge in censorship (Wells 1987a).

Censorial activity by the government intensified in 1988. In February it attempted to prevent the publication of extracts from *Inside Intelligence* by former MI6 officer Michael Cavendish and Channel 4 cancelled the showing of *Fireraiser* - a film about the saturation bombing of Dresden in the Second World War. This was also the year of the homophobic Clause 28, which became part of the 1988 Local Government Act. It followed tabloid "outrages" over one or two Labour councils giving small grants to Gay and Lesbian centres and a book called *Jenny Lives With Eric and Martin*(4). The clause forbade local councils from "promoting" homosexuality and teaching it as "normal" in schools.

An attempt to stifle terrorism which had little effect on it, but curtailed freedom of expression, also came in 1988. This was the October broadcasting ban on statements giving support to terrorist groups. It directly hit pop leading, amongst other things, to the banning of The Pogues' *Birmingham Six* track by the IBA. It was widely felt that any songs dealing with Ireland would also be unlikely to get an airing and meant that Sinn Fein, a legal political party, was banned from the airwaves until autumn 1994.

In 1989 Salman Rushdie, author of *The Satanic Verses*, was forced into hiding after a fatwa (death sentence) was passed against him by Iran's Ayatollah Khomeini. Some British Muslims demonstrated against the book, but booksellers' reactions varied. W. H. Smith stopped stocking it, whilst Collets in London was firebombed for continuing to stock it. In 1995 Rushdie is still in hiding and the printed word is still far from the freedom envisaged after *Lovelace*.

Instead a new type of religious intolerance appears to be rising. The Rushdie case saw calls to bring Islam under the protection of British blasphemy law, which at present covers only the Christian faith. The alternative - of treating religions equally by abolishing all blasphemy laws - was never seriously considered. Instead in December 1989 the BBFC refused a certificate for the film *Visions of Ecstasy* - which dealt with a 16th Century Spanish Nun, St. Teresa, and included scenes of her erotically caressing Christ. This was the first time a film had been refused a certificate on grounds of blasphemy (*IOC* Vol.19 No.2 February 1990, pp.3-4).

1990 saw further broadcasting legislation, part of which placed on a statutory footing a new watchdog body, the Broadcasting Standards Council (BSC). *The Sunday Times* and *The Independent* had fines imposed for publishing extracts of *Spycatcher* dropped, but were still held to have been in contempt of court for publishing them. 1990 also brought Graham Bright's moves against raves via the Entertainments (Increased Penalties) Act (see below). However a spokesman for the record industry's umbrella organization, the BPI, also said in this year that censorship was not a major issue for the industry (*NME* 9/11/90).

In 1991 much debate surrounded denial of information to the media in the Gulf War (see Simpson 1991). In the run up to the war Mark Elder, conductor at the Last Night of the Proms, was sacked for suggesting he might not play *Land of Hope and Glory* and *Rule Britannia* if the war had started by the time of the Proms (*NME* 2/3/91). By this time the BSC was publishing its third annual report and the BBC had decided not to show the highly acclaimed film, *The Last Temptation of Christ*, following pressure from clerics, pressure groups and MPs.

1992 saw controversy over plans to publish the Maquis de Sade's *Juliette*. It went ahead, but many bookshops refused to stock it. A documentary on the economy, which was potentially damaging for the Government, was dropped by the BBC on its scheduled day of broadcast, 9 March, the eve of the last Budget before the General Election. The BBC denied that this was a political decision and showed it two months later. The ban on Sinn Fein was lifted during the general election, but the BBC censored the words of Northern Irish civil rights campaigner Bernadette McAliskey from a television interview in September (see McAliskey 1992). The destruction of literature returned when Manchester's Savoy bookshop had copies of a magazine called *Mengs and Ecker* destroyed on the grounds of obscenity (see *The Daily Telegraph* and *The Guardian* 31/7/92). The year ended with a debate on restricting the press following concern over its treatment of the Royal family and general invasions of privacy.

Bringing it all back home

The history of British censorship in general helps to contextualize the censoring of pop, where several factors need to be borne in mind. Pop has an important place in British culture. Britain buys more singles per head of population than any other country (*NME*

12/12/92 and *The Independent* 2/12/92). A 1990 report showed that 87% of 20-24 year olds listened to records and tapes, 92% of them listened to the radio and 38% of 11-25 year olds went to discos (Willis 1990, p.ix). In 1992 76% of people listened to records or tapes - up from 62% in 1977 (*The Guardian* 2/3/92). Britain also spends more on entertainments than any other country in Europe (*The Daily Telegraph* 23/1/92) and is a country where pop is a passion (see Morrison 1992). Interfering with it therefore impedes the pleasures of a substantial part of the population.

In 1972 O'Higgins (p.155) noted that British censorial practice was seldom open to scrutiny for social justification and twenty years later this remained the case. This book raises the issue of whether censorship of pop in this country has thus far proved to be "socially justified".

Robertson and Nicol (1984, p.69) describe Britain as having a 'vague law and a swinging moral pendulum' in the realm of censorship and in 1992 this pendulum appeared to be swinging once again towards the censors. Muslim and Christian fundamentalists, feminists, Tory MPs and moralist pressure groups all called for more censorship. They were countered by anti-censorship groups such as Article 19, the National Campaign for the Reform of the Obscene Publications Acts (NCROPA), the Campaign Against Censorship (CAC), the National Campaign For Civil Liberties (Liberty) and the Campaign For Press and Broadcasting Freedom (CPBF).

Nevertheless it is somewhat premature to claim, as Smith (1991, p.53) does, that Britain's pop censors have now realized that 'censoring almost always backfires'. When a parliamentary question was asked about the possibility of tightening up the law in the light of a failed prosecution of NWA's *Efil4zaggin* album in 1991, it was rightly pointed out that such moral legislation often comes via Private Members' Bills (*Hansard* Written Answer 12/11/91). The tendency of such legislation to follow moral panics (as in the cases of video "nasties" and raves) and the possibility of pop causing such a panic means that pop is far from in the clear. This was evidenced in April 1993 when more moves to restrict raves were announced (*NME* 10/4/93). Moreover, pop could also be the indirect victim of an attempt to clamp down on other mediums. In the debate on the current Obscene Publications Act pop was not mentioned - but that law **has** been used against it.

Legislation such as Clause 28, the Video Recordings Act and the

Public Entertainments (Increased Penalties) Act suggest that the liberals have been fighting a losing battle. In 1984 Calder wrote that: 'We are now witnessing the reversal of the gains that were achieved from the late fifties to the early seventies' (Calder 1984). This continued and in 1988 Harding (1988, p.25) wrote that 'Britain is a far more censorious place than it was five years ago'.

So the picture is of increasing censorship from which pop has not been immune. British censorial practice has been characterized by local and pressure group intervention. It has ebbed and flowed and has intervened with pop almost randomly. O'Higgins (1972, p.156) noted that much of British censorial practice was 'an extraordinary mixture of sense and nonsense, of enlightenment and cruelty, of stupidity and absurdity'. This has been as much the case with pop as it has in general. Why this should be so will become clearer once I have outlined the general characteristics of censorship and debates surrounding it.

Notes

1. Frith 1983, p.254 also notes the importance of local regulation and argues that this has been more important than outright repression in Britain. O'Higgins 1972, p.44 notes the plethora of local obscenity laws. For more on the importance of local censorship see Benedictus 1979, p.996, Robertson 1974, p.243, Sutherland 1982, p.163 and Wistrich 1978, pp.122/123.

2. For example see Cheshire 1974, p.54 for how the Halls were used to whip up anti-German fervour.

3. Other people excluded from Britain include comedian Lenny Bruce in 1963 and Louis Farakhan, black separatist preacher much admired by Public Enemy and others, in 1986. Such exclusion orders have not been used against popular musicians, but were called for by MPs Leo Abse, with regard to Alice Cooper, in 1972, (see below) and Peter Brunivels, over The Beastie Boys, in 1987, (see below.)

4. For details of *Jenny Lives With Eric and Martin* see *IOC* Vol.17, No.8 September 1988, pp.37-39. For Clause 28 see ibid, p.39 and Newburn 1992, pp.188-189.

2 Censorship: some characteristics of the debate

This chapter examines the debates surrounding censorship, its characteristics and the arguments of censors. Before this, however, a definition of censorship is necessary. For my purposes censorship is: the attempt to interfere, either pre- or post-publication, with the artistic expressions of popular musicians, with a view to stifling, or significantly altering, that expression. This includes procedures of marginalization, as well as the overt banning, of such expressions. Note that this includes market, as well moral, censorship.

The censorship debate has generally been polarized around "liberals", who have stressed the right to free expression, and "conservatives", who have appealed for "responsibility" in artistic, and other, endeavours. To this divide has recently been added a third viewpoint - that of radical feminism (see *New Statesman* 1991, p.29) which, at its most extreme has, for example, seen pornography **as** rape and the debasement of women, rather than being a contributory factor to these phenomena[1].

The debate has consistently featured a number of elements. The concept of free speech has been prime amongst these but few, if any, have seen this right as being absolute. In a famous example, the right to free speech does not entail the right to randomly shout "Fire!" in a crowded theatre (Cline 1974, p.8). The question centres on **where**, rather than **whether**, to draw the line. Birmingham councillor Alan Blumenthal neatly illustrated this tension when he said of NWA's *Efil4zaggin* album:

> I'm a great believer in free speech, I don't believe in censorship, but one does have to have certain standards ... and if you go

beyond a line, then you have to be stopped (Radio 1 interview 5/6/91).

It is a misconception to see the history of British censorship as one of ever increasing liberalization as the reality is that of a constant renegotiation of boundaries. For example, it may be the case that records with swearing on them were commonplace in 1992, but it was also true that, as the BSC noted, the word "nigger" was less likely to be acceptable on television than it had been years before (BSC 1991, p.13). In other areas liberalization **has** taken place and in retrospect some censoring of pop seems quaint. For example, *Great Balls of Fire* was shocking in the 1950s, but used in a cheese advert in the 1980s (Street 1986, p.91), *Relax* was banned by 1 in 1984, but used in an advert a couple of years later (*NME* 20/6/87) and *If I Had A Hammer* was a dangerous, politically charged song in 1949 but a night club favourite by 1964 (Denselow 1989, p.13).

This ebb and flow, rather than increasing liberalization, means that records previously held to be innocent can **become** offensive. Lennon's *Imagine* was innocent until the Gulf War, The Pogues' *Birmingham Six* was fine until the Government ban on statements supporting terrorism in 1988 and Ice T's *Cop Killer* only became an issue after the LA riots of April and May 1992. But the idea that rampant liberalization has taken place may be a motivating factor for Whitehouse et al, whilst the apparent arbitrariness of censorship (such as 1 banning Judge Dread records, but allowing Lou Reed's *Walk On The Wild Side*) is often a reflection of changing social mores.

Crucially, the censorial climate is also bound up with contemporary events. In 1973 concern over the effects of the film *Clockwork Orange* followed the IRA bombing of Aldershot and disturbances in Ulster (Wistrich 1978, p.21). Raids on sex shops in Oxford and Cambridge followed the arrest of the Cambridge rapist in 1975 (Sutherland 1982, p.145). Similar clampdowns occurred around the drug scare in 1967, the press reaction to punk during the 1977 Jubilee celebrations, the video nasties scare of 1983/4 and the wars in the South Atlantic, the Gulf and Ireland. In pop 1's Mike Smith tried to ban the Jesus and Mary Chain's *Some Candy Talking* in 1986 as it was allegedly about cocaine and at this time Boy George's drug problems were receiving widespread press coverage (see below).

Censorship also brings up issues of control and one way in which pop adds to the censorship debate is that it soon leads into areas of social control (in a way that, for example, books do not) especially once it enters the live arena. Indeed it soon becomes evident that no clear dividing line between regulation and censorship in pop exists.

The processes of deciding who gets signed or played on the radio are in some ways censorial ones. Here the market acts as a censor to those who are unlikely to sell and adds another, recurrent, dimension to the censorial debate. For example, Q noted that it was small bands that suffered in times of recession and were effectively economically censored by not being able to get a market for their music[2], whilst Attali (1977, p.70) notes that with the onset of capitalism: 'It was necessary to sell oneself to have the right to create' and cites Mozart as an example of this. Suffice to say here that matters of artistic control in the industry **do** have censorial implications. Meanwhile calls for more direct censorship are underpinned by certain arguments.

Justifying my hate - arguments for censorship

Proponents of censorship broadly postulate two sorts of arguments to substantiate their case. These are the causal and the offence arguments.

Causal arguments propose that the medium in question can cause behavioural or attitudinal changes in its audience. With pop such arguments are primarily forwarded against its recorded format, with the most notorious causal arguments centring on attempts in America to blame music for being the decisive factor in suicide and murder cases[3]. In the live arena, as we shall see, censorship is more often, though not exclusively, motivated by fears about crowd control rather than by the music.

But there are a number of problems with causal analyses. First, reception of music is not a simple process. Music has no given meaning or effect. Its "meaning" to an individual listener will be mediated by a number of factors such as age, ethnicity, sex, sexuality, class, knowledge of musical conventions and so on. Moreover, pop is not just music and, as Negus (1992, p.79) notes, 'Music is not simply received as sound, but through its association with a series of images, identities and associated values, beliefs and affective desires'. Furthermore, doubt has been cast over the possibility of determining the causal effects of **any** media. Simpson (1982, p.246) has argued

25

that 'it is by no means certain that causal explanations of social phenomenon are in principle possible'(4) and Wistrich (1978, p.88) writes that few professionals now take causal arguments seriously, although there is some evidence, for example, that the use of pornographic material **may** exacerbate preexisting problems and, if used in crime, that it can mediate the **type** of crime committed (*The Guardian* 20/3/93).

Causal arguments have plagued pop throughout and one feature of the arguments used by the censors I document is the preponderance of unsubstantiated causal claims. Laurie (1965, p.102) writes of a letter from a teacher in *New Statesman* claiming that The Beatles were turning his pupils into homosexuals and in 1967 letters to *M M* blamed pop for drug usage (*M M* 18/3/67). By 1992 rap was being blamed for the LA riots(5) and 1993 saw ragga blamed for attacks on gays (see *The Guardian* 20/11/93 and *The Independent* 1, 4 and 8/10/93).

But such attributions have failed to stand up to objective tests. Wistrich (1978, p.144) noted that 360 surveys of the impact of film had failed to establish any firm conclusions on their impact. Three different American commissions on the effects of pornography came to three different conclusions (see Hawkins and Zimring 1988, especially pp.75 and 276). The debate appears hopelessly polarized around "liberals" who want scientific "proof" and "conservatives" who lay claim to "commonsense" and call for "responsible" artists.

But causal debates have made a comeback in recent years. Bloom's *The Closing of The American Mind* attempted to give academic credence to causal claims in 1987 and in 1992 *The Sunday Times* serialized the work of Medved who varied the causal argument by saying: 'I do not claim that media messages **cause** destructive behaviour, but I do contend that they **encourage** it' (Medved 1993d, p.23)(6). He advises boycotting Capital because WASP are on the label, sees popular culture as the cause of America's moral malaise and campaigns for more "responsibility" in the media. Censorship, he says, does not work, it merely makes heroes out of "thugs" like 2 Live Crew. Best to get in right at the point of production rather than have to fight a marketplace battle (see Medved 1992 and 1993a-d and *The Sunday Times* 7/3/93).

Whilst causal and offence arguments are the two poles around which debates on censorship tend to gravitate, they are **not** mutually exclusive. However, claims based on offence tend to be the most common. They are easier to maintain as the protagonist does not have to prove effects, merely show repulsion. Thus records containing swearing are barred from daytime radio, not because they will **cause** crime, but on grounds of offence to listeners.

But one can be offended and enjoy it (Williams Committee 1979, p.97 and Laing 1985, p.81). Offence in art can also be a safety valve, whilst AIDS and VD advertisements have shown the beneficial uses to which "offensive" material can be put (Smart 1982). Moreover "offensive" language can be an important part of artistic expression. Redmond (1991, p.47) has said that there is no phrase quite like "Shut the fuck up" for getting a point across and songs such as Neil Young's *Fuckin' Up* and NWA's *Fuck Tha Police* would not make sense without the key words. For Whitehouse (1982, p.61) swearing simply debases our culture, but Feinberg (1985, p.277) has argued it can be beneficial for children as it is simply part of growing up. Such benefits are not easily seen by potential censors who have a number of motivations.

Fighting the right to party - common themes in censorial thinking

When the arguments of rock's opponents are examined several common features emerge.

(1) The assertion, noted previously, that the pop audience is the hapless dupe of the cynical and amoral men who run the record industry. In 1964 Johnson (p.326) spoke of Beatles fans as 'fodder for exploitation' and saw that: 'Behind this image of "youth" there are ... some shrewd older folk at work'. After the Sex Pistols' television debacle (see below), Butt called for EMI to drop them and wrote:

> Exploitation comes in many guises. The masses were once exploited by being made to work too hard for too little cash. Today it is their children's minds which are exploited, to make quick bucks by the million for the record companies (Butt 1976).

This was a particular nonsense, as at this time only three punk bands had been signed by majors and no millions had been made. But even the more enlightened Cosgrove (1988b) warned, at a time of scares over the links between raves and ecstasy, of 'unscrupulous record companies which are marketing themselves in the most sickeningly opportunist ways'.

The idea of the industry foisting rubbish more or less at will on to a totally passive audience is facile. If it could do so it would, but it can not. Most records are **not** hits, the industry is notoriously slow in picking up on crazes and audiences soon tire of artists who are hyped into the charts. Even the apparently malleable teen audience is not an easy target. Rimmer (1985, p.108) has written of young pop fans that 'all the media manipulation in the world isn't going to sell them something they haven't any use for'. As an example he quotes the failure of the Roaring Boys in 1985. To that we might add 1970s television hosts Flintlock and 1980s hype Sigue Sigue Sputnik. Rimmer concludes that 'the pop market remains notoriously difficult to control' (ibid, p.144) and the capitalist's Bible, *The Economist*, has agreed with this (*The Economist* 21/6/86)[7]. Meanwhile the theme of exploitation is closely linked to another:

(2) "Doing it for the kids" - When called upon to defend their actions all censors, or would be censors claim to be protecting children (see Newburn 1992, p.78 and Durham 1991, p.95). Because pop's audience is, often wrongly[8], seen as being made up of innocent children attempts are made to justify censorial action on the grounds of defending that innocence. So Whitehouse claims that in pop songs such as Presley's *It's Now Or Never*: 'Children accept many of these words at face value but are nevertheless being brainwashed by the pornographic ideas behind them' (Tracey and Morrison 1979, p.42). Tory MP Peter Brunivels said of a proposed Beastie Boys tour in 1987: 'Our children will be corrupted by this sort of thing' (*NME* 25/4/87)[9]. Note that these are unsubstantiated causal claims.

Such censors also tend to present children as obsessed with pop (see, for example, Larson 1988, p.86), but this is true only for a small minority[10]. Protecting children recurs throughout this book and, whilst obviously respecting this motive, I was often left with the unprovable notion that children are being used as an excuse for censoring material which the censors themselves find aesthetically offensive. Others have also drawn this conclusion. Barker (1984b) noted the use of children as an excuse to mask political censorship in the video "nasties" scare[11] and *Rolling Stone* editorialized that the PMRC were using "protect the children" rhetoric to impose their morality (Garofalo 1987, p.88)[12].

(3) Aesthetic critiques: Proponents of pop censorship often seem

compelled to prove pop's cultural worthlessness. Pop not only has to be dangerous, it also has to be, in the words of Dr. Donald Soper, "artistic suicide" (*M M* 29/3/58). Obviously not all aesthetic critiques of pop are calls for censorship, but censors frequently use aesthetic critiques to substantiate their case. Johnson (1964, p.327) compounded his critique of Beatles' fans by saying that their concerts featured 'the monotonous braying of savage instruments'. In *The Daily Telegraph* Simple followed his praise of the ban on McGuinness Flint's anti-internment song, *Let The People Go*, by commenting on its 'matchless idiocy, inanity and feebleness' (*M M* 11/3/72). Such feelings were backed up by the classical world in the mid-1970s when Dr. Ruth Gipps, conductor of the London Repertoire Orchestra, mixed causal and aesthetic arguments by saying that: 'amplified "pop" is evil and injures those who partake in it' and that: '"Pop" is not music ... it is an ugly blasphemy' (Gipps 1975a). Her censorial intent was also clear - 'It is time pop festivals were outlawed for good' (Gipps 1975b)[13].

One effect of pop being seen as irredeemably "low" art has been that censorship of it has been seen as unimportant, as it has been felt that nothing of social importance will be lost. In this context it is interesting to note that in 1991 Island defended NWA's *Efil4zaggin* not on artistic grounds, but on grounds of free speech (see Marot 1991a). Even those within the industry seem reluctant to defend their products on aesthetic grounds.

(4) Miscellaneous other themes: (a) Xenophobia: Initial reaction to rock 'n' roll in Britain was clouded by fear of "Americanization" and the replacement of a genuine national culture with crass commercialism[14]. Xenophobia was apparent in the *Daily Mail*'s response to rock (see below), MP Leo Abse's comments on Alice Cooper (see *M M* 26/5/73 and below) and Brunivels' comments on the Beastie Boys (see *NME* 23/5/87 and below). If patriotism is the refuge of the scoundrel, then xenophobia may be that of the censor and Pearson has shown a long tradition of blaming foreigners for domestic problems - for example by giving young troublemakers an Irish name - hooligan (Pearson 1983, pp.x and 75).

(b) Religious motivation: I deal with the attitude of various religious sects to pop below (see Chapter 11), but it should be noted that many of pop's would-be censors come from religious backgrounds. Examples of this include Whitehouse, former Manchester police Chief James Anderton and Brunivels (a member of the Church of

England's General Synod).

(c) Much censorial activity concerns pop's attendant features, especially fans' behaviour, rather than the music itself. This is most obviously the case with live music and raves, but it also occurs elsewhere. The chapter on religion will show that many of pop's opponents make much of stars' lifestyles as, for example, when moralists attacked Mick Jagger for living with Marianne Faithfull outside wedlock (Wyman 1991, p.597 and Lady Morrison 1978). Attempts to prosecute T-shirts (see below) also fall into this category and the links between pop and drugs are often picked up on by moralists (for example see Whitehouse 1977, p.38).

(d) Many would-be censors have bigger agendas. For example, Whitehouse aims to make Britain a theocracy (Tracey and Morrison 1979, pp.188 and 198) and the reactions of many MPs to pop are often motivated by the desire for publicity and votes, rather than any moral agenda. Similarly objections by feminists to some of rock's imagery, such as the name Rapeman (see below) and the depiction of women on covers (see Stallings 1984, p.157) are part of a more general campaign for equality. So often pop is not attacked **as** pop, but as part of a cultural and moral malaise. But noble aspirations do not lessen the censorial impact or intent.

(e) Many of these critics are also nostalgic - pop and the country are to be returned to a previous, often mythical, golden age (see Whitehouse 1971, p.21 and Pearson 1983, pp.9-10).

(f) There is also the perennial problem of self censorship - for whatever reason. Unfortunately this is hard to document and will therefore be somewhat under represented here[15].

These features and themes of censorship recur throughout these pages. I noted earlier that virtually the only British commentator on censorship of pop is *NME* writer Steven Wells who believes that rock's opponents 'are all conservatives' (Wells 1990a, p.19), but I shall demonstrate that this is somewhat simplistic and that opponents of pop have been drawn from across the political spectrum. However, with a medium such as pop it appears that the odds are stacked against the would-be censors. So why bother to censor pop? What particular characteristics does it have that arouse censorial ire?

Why pick on pop? - The particular censorial problems of popular music

To avoid the impression that pop is an innocent victim of censorship it is necessary to recognize that it is an active medium with the power to antagonize and thus provoke censorship. As a non-verbal form of communication, music is a medium which has a long history of attracting suspicion and occasional vehement opposition. Plato believed that music's power was that:

> By gradual infiltration it softly overflows upon the characteristic pursuits of men and from those issues forth grown greater to attack their business dealings, and from these relations it proceeds against the laws and constitution with wanton licence till it finally overthrows all things public and private ... (Attali 1985, p.33)[16].

For these reasons, Plato believed that censorship was justified.

In Britain, Blom (1943, p.17) reports that Welsh harp music 'became subject to official regulation' in the twelfth century, whilst Cromwell suppressed the use of choirs and organs in church in 1644 (ibid, p.61). In the eighteenth century *Polly*, Grey's follow-up to *The Beggars Opera*, was suppressed by the Lord Chamberlain for its political content (ibid, p.97).

Nineteenth century Britain saw attempts to promote some forms of music, such as brass bands and tonic sol fa (Russell 1987, p.31) at the same time as clamping down on others, especially Music Hall[17]. The arrival of jazz in the early twentieth century provoked accusations that 'the music is impertinent and hath no respect for persons' (Godbolt 1984, p.10), whilst 1951 saw Rowntree and Lavers worrying that youth were being corrupted at dance halls where dancing could 'easily degenerate into a sensuous form of entertainment' leading on to 'unruly behaviour and not infrequently to sexual immorality' (Frith 1983, p.203). The power of music to promote hedonistic behaviour has thus long been a concern of moralists.

The arrival of rock and roll in Britain caused a moral panic as youths denied the opportunity to jive to the *Rock Around The Clock* film took revenge by cutting up cinema seats (Rogers 1982, pp.16-17). Beatlemania engendered Johnson's poison pen, whilst 1967 saw *Sergeant Pepper* and the beginnings of the "Is rock art?" debate. Punk raised questions of whether it was even music, but this had also been asked of jazz and rock and roll before. By the 1990s Redhead (1990, p.8) was pointing out that pop in Britain was part of an ever more heavily regulated leisure arena.

Pop certainly goes beyond mere notes, chords and vocals and involves image, covers and so on[18], as movements like punk show. As already noted, one consequence of this is that popular music censorship can be differentiated from that of most other art forms by the way that it soon becomes embroiled in questions of social control, primarily because of its live context. Dunaway (1987, p.50) has noted that performance is a vital part of pop's meaning, so attempts to control live pop also involve attempts to control pop's meaning. Reviving unsubstantiated causal claims, Medved (1993d) argues that behaviour at gigs has worsened because of the worsening moral depravity of the music. The ahistoricity of this is shown by Russell (1987, p.182) who notes many examples of bad behaviour by brass-bandsmen in the Victorian era.

Pop also antagonizes because it is a particularly intrusive medium. For example, music caused a third of all complaints about household noise in Britain in 1991 (*The Daily Telegraph* 23/1/92). It is often the very **sound** of pop that offends, again linking aesthetics with calls for restraint. Frith (1983, p.56) alleges that it is lyrics which cause censors most concern, but this analysis misses the aesthetic critiques that censors often use to supplement their arguments. Lyrics are often a prime motor for censorship[19] but: (1) One is also left with the feeling that music itself upsets many of the censors (for example see Leonard 1964, p.2) and (2) it is often noted that few fans listen to lyrics with any great attention (see Lull 1982, p.122). In this sense concentration on lyrics misrepresents the case[20].

One problem for pop is that it is harder for singers to distance themselves from the sentiments of the character in songs than it might be in a novel or film. Too often pop artists are held to straightforwardly advocate the sentiments they express in song, when they may be assuming a persona to sing with which does not necessarily reflect their personal views. There is also the perennial problem of text and context[21] and misinterpretation[22]. Much of the criticism of heavy metal, for example, misses the pathos and humour in the genre. The humourless tracts of Medved et al are full of examples of irony being taken at face value[23].

Reaction to pop centres around how its "meaning" is perceived. Those who see pop as harmless are unlikely to call for its censorship.

But pop's meaning is not fixed, it has been a notorious battleground over the years. Frith (1983, p.10) points out that music's meaning is socially conditioned, so that it has different connotations in America from those it has in Britain and Wicke (1990, p.xii) notes that the "meaning" of pop has constantly changed throughout its history. Hence the ability I mentioned earlier of previously "innocent" pop to become "offensive", again showing that pop's "meaning" is not etched in stone, but open to negotiation.

Pop also causes concern and suspicion because it is essentially a mass medium(24) and the effect of **all** such media have been subject to suspicion. As little research has been done specifically on the effects of pop, one is forced to look into other research into other media for guidance. This soon returns us to causal arguments, as most research has centred on the alleged links between various media and subsequent audience behaviour. McQuail (1977, p.83) has suggested that:

> ... most dependable research so far available has not supported the thesis of a general association between any form of media use and crime, delinquency or violence.

Overall, he says: 'The results remain confusing and contradictory' (ibid, p.85). Frith (1983, p.268) also notes that it is hard to attribute causal influences to an industry which is itself an **effect**, 'of postwar social changes'. Perhaps the one conclusion to draw is to treat all causal claims with caution.

Pop's omnipresence has also been held to be damaging. For example, Medved (1993d) posits an argument based on the **accumulated** impact of exposure to film and pop, but Barker (1984, p.134) has argued that repeated exposure leads to knowledge of conventions rather than ever more danger.

British censorship of pop has tended to be sporadic and pop generally has an easier time of it in Britain than it does in, for example, America. But the fact that America may have been more censorious up to 1992, does **not** mean that this situation will continue come what may. But, as noted previously, those who oppose pop in America can affect its dissemination in Britain, as the dropping of Ice T after *Cop Killer* shows (see below).

St. John-Stevas (1965, p.xi) wrote that: 'The books we battle about are nearly always rather a bore'. This is also the case in pop. Much of the material that is deemed offensive, I personally find musically uninteresting. But I also recognize that it is such music that often makes life worth living for significant numbers of people and that artists have some right to offend. Pop's "offence" can bring to light problems that might otherwise not gain attention. To call an album *The Fucking Cunts Treat Us Like Pricks* is not only offensive, but also a call for attention and action. Whatever else NWA do, they keep the issue of black ghettos in America alive[25]. Wicke (1990, pp.13-14 and 22) has also seen a democratic potential in pop, the censorship of which therefore must, logically, be **anti**-democratic.

That pop has the potential to offend is undoubted. That censors have increased their efforts is also true, as the Ice T case in America and NWA case in Britain show. Street (1986, p.115) was premature in declaring that all pop censorship is ineffective as not being able to buy *Cop Killer* **is** of some effect. The impact of American censorship on British fans may be part of the effects of the "global village". The increasing role of the EC in British law also gives scope for further action. But to mention all this is, in some respects, to jump the gun and to move from offence to action. So let us return to the beginning of the pop process, to the point of production, and examine censorial problems there.

Notes

1. See Chester and Dickey 1988 and Itzin 1992. For radical feminist approaches see Brownmiller 1976 and Dworkin 1981. For anti-radical, feminist, approaches see Segal 1991 and Rich 1983.

2. See Garofolo 1987, p.81, Jansen 1988 and Street 1986, pp.107-8 for more on the market as censor.

3. For attempts to blame rock for deaths see S. Jones 1991, Cosgrove 1986, Wells 1991a and Walser 1993, pp.145-151.

4. Grossberg 1987, pp.177-178 pointed out that 'millions of us have listened to Ozzy Osbourne's *Suicide Solution*, Van Halen's *Jump* and Blue Oyster Cult's *Don't Fear The Reaper* without following the rather demented example of a small number of already suicidal fans.'

5. For example, actor Mickey Rourke said: 'The blood of Los Angeles falls on those who instigated this revolt - the malicious prophets of black cinema and rap music ...'. *NME* 16/5/92. Medved 1992, p.341 portrays Ice Cube as a causal factor in the riots.

6. For Bloom as a causalist see Grossberg 1992, p.5. For the machinations of Medved and Rupert Murdoch's media empire see Lennon 1993, M. Walker 1993 and Martin 1993.

7. See also *Vox*, March 1992, pp.30-31 for hyped bands who failed. Harker 1980, pp.9-10 notes that far from being passive it is the audience which gives music meaning.

8. See Negus 1992, p.68 for the declining importance of the younger audience. *The Observer* of 14/3/93 noted that in pop 'the average punter is growing older'. Morrison, 1992, confirmed this, see summary. See Pattison 1987, p.96 for similar findings in the USA.

9. Brunivels also claimed the Beasties 'undermine family values',

NME 23/5/87.

10. See *NME* 15/10/91 where a Gallup poll found that only 7% of teenagers put pop as the most important thing in their life. In a 1978 poll of 15-21 year olds two thirds listed their parents as their greatest influence, only 6% listed pop stars, Roberts 1983, p.38. See also *The Observer* 9/10/94, p.3.

11. See Barker 1984b for how rational debate is impossible once children enter in. See also A. Walker 1984, p.5.

12. See also BSC 1991, p.68 and Newburn 1992 p.130 for children as an excuse for censorship.

13. Flashman 1992, p.14 shows a religious censor being motivated by a cultural dislike of rock.

14. See Wicke 1990, pp.55-58, Pearson 1983, p.20 and Chambers 1986, p.23 and 38-40.

15. For an early example of self-censorship in the Music Halls, see Russell 1987, p.97.

16. Christian fundamentalist Noebel also noted Plato's remarks, see M. Sullivan 1987, p.315.

17. For attacks on Music Hall see Chambers 1986, p.130.

18. See Negus 1992, p.70 and Street 1986, p.5 for pop as more than just music.

19. See F. Hoffman 1989, pp.120-122, 136-137, 197-205 where most pop censorship cases concern lyrics and, to a lesser extent, backmasking.

20. Street 1986, p.159 notes that it is pop's **sound** as well as its lyrics which give it its meaning. For concentration on lyrics see publications by Whitehouse and the PMRC.

21. Chambers 1985, p.211 also notes how the same song can have

different meanings in different circumstances.

22. See, for example, below for courts misinterpreting songs. Wicke 1990, p.ix notes that meaning is also tied up with use.

23. For Medved misunderstanding films see Lennon 1993 and Martin 1993. For the ignorance of pop's censors see Wells 1990a.

24. Chambers 1985 notes the early British discussions of rock as **American** mass culture and Frith 1983 notes that pop is **essentially** a mass medium.

25. See Chapter 4 below for *The Fucking Cunts Treat Us Like Pricks* and NWA.

Part Two
Industry and the law

3 'Not here you don't' – censorship by record companies

One of the least reported, but probably most frequent, forms of pop censorship occurs at the point of production when record companies decide a particular track or video is "unsuitable" for the market. Details of such decisions are hard to come by, but enough emerge to illustrate that a lot of "offensive" material never reaches the public. Various examples span the years this book is concerned with. In 1967 The Game's *The Addicted Man* was withdrawn by EMI following Juke Box Jury's condemnation of its theme of drugs (*MM* 14/1/67) and the label also made Smoke change their lyrics to their *My Friend Jack Eats Sugar Lumps* single before they would release it (*NOTW* 12/2/67). In 1992 Warner Bros made REM change the title of a track from *Fuck Me Kitten* to *Star Me Kitten* (*NME* 3/10/92) and also instituted a worldwide ban on Ice T's *Cop Killer* track after the LA riots (see below).

To simplify matters this chapter presents most cases as being examples of artists against companies, of artistic expression versus commercial expediency. The truth is more complex than this, involving disputes **within** both bands and labels, as well as **between** them, but the main aim here is to illustrate overt label censorship rather than internal industry machination.

However, it is first necessary to give some detail of the relationship between artist and label. There are various permutations of this, dependent on such factors as the status of the act, size of the company, likely audience, sales of previous records and so on (see Negus 1992 and Chapple and Garofolo 1972, p.179). The most important characteristic of the relationship is that the artist's product is owned by the label (see Negus 1992, pp.5, 6 and 156-7). By 1992 the world's record industry was dominated by six major companies - EMI Music, MCA, Polygram, Sony Music Entertainment, Warner Music International and the BMG Music Group. These companies are themselves owned by larger multinational corporations. One problem of this diversity is that companies can be open to consumer boycotts of other products should one of their pop products offend.

One of my themes is that the market is in a sense inherently censorious, and record companies are generally run according to market criteria. Normally only that which is likely to cover its costs is released. It has been variously estimated that between 5% (Eliot 1987, p.249) to 12% (Negus 1992, p.40) of artists signed will prove profitable. This has been held to have bred conservatism. Repeating successful formulas rather than risking something new may often be tried, especially in time of recession[1]. The industry ultimately conforms to the logic of capitalism[2]. This need not involve overt censorship, but the market's influence inevitably means that artistic expression is compromised by the need to make that expression sell. Labels dropping artists, as happened to such acts as Julian Cope (Island), Public Image Limited (Virgin) and Pop Will Eat Itself (RCA) in 1992[3], means the public is deprived of the chance to hear them in recorded form - which is often the only form available to many.

When a label signs an artist it generally acquires the right to do what it wants with their work. It **owns** it and so can decide whether or not to market it. So labels, along with artists themselves, become the **only** ones with the capacity to **pre**-censor recorded pop. Other censorship cases involve attempts to censor a product which is already on the market.

Profit, not artistic expression, motivates the industry. Police manager Miles Copeland admitted: 'We're not in the music business ... We're in the commodities business' (Rimmer 1985, p.141). But artists can resent their commodification. In 1992 George Michael stopped producing any new material in a row with his Sony label and initiated legal moves to get out of his contract (see *NME* 21/11/92 and 5/12/92). The case came to court in the summer of 1994 and resulted in a victory for Sony[4], although as I write Michael is due to appeal. Before the case Dire Straits manager Ed Bicknell said a victory for Michael:

> ... could mean that for the first time the artists will have the record companies in a stranglehold ... but this could prove

disastrous for new bands who already find it hard to get a deal. Companies won't be prepared to take a risk on new talent (Garfield 1992).

Changes in the relationship between artists and labels could have the censorial implication of giving the superstars greater control, whilst making it harder for the nobodies to get their voice heard.

The point to note here is that not only is control of music **not** with the consumers, it is also seldom with the producers. It is with, in Frith's (1983) term, "gatekeepers". The record company is the most important "gatekeeper" (and thus potential censor) of all, as it decides what reaches the market.

Music press interviews often feature questions about the relationship between artist and label. Liam of Flowered Up explained the band's relationship with their label in 1991:

> It's not like we've been having big arguments with London ... but they talk units and you talk passion ... Virtually every song we've done we've had to chop up to get on the radio ... I fucking hate it, you're dissecting your songs, but if it's got to be done, you gotta do it (*NME* 7/8/91)[5].

The latter part of this quote reflects a problem that has dogged musicians for years - the compromise between playing what they want and the need to have commercial success in order to live. Becker (1963, pp.82/3) noted this form of self-censorship in his *Outsiders* study in 1948 and Laurie (1965, p.75) confirmed it in 1965. Negus (1992, p.150) suggests that the struggle is not so much of art versus commerce, but one to control the fate of the art and pop musicians know the rules. As Joe Elliott of Def Leppard put it: 'We wanted to be the biggest band in the world and you don't do that by sounding like Napalm Death' (*NME* 21/1/89).

No artist wants **not** to sell, but the point is that record companies may be able to exploit artists' vulnerability in order to make them put out a product which is (self) "censored" inasmuch as it is not that which the artist would rather issue. For example, Shane MacGowan spoke of his songs not being recorded by The Pogues because their record label wanted to "clean up" the band's boozy image (*NME* 28/11/92). Such intervention can happen to even the most radical of artists, as Street (1986, p.102) notes that SWP members The Redskins were told which producer to use by their label, London.

Signing policies are also a contentious issue. Labels look to artists who are likely to have an international appeal and Negus (1992, p.57) suggests that the culture of those doing the signing, mainly young university educated men from a rock tradition, militates against other forms of music. Likely appeal to radio formats is also crucial, especially to American signings (Negus 1993, pp.61-63). Looks can be as important as music - as the remarks of an American label that female duo The Banderas were 'too fat and too ugly for America' (C. Sullivan 1991) show. Street (1986, p.108) suggests that not signing bands is censorship and as far as freedom of expression is concerned it is, although it is hard to envisage a situation where **all** artists got signed.

The examples thus far add up to a type of subliminal censorship, based on industry control and market expectations, but there have been numerous occasions when a product has either never been released or has been withdrawn for more overtly censorial reasons.

Stopping the rot

Leonard (1964, p.99) notes that the industry tried to censor itself in America during the 1920s and in the early 1950s The Weavers were dropped by Decca Records after singer Pete Seeger appeared before McCarthy's House Un-American Activities Committee. In the early 1960s Decca refused to release Ray Peterson's American hit *Tell Laura I Love Her*, based on the dying words of a stock-car racing crash victim, because it was 'too tasteless and vulgar'. They scrapped 20,000 copies of the record which had already been printed. EMI-Columbia then released a Ricky Valence version of the song, which topped the charts (Martin and Segrave 1988, p.107). Perhaps more understandably a Phil Spector song written for The Crystals, *He Hit Me (And It Felt Like A Kiss)*, was withdrawn in 1962 (Chapple and Garofolo 1972, p.272).

The ability of censorship in one country to have effects on another became apparent at this time when CBS made Bob Dylan keep *Talkin' John Birch Society Blues* and another track off his second album (Gillett 1983, p.301) and various other American artists also suffered censorship which had implications for UK fans. Attali (1977, p.105) notes that in the business in the 1960s: 'Explicit censorship played a very prominent role'[6] - which undermines the decade's reputation as one of permissiveness.

Record companies are also prone to the ebb and flow of the censorial tide, which is itself tied to contemporary events. This was illustrated by a 1967 case mentioned above. I noted earlier the year's moral panic surrounding recreational drug usage and it was into this climate that The Game's *The Addicted Man* came. After its drugs theme was criticized on Juke Box Jury, EMI made the decision to withdraw it. A spokesman explained that:

> We believe in all sincerity that this is an anti-drug record and no one is sorrier than us that it has had such repercussions. The very last thing we want to do is cause offence however, and so ... we will do everything we can to restrict sales (*M M* 14/1/67).

The record's withdrawal shows the censorial climate within which labels sometimes have to work. At that time **any** reference to drugs might have caused "offence" and so EMI dropped the song. The Game, as far as I can tell, were never heard of again.

Ireland remained a contentious issue at this time and Pye took steps to make sure that a record by The Tinkers called *The Reluctant Patriot*, which made references to Princess Margaret and Lord Snowdon joining the IRA, was only available in the Irish Republic (O'Higgins 1972, p.158).

Again, even the most radical could suffer and succumb. The MC5's refrain of "Kick Out The Jams Motherfuckers" became "Kick Out The Jams Brothers and Sisters" for the single version of the song (Neville 1971 pp.65-66). Peterson (1972, p.269) also notes that RCA censored virtually all of Jefferson Airplane's early records - primarily because of swearing.

Drugs continued to cause some industry paranoia and MGM's president, Mike Curb, threatened to sack any band using drug references in their lyrics. He claimed to have done so to 18 unnamed bands, but it appears that this was more a publicity stunt than a policy as the label did not drop known drug user Eric Burdon whose MGM albums included *Sandoz* - the name of a Swiss LSD manufacturer (Martin and Segrave 1988, pp.206-7). Martin and Segrave (ibid, p.149) also say that the label 'censored the lyrics on Mothers of Invention songs without telling them'. Again censorship in one country affected another, as American censorship meant that these records either did not appear, or were altered, in Britain too.

By 1969 at least one record company had adopted a more liberal approach to artistic expression. The first "fuck" on a British record came that year, some four years after its television debut[7]. This was in the title track of Al Stewart's *Love Chronicles* album. CBS' Derek Everett commented that: 'this word is very much in the context with the lyrics. If it was used in a sensationalist way I would have said no' (*M M* 1/2/69). So **the** swear word became acceptable in some circles if it was not used gratuitously. Slowly, it seemed, labels were pulling the censorial curtains apart.

But things are never that simple. As argued earlier, censorship is not a process of continually rolling back the boundaries, but one of their constant renegotiation. The same year Serge Gainsbourg and Jane Birkin's *Je T'Aime* was a big hit, but it was dropped by Phillips when No. 3 in the charts. The company explained that:

> Recordings on the Phillips label are only released if they measure up to our high standards of artistic and technical quality.
> This record is no exception. However certain sections of the press and general public have seen fit to make a controversy over the contents of this recording. And as Phillips does not intend to allow any of their products to be the subject of controversial matters the record is being withdrawn from our catalogue (*M M* 20/9/69).

The mention of the press here illustrates the surveillance the industry is often under. The record was subsequently re-issued by the Major Minor label and carried on selling well, rising to No. 2.

The debut album by John Lennon's Plastic Ono Band caused problems in 1970. The track *Working Class Hero* included a few "fuckings" which caused EMI, the distributors, some concerns. It was released, but the lyrics on the inner sleeve omitted the offending word (Harker 1980, p.214).

EMI took a more censorial stance in 1971 and refused to distribute Eric Burdon's *The Black Man's Burdon* album because one track, *PC3*, contained a reference to the Queen being caught with her knickers down. EMI believed that such an idea 'could clearly sound offensive to many people.' Eventually the album was issued in two formats - one with the offending track, which independent distributors distributed and one without, which EMI happily distributed (*M M* 30/1/71). EMI turned censor again weeks later when it refused to release Lennon's *Power To The People* because the B-side, Yoko Ono's *Open Your Box*, was considered 'distasteful' by Philip Brodie, EMI Records' MD. A spokesman for Apple, Lennon's label, explained that:

> The original lyric said: "Open your trousers, open your skirts, open your legs and open your thighs".
> The last words in each case have now been been changed - with the consent of John and Yoko - to "houses", "church", "lakes" and "eyes"' (*M M* 13/3/71).

The same month Pye deleted the words "And Your Ass Will Follow" from its advertising campaign for Funkadelic's *Free Your Mind And Your Ass Will Follow* album. Pye International repertoire manager, Dave McAleer, explained that this was because: 'Pye wanted to keep an image of good, clean family fun' (*M M* 27/3/71). A "family image" was seemingly incompatible with the word "ass".

The same year also saw allegations that Polydor were interfering with Slade's lyrics. *M M* reported that:

> ... for the third time, the group had to make the trip to Olympia studios in Barnes, London, to alter the words on a recorded song ... Polydor ... had objected to the "suggestive" lyrics on a number called *Do You Want Me*. Each time they made an alteration, Polydor said no - until finally an acceptable version had been produced (*M M* 1/5/71).

The band's singer, Noddy Holder, commented that: 'John Lennon got away with much worse on his solo album ... but we're not John Lennon' (ibid).

This comment links an artists' stature with the amount of censorship they are likely to encounter[8]. Once established, with a loyal market to guarantee profits, artists may be in a stronger position to determine what gets released and labels may be willing to court controversy if profits are practically guaranteed. Thus "artistic expression" is again mediated via the market. However it should be noted that REM were censored by having to change the name of *Fuck Me Kitten* - presumably so as not to offend their newly found mass audience. Previously The Rolling Stone's *Starfucker* had appeared on their 1973 album *Goats Head Soup* as *Star Star*. Thus it is by no means the case that commercial success **always** engenders more artistic freedom.

Meanwhile disputes between artist and label continued. Warner Bros sued Alice Cooper for not making enough "commercially acceptable" material during their contract with the label (*NME* 9/8/75) and Neil Young was sued by Geffen for making "unrepresentative music" (*NME* 4/5/91). These are not examples of overt censorship - but they have implications for artistic expression and illustrate labels' power to determine what the public gets to hear.

By the time of punk censorship by labels was nothing new - but sacking a band because of public misbehaviour brought a new dimension to the equation. The Sex Pistols were sacked by EMI after their television swearing and an alleged incident involving them spitting and vomiting at Heathrow - which they always denied. When they signed to EMI, on 8 October 1976, its A&R director, Nick Mobbs, enthused that:

> They are a band who are shocking up the music business ... I don't think there'll be any problems with their lyrics because I've got more than a little sympathy with what they are doing (Vermorel 1978, pp.208-9).

But from Grundy (1/12/76, below) onwards pressure was applied to EMI as the press speculated about the band's future(9). Initially the label appeared to be standing by them. At EMI's annual general meeting on 7 December 1976 chairman Sir John Read said that:

> During recent years in particular, the question of acceptable content of records has become increasingly difficult to resolve ... Throughout its history as a recording company, **EMI has always sought to behave within contemporary limits of good taste,** taking into account not only the traditional rigid conventions of one section of Society, but also the increasingly liberal attitude of other (perhaps larger) sections of Society (sic) at any given time ...
> **It is against this present-day social background that EMI has to make value judgements about the content of records in particular. EMI has on a number of occasions taken steps to ban individual records, and similarly to ban record sleeves or posters or other**

promotional material which it believed to be offensive.

After noting the 'disgraceful interview' and the 'vast amount of newspaper coverage' the group had attracted, Read continued:

> EMI will review its general guidelines regarding the content of pop records ... Our view within EMI is that we should seek to discourage records which are likely to give offence to the majority of people. In this context, public attitudes have to be taken into account.
> **EMI should not set itself up as a public censor,** but it does seek to encourage restraint ... (Wood 1988. Emphasis mine. This book has no page numbers).

I have quoted this at length because it shows a company acting not by some eternal moral code or abstract theory of taste, but by what they think the public will accept at a particular time - again illuminating the link between censorship and contemporary mores. Read also admits EMI's past censorial role and hints its future one. It will not set itself up as public censor, but ... well, we shall see.

By this time EMI had released the band's first single, *Anarchy In The UK*, which was selling around 1,500 copies a day (Savage 1991, p.271). Its lyrics were confrontational but unlikely to 'give offence to the majority of people'. However, it was soon to be censored, after selling around 50,000 copies - which undermines Street's (1986, p.107) argument that the business 'censors only when the market is offended'. Pressure on it was maintained by the press and certain MPs, as well as radio bans. The alleged "puking" incident at Heathrow on 4 January (see *NME* 15/1/77) was apparently enough for EMI.

The end came on 6 January 1977 when the label issued a statement saying, in part, that:

> EMI and the Sex Pistols group have mutually agreed to terminate their recording contract.
> EMI feels it is unable to promote the group's records **internationally** in view of the adverse publicity which has been generated over the last two months, although recent press reports of the behaviour of the Sex Pistols appear to have been exaggerated (Wood 1988. Emphasis mine).

The single was also withdrawn. Leslie Hill, EMI's MD, continually cited press pressure as the reason for the termination (Vermorel 1978, p.63), which came officially on 22 January. Unlike Hill (ibid) and Butt (1976), I class this as a case of censorship and a very important one. The band was then the most exciting in the country and it was denied the chance to issue records. *Anarchy in the UK* was censored just as it started to make its impact.

It was noted earlier that matters have been simplified here into artist against label, but in this case it seems that the A&R department at EMI wanted the band to carry on (*NME* 15/1/77)(10), while those higher up decided they had to go. The appearance of the band on the front of the *Los Angeles Times* had put in jeopardy an EMI brain scanner project (Savage 1991, p.285) and the earlier quote noted potential problems regarding marketing the band abroad. Thus EMI's corporate and multinational structure made it vulnerable and more inclined to censor. Others claimed that EMI dropped the band because it held shares in Thames, the company which broadcast the Grundy interview (Wood 1988), again showing the censorial pressures which can accompany corporate multinational diversification.

The Pistols moved on to A&M, signing outside Buckingham Palace on 10 March 1977. In the early hours of 12 March members of the band were involved in a scuffle with *OGWT* presenter Bob Harris at London's Speakeasy Club. A&M's English director Derek Green, who had signed them, was appalled at this violence and, despite the fact that 25,000 copies of *God Save The Queen* had already been pressed, he phoned the label's American half owner Jerry Moss. Within an hour the other owner Herb Alpert had called back and the decision was made to sack them (Savage 1991, pp.307-321). The company issued a statement which read:

A&M Records wishes to announce that its recording agreement with the Sex Pistols has been terminated with immediate effect. The company will therefore not be releasing any product from the group and has no further association with them (Wood 1988).

A&M denied, as EMI had done, that they were acting as censors (Vermorel 1978, p.86). Pressed copies of *God Save The Queen* were subject to the censorial martyrdom of being melted down. Pistol's vocalist Johnny Rotten claimed that:

They've given us up through fear and business pressure. They've kicked us in the teeth. A record company is there to market records - not dictate terms (*M M* 26/3/77).

His tone echoes that of the punks' supposed enemy, Mick Jagger, years previously in a dispute with Decca over the cover of *Beggars Banquet* (see below). Malcolm McLaren, the band's manager, tried to blame the sacking on objections from other A&M artists but this appears now to have been a "scam" (Savage 1991, p.339). Green later said the sacking 'was nothing to do with pressure from any other quarter. I just didn't want to be involved in the things they were involved in outside their music' (*NME* 16/7/77). Alpert cited the band's rudeness as the reason for their sacking (*NME* 20/6/77). Notably the band's music was not mentioned, again showing how pop's attendant features are often the reason for its censorship.

The Sex Pistols moved on to Virgin, signing on 13 May. There they finally released *God Save The Queen* - but not until a strike threat at the CBS plant at Aylesbury, which pressed records for Virgin, had been overcome (Wood 1988). It was subsequently released - to suffer further censorship - on 27 May. Despite various hassles, some of which are detailed elsewhere in this book, Virgin was willing and able to release a series of Sex Pistols records from then on.

But the Sex Pistols were far from being the only punk band to suffer label censorship. The Ramones' problems with the track *Now I Want To Sniff Some Glue* is referred to below and they also had problems with their second album, *The Ramones Leave Home*. American copies of this featured the track *Carbona Not Glue* (Carbona is a typing fluid), but the band's British distributors, Phonogram, forced their label, Sire, to drop the track from British copies. The connection between censorial action and contemporary events in this case was a moral panic around glue sniffing (*NME* 5/3/77).

But this was not a clear cut case. Tony Morris, managing director of Phonogram in England, wrote to Sire president Seymour Stein saying:

> I'm sorry, but I have to say we cannot promote product which extols the virtues of "dope". As you know, we had correspondence with the Home Office about "Glue sniffing". Carbona is apparently available, and more dangerous than glue.

... we will have to omit the offending track. Please ensure that the Ramones record responsible lyrics if you wish us to release in the future.

Note here the word "responsible" - a very censorial term (see below). Stein replied:

You're entitled to your feelings about the use of drugs of any sort. But what you're attempting to do is set yourself up as judge and jury. This is censorship, a far greater evil than either Carbona or glue, and something that in good conscience I cannot be a party to (*NME* 12/3/77).

Nevertheless the album subsequently appeared in Britain without the offending track.

Hypocrisy also appears in corporate censorship. In July 1977 advertisements appeared in the music press for an album called *Live At The Roxy*, which claimed that:

Between January and April this year, The Roxy Club devoted itself entirely to new wave music. There was nowhere else for the groups to play. This is the album of the club (*NME* 2/7/77).

Attentive readers might have noticed the words 'distributed by EMI' on initial advertisements, although this was later dropped (*NME* 2 and 16/7/77). In fact the album was on Harvest - an EMI subsidiary. Ironically EMI, who had sacked punk's leading lights, placed advertisements bemoaning the lack of punk venues. Moreover, whilst EMI had sacked the Pistols following their television swearing, this album was full of swearing (*NME* 20/8/77).

Laing (1983, pp.37 and 49) notes that labels often had a contradictory attitude to punk - they would not promote bands as punks, but the Pistols were the only ones to suffer sacking. But others also suffered label censorship and the Rough Trade distribution network refused to handle Raped's *Pretty Paedophiles* EP (ibid, p.138).

But it was the majors who were the most censorious. CBS released The Clash's *Remote Control* as a single without the band's consent and the band issued a statement deploring this (*NME* 10/9/77). The Clash were censored by not being allowed to make and release records for the British market the way they wanted. When the time came to market them in America, the situation worsened. Release of their debut album was delayed for two years as it was felt to be too raw for American ears. When it was finally released it was with track changes. CBS were determined that no such problems would beset the next album and hired successful producer Sandy Pearlman to tone down the band's sound. Pearlman said that:

> There is a real revolutionary, anti-authoritarian, subversive consciousness in The Clash's songs. I've been asked to produce their next album to bring their sound more into line with what's acceptable to American ears (*NME* 25/2/78).

The censorial agenda of a major record company was seldom so boldly stated. Other censorial actions by labels around punk included CBS' refusal to continue printing an album by porn star Xavier Holland after complaints from a worker (*NME* 7/5/77), major distributors refusing to handle Wayne County and The Electric Chair's *Fuck Off* single (*NME* 22/10/77) and CBS refusing to continue distributing Derek and Clive's *Come Again* album for Virgin in October (*NME* 29/10/77).

EMI's A&R department seemed to reassert itself in 1978 when it signed the Tom Robinson Band - a controversial decision because of Robinson's espousal of gay rights and various other causes. Virgin had apparently rejected the band because of this (Denselow 1989, p.149). There was much speculation as to how EMI, having sacked the Pistols, would handle them, with the fate of live favourite *Glad To Be Gay* the centre of most interest. *NME* soon reported that 'executives are reluctant to release ... *Glad To Be Gay* as a single' (*NME* 20/8/77). By January 1978 the label announced that: 'We're treating it like any other release' (*NME* 14/1/78). This was not exactly the case. Rather than being a single in its own right, the song appeared as one of four on the band's *Rising Free* EP(11).

EMI also continued its role as "public censor" elsewhere, despite Read's words that it should not. In January 1978 it refused to press The Buzzcocks' debut single for United Artists, *What Do I Get*, because of the "B" side, *Oh Shit* - a song reflecting the mood of a jilted lover (*NME* 21/1/78). Later that year EMI refused to manufacture Ivor Biggin and The Red Nosed Burglars' *The Winkers Song*, although they were willing to distribute it (*NME* 1/1/78).

53

Other censorship was undertaken for radio. The lyrics to The Jam's *This Is The Modern World* had the words "two fucks" changed to "a damn" when it was released as a single by Polydor in February 1978, whilst Rough Trade issued Stiff Little Fingers' *Suspect Device* with the words "fuck all" changed to "sod all".

In June 1978 the Sex Pistols returned to controversy. With Rotten gone, they released a single featuring great train robber Ronnie Biggs. This was originally to be called *Cosh The Driver* (the train driver attacked in the robbery eventually died of his injuries), but after protests by workers at a CBS pressing plant it was changed to *No One Is Innocent* (*NME* 24/6/78)[12].

Record companies also seemed sensitive to criticism. In February 1979 Graham Parker planned to issue a song called *Mercury Poisoning* as the "B" side to his *Protection* single for Phonogram. This was his reaction to what he felt was poor treatment by Mercury, his American label. However Phonogram were affiliated to Mercury and vetoed the release of the song. Parker replaced with a cover of the Jackson Five's *I Want You Back* (*NME* 10/2/79).

By 1980 the women's movement had begun criticizing the sexist nature of much of the advertising and imagery around rock. The advert for the Rolling Stones' 1976 album *Black and Blue*, depicting a bound and bruised half naked woman, provoked particular anger. The Los Angeles based Women Against Violence Against Women (WAVAW) then launched a campaign against sexist imagery in the industry (Stallings 1984, p.153). Three years later Warner Bros announced a new policy opposing 'the depiction of physical and sexual violence against women on record sleeves and promotional material' (*NME* 2/2/80). Although this was heralded as a breakthrough at the time, it seems to have had little effect.

In 1981 came Oi. After the arson at the Hamborough Tavern in Southall whilst it was being used as an Oi venue (see below) the press, particularly the *Daily Mail*, became interested in pop's latest "cult". One result of this was the withdrawal of the *Strength Through Oi* compilation album by Decca's subsidiary, Deram (*NME* 11/7/81). Another, unspecified, label said that: 'In future all bands will be screened; we're not imposing censorship but we don't want to give out contracts and money to fascists' (Coren 1981). This attitude generally continued throughout the industry up to 1992 and records by confirmed supporters of the far right such as Skrewdriver were only available through networks such as Blood and Honour[13].

1981 also saw hunger strikes in Northern Ireland and into this climate The Au Pairs released an album, *Playing With A Different Sex*. This featured the track *Armagh*, a criticism of the treatment of women in that prison. *NME* reported that:

> The major record distributors in Northern Ireland have refused to handle the LP because of this track - a case of virtual, undeclared, censorship (*NME* 11/7/81).

The year was also the International Year of The Disabled. In sympathy with this polio victim Ian Dury released a single called *Spasticus Autisticus*. This was effectively vetoed by radio because of the word "spastic". So it was deleted by Polydor - but with the permission of Dury, although it remained on his *Lord Upminster* album. A joint statement from Dury and Polydor said that 'it was made impossible to function as a normal record' (*NME* 26/9/81).

In 1983 Dury was involved in another censorship case. This concerned the track *Noddy Harris* or *Fuck Off Noddy*, the lyrics of which Polydor wanted to change. It was eventually dropped, with Dury's agreement, after it was pointed out to him that the tabloids might connect lines like "Winnie The Pooh is having a wank" with paedophilia (*NME* 1/10/83). Dury's acceptance of the decision is a rare documented example of self-censorship, but it also illustrates the atmosphere within which pop often works. Not wishing to encounter "shock horror" headlines resulted in censorship. A similar attitude lay behind the decision by WEA not to release a Jesus and Mary Chain track called *Jesus Suck* in 1985 (*NME* 21-28/12/85).

By the early 1980s video was an important marketing device and brought disputes between artists and labels over what was marketable. Marc Almond is a prime example here. In 1982 he had problems with the violence in the video of his band, Soft Cell's, *Sex Dwarf* song (*NME* 19/6/82). By 1986 Almond was with Virgin and presented them with a video for his *Ruby Red* single. This was generally of a "camp" nature, featuring male buttocks and "romping" devils. However Virgin ordered cuts to it to make it suitable for television - again illustrating that often disputes are not simply between artist and label, but can involve consideration of third parties. Virgin's head of promotions, Chris Griffin, said that he liked the video but:

55

It's just not the sort of thing Saturday Superstore would show and it would be very hard to convince any TV producer when the subject matter is so risque ... As a video it was very well made, but as a marketing tool it doesn't work (*NME* 18/10/86).

This comment makes some interesting points. First there is Almond's desire for artistic freedom clashing with Virgin's need for a suitable marketing tool acceptable to television companies. Secondly an undercurrent of homophobia was assumed on behalf of television. The objections seemed to be that the buttocks featured all belonged to men and that the video was generally too "camp". Almond believed that: 'If the video contained scenes of near naked women then that would have made it acceptable' (ibid). The third point is the way "children's television" is used to justify censorship.

Polydor made a similar, homophobic, stand in 1983 when they ordered cuts to the video for The Style Council's *Long Hot Summer* single as they feared that scenes of band members Paul Weller and Mick Talbot tickling each other's ears might be "misinterpreted" (Martin and Segrave 1988, p.277). Boy George's video for his band Jesus Loves You's *Generations of Love* single was also vetoed by Virgin in June 1990. It featured an erect penis and scenes from Soho (*NME* 16/6/90). George had previously complained in 1988 that Virgin had not promoted his *No Clause 28* single - a protest at the Government's proposed homophobic legislation - as enthusiastically as they had done with other singles[14].

The same year as Almond's *Ruby Red* affair, 1986, also saw censorship of a more overtly political nature when the Orlake pressing company refused to complete *Voices*, an album by singer-guitarist Maria Tolly, because of its lyrics. Four of the twelve tracks on the album were about the political situation in Northern Ireland including strip searching of women, plastic bullets and the need for a "troops out" policy. Orlake saw this as "too controversial" and Tolly had to go elsewhere to get the disc pressed (*NME* 26/6/86).

Meanwhile in America the PMRC gained its first victory when the Record Industry Association of America agreed to place warning stickers on albums containing "explicit lyrics" (Denselow 1989 pp.286-287). Soon it was reported that MCA were carefully vetting all material that was released (Wells 1990a) and *NME* wrote of a "chill factor" (Wells 1987) where American companies were unwilling to sign acts that were likely to get "stickered" and thus face consumer boycotts (*NME* 27/10/90). Again the censorial point is that if American labels do not sign acts then British fans are unlikely to hear them.

In Britain an attempt was made to test the censorial waters. Manchester's Savoy Books had endured various censorship problems(15) and in revenge it issued a cover of New Order's *Blue Monday* in November 1987 under the name of the Savoy-Hitler Band. Its cover featured a cartoon of Manchester Chief Constable James Anderton with the back of his head blown off speaking the words "fucking suckarse nigger Jew". The record received a total blacking by distributors. A spokesman for Savoy admitted that the reason for the record was 'to test out the climate as regards how far you can go with extremity in this country ... it took us six months to get the cover printed' (*Sounds* 24/11/87). Artistically the record meant little, but it illustrated that limits were definitely in place.

Another label interested in exposing limits was Fierce Records of Swansea. Their first issue, in 1985, was a Charles Manson bootleg under the title *Love Terror Cult*. It resulted in the Revolver distribution chain refusing to work with them. Fierce then upset the Jesus and Mary Chain by issuing the single *Riot* - a recording of the crowd's reaction to an unduly short set at North London Polytechnic. Although the band threatened legal action none came because, as it contained no music, no copyrights were breached. A later plan to feature John Lennon's killer Mark Chapman singing a version of his *Imagine* was dropped after objections from Yoko Ono (*NME* 20/2/88 and Gregory 1991)(16).

By the late 1980s rap had become of major importance with Public Enemy at the forefront of this. Their label Def Jam, a CBS affiliate, often censored their lyrics, especially on singles. In December 1989 the word "nigger" was bleeped out of their *Welcome To The Terrordome* single (it remained on the album version). In the summer of 1991 the words "kiss my butt" were cut from the *I Can't Do Nothing For You Man* single (again remaining on the album version) and in October 1991 part of their video for the *Can't Truss It* was cut by Def Jam. The scenes included hanging, rioting and rape (*NME* 12/10/90).

The word "nigger" was also alleged to have got Birdland dropped by their American label, RCA, in September 1990 as it was rumoured to have been because the company was unhappy at them recording a version of Patti Smith's *Rock 'n' Roll Nigger* (*NME* 20/9/90). The same word was also cut from Arrested Development's *People Everyday* single in Britain in 1992.

Island Records UK was involved in the major censorial case of 1991, the attempt to prosecute NWA's album *Efil4zaggin* (see below) when it stood resolutely against censorship. But a few weeks later Island turned censor itself and decided that it would only release Ice Cube's *Death Certificate* album if two tracks were omitted. The first, *Black Korea*, threatened Korean shopkeepers who discriminated against black shoppers in LA. The second, *No Vaseline*, was an attack on NWA's Jewish former manager Jerry Heller. To their detractors these tracks were racist and, in the latter case, homophobic (*NME* 25/1/92). British fans could only find out by buying import copies of the album. Marc Marot, MD of Island UK, argued that Island was merely deciding where it drew the line. For Marot the Ice Cube album was offensive, because it advocated racism, in a way that the NWA did not, as their album was reportage (Marot 1991b). Island offered to let Ice Cube release the album on another label, but he agreed to leave the two tracks off. To Marot this made it a case of self-censorship (ibid).

By 1992 censorship was still causing even major stars problems and again showing the capacity for events in one country to shape the censorial climate in another. After the LA riots attempts were made to link the violence with the lyrics of rap artists (*NME* 19-26/12/92 and Medved 1993d). By this time the *Body Count* album, by Ice T's band of the same name, had been out for some time. Members of the Los Angeles Police Department (LAPD) took exception to a track on the album called *Cop Killer* and threatened various actions against Time Warner, Ice T's label, including a boycott of its film *Batman 2* and refusing to cover its premises. After Warner's received death threats to its employees, it withdrew the track on a worldwide basis. So the unelected forces of law and order deprived fans the world over of hearing the track - although copies of it were to be given out at Ice T concerts[17].

In comparison to the Ice Cube case where an album containing a great deal of sexism was defended whilst two racist songs were vetoed, it is worth pointing out that the track *KKK Bitch*, which features the sodomizing of a Grand Duke's daughter was allowed to stay on *Body Count*. It was also noted that not until a white male bastion, the LAPD, was threatened did the company take action (*NME* 8/8/92).

A number of censorship cases followed in the wake of the *Body Count* affair. Intelligent Hoodlum dropped a track called *Hoodlum*, which called for a shoot out with police, from an album for A&M. WEA were alleged to have pressurized the Boo Yaa Tribe into dropping a track called *Shoot 'Em Down* from their debut album (*NME* 19/9/92). It was also reported that the rapper Paris had problems getting a US release for his *Bush Killa* album (*NME* 9/1/93).

In November 1992 Soho claimed that their *Thug* album, released in America the previous March, was not being released in Britain by the record company Savage Records (whom they had left in September), because one of the tracks concerned an alleged affair between a senior Cabinet Minister and the owner of a catering company, whispers of which were widespread(18). The band reported being under surveillance and a break-in at their London home (*The Independent* 8/11/92 and *NME* 7/11/92). Savage Records said that by September they did not want to take up their option on the album - for reasons they would not disclose (*The Independent* 8/11/92). So it remained unreleased in Britain, where an air of mystery surrounded it.

Such an air surrounds much internal music business censorship. The day to day disputes between artists and company remain the subject of gossip and rumour (but see Negus 1992 for some details). Companies ultimately treat artists as product - the reality of labour under capitalism. But some of the labour's product is not deemed suitable for the market, or, worse still, unmarketable. In such cases labels try to ensure that the product does not reach the market. This struggle is not without its ironies. In 1992 EMI bought Virgin Records, and is now the proud owner of the Sex Pistols back catalogue. *Anarchy In The UK* had succumbed to the anarchy of the market.

Covered up

Censorsial problems around record covers take the issue away from music *per se* but covers play an important part in pop's overall message. As Fabbri (1982, p.139) argues, 'the record sleeve contributes to determining the meaning not only of the record object but also of the very music found itself'. That "meaning" has often been a matter of dispute between companies and artists. The Rolling Stones' numerous disputes with Decca are illustrative here.

In 1965 the cover of their *No. 2* album was changed after complaints about Andrew Loog Oldham's sleeve notes, which talked of robbing a blind man in order to be able to buy it (Wyman 1991, p.359). The following year Decca vetoed a plan to release an album titled *Can You Walk on Water*, which eventually became *Aftermath* (ibid, p.431).

September 1968 saw the band's *Beggars Banquet* album delayed because Decca objected to the cover, which depicted a toilet wall. They rejected a compromise solution of putting it out in a plain brown envelope. Predating Rotten by some nine years, Mick Jagger commented that: 'The job of a record company is to distribute records ... not dictate how they should and should not look' (Stallings 1984, p.152). Despite Jagger's protestations that 'I am opposed to all forms of censorship' (Wyman 1991, pp.595-596) and that 'You can't have entrepreneurs making moral judgements' (*M M* 14/9/68), the album eventually appeared on 6 December 1968 in a plain white sleeve. The original sleeve appeared on the CD version some years later.

Decca had more problems with graphics in 1973 and blocked a plan for a naked woman to adorn the cover of Caravan's *For Girls Who Grow Plump In The Night* album. The company's Charles Webster said:

> W. H. Smith would not have carried it if it went out with a naked lady. A certain amount of moral judgement comes into this. If we think a dealer is unlikely to stock something we take a straight attitude (*M M* 8/12/73).

The idea of a "moral judgement" undermines any notion of financial considerations determining all label censorship. The passive censorial role of major retailers here should also be noted.

The cover of Gong's *Angel's Egg* album was objected to in 1973, by its distributors, EMI, because it depicted a naked woman. Gong's label, Virgin, offered to cover up the offending parts, but EMI refused this. *M M* also reported that:

> It was also planned to include a booklet containing the complete libretto, but due to the large number of four-letter words contained EMI have refused to have anything to do with this (*M M* 15/12/73).

The album was eventually released without the offending articles.

In 1980 Iron Maiden planned to feature a cartoon of their "mascot" Eddie having stabbed Margaret Thatcher for pulling down a poster of the band as the cover of their *Sanctuary* single. But its release coincided with physical attacks by skinheads on establishment figures Lord Home and Lord Chalfont and so the band and their label, EMI, imposed self-censorship and changed Thatcher's face to a more anonymous one (*Sounds* 10/5/80). In 1986 the cover of a cassette version of Elvis Costello's *Blood and Chocolate* album in the shape of a Bournville chocolate bar was changed after complaints by Cadbury's (*NME* 11/10/86).

The link between contemporary events and censorship was further highlighted in November 1987 when The Stranglers wanted to feature Monica Coughlan, the prostitute then at the centre of allegations surrounding Jeffrey Archer, on the cover of their single *All Day and All Of The Night*. The 12" version of this was to have had the catalogue number VICE1 and to feature a *Jeff Mix* of the track. Here their label, Epic, drew the line, fearing libel by association (*NME* 7/11/87). The single was held up for a month whilst a new sleeve was designed, a delay which the band later claimed hampered the single's chances of success (*NME* 23/7/88).

In 1988 Epic also vetoed a sleeve suggested for The Godfathers' *Cause I Said So* single, which featured Margaret Thatcher with a Hitler moustache. The cover change delayed the single for two weeks. Epic gave no official reason for the ban, but the possible reaction from retailers such as W. H. Smith and Boots was mooted (ibid).

Covers caused more problems in October the same year when Geffen vetoed a sleeve for Slayer's *Mandatory Suicide* single. This depicted a youth hanging from his bedroom door after receiving his call-up papers. The label seemed wary of upsetting anyone in the wake of legal action taken against Ozzy Osbourne in America (*NME* 1/10/88)[19]. But overall the censorship of covers is again illustrative of the censorial power that record companies have over what the public gets to see and hear.

Conclusion

This chapter has illustrated that companies censor for various reasons, ranging from dislike of content, covers or lack of commerciality. During punk EMI said that: "We don't release a record **only** if we feel it isn't commercial' (*The Guardian* 4/12/76), but a mixture of market and moral forces is generally in play. If the market is dominant, the acceptability of material to those who constitute the market also has to be considered. Meanwhile artists vary in the amount of intervention they will allow or need. Some will do anything to sell records, others may want more control.

The aim here has been to show the censorial outcomes of artist/company relationships. If a confusion emerges between intervention and censorship it is because there is no clear dividing line. Cutting an eight minute track down to three for the radio may be censorship if the artist is unhappy about it, but may not be if they do not mind. Clearly problems such as racism (see Hewitt 1986) and sexism (see Negus 1992 and Steward and Garratt 1986) can have a more detrimental effect on artists on a day to day basis than overt censorship does, but cases of censorship by companies need documenting in order to show that censorship occurs not only **in** the market place, but **prior** to it. The next chapter deals with problems that records can have once they reach the market place.

Notes

1. 1992, the year of the cover version, may be a paradigmatic case here. See *NME* 19/26/12/92.

2. See Harker 1980, p.104, Frith 1983, p.184 and Negus 1992, p.137 for the nature of the industry.

3. See O'Brien 1992 for more on sacked bands.

4. See *The Guardian* and *The Independent* 11/10/93 for more details of the case and ibid 19/10/93 for the case starting. See press of 22/6/94 and *NME* 12/7/94 for its conclusion.

5. See *Vox* November 1992 for Radiohead having to re-record *Creep* without the word "fuck" for its release as a single.

6. CBS also claimed to have "The Revolutionaries" on its roster, Goodwin 1988.

7. See Tynan 1988, pp.236-242 for the first televised "fuck".

8. Radio 1 producer Tim Blackmore said that Madonna was able to get away with swearing 'because she has enormous commercial power', Radio 1 1993a. Frith 1983, p.135 and Negus 1992, p.158 note the great disparities in earnings (and thus power) within the industry.

9. For example see both *The Daily Telegraph* and *Daily Mirror* 8/12/76.

10. See Negus 1992, pp.48, 148 and 149 for the relationship between A&R and marketing departments.

11. Robinson later said that EMI made the decision in order to get radio plays, Radio 1 1993a.

12. *No One Is Innocent* is also known as *The Biggest Blow - A Punk Prayer*. See Savage 1991, p.565.

13. For more on Blood and Honour see G. Marshall 1991, p.140 and *The Guardian* 14/9/92 and 30/10/93.

14. I am grateful to Keith Negus for this reference.

15. For an example of Savoy's censorship problems see *IOC*, Vol.20, No.10, November/December 1990, p.53.

16. For more on Fierce see *NME* 9/4/88 and 2/7/88.

17. See *NME* 8/8/92 for Ice T leaving Warners. See *NME* from May 1992 until the end of the year for the *Cop Killer* controversy.

18. The Minister was John Major, who later instigated libel proceedings against the *New Statesman* and *Scallywag* for printing the allegations.

19. For cases involving Osbourne see Cosgrove 1986, p.13, *NME* 1/6/91 and Walser 1993, pp.145-151.

4 'I'm sorry sir, we don't stock that' – retail policy towards popular music

By 1992 Britain's record shops were divisible into three categories; the major chains specializing in music related products (e.g. HMV and Our Price), the generalist chains selling music alongside a variety of other products (e.g. Boots and Woolworths) and the independent record shops of various sizes (e.g. Manchester's Eastern Bloc and Liverpool's Probe). The last group contains those shops where the consumer will be able to buy various non-chart artists which the larger stores may not stock.

This division incorporates market censorship, as the chain stores often offer a limited form of consumerism and make deliberate decisions not to stock various artists. Often "choice" involves only records which are already in the charts. The "generalists" guard their reputations as "family stores" and will refuse to stock a product which carries warning stickers about "explicit lyrics". For example, Boots do not stock such product as: 'We do not consider it ethical to stock merchandise which would offend the families that shop at Boots' (Boots 1991).

This attitude is typical of the major chain stores. For example, in 1980 HMV explained their decision not to sell Crass records by reference to the market. A memo to staff said: 'The question is does the commercial advantage of selling Crass records outweigh the risk of prosecution?' (*Sounds* 7/6/80). But the slight risk of being prosecuted was not the primary concern of HMV - their image, and hence profit margin, was. The market enters as censor because had Crass been likely to sell more records then perhaps "the commercial advantage" **would** have outweighed the risk of prosecution.

The previous chapter noted labels' censorship of covers and covers have also lain behind decisions by retailers not to stock records. In November 1968 *MM* reported that 'a number of record shops ... in various provincial towns' (*MM* 9/11/68) had refused to stock Jimi Hendrix's *Electric Ladyland* album, because the cover featured 21 nude women. Note again here the importance of locality. The same year John Lennon's *Wedding Album* was only available by mail order to avoid retailer objections to its cover, which featured him and Yoko Ono nude (*MM* 21/12/68). In January 1976 Boxer released their first album. The cover featured a naked spread-eagled woman with a boxing glove over her crotch. The band's label covered up parts of the cover, but *NME* reported that 'some multiple stores are adamantly refusing to stock it' (7/2/76).

In 1985 a single by The Ex Pistols, some of the Sex Pistols' former associates, called *Land of Hope and Glory* was banned by HMV and Woolworths because of obscenities on the back cover (*NME* 16/2/85). 1987 saw Guns 'n' Roses' *Appetite For Destruction* banned by W. H. Smith because its cover featured a robot raping a woman (*NME* 1/8/87). The Beautiful South had problems with the cover of their 1989 eponymous debut album, featuring a woman with a gun in her mouth and a man smoking a joint. This was replaced with a picture of two teddy bears cuddling because 'several shops' had declined to stock the original cover (*NME* 11/11/89). In 1992 some stores made Chrysalis obscure a reference to condoms on the cover of Carter The Unstoppable Sex Machine's *Only Living Boy in New Cross* single (*Vox* June 1992) and several shops refused to stock Sonic Youth's *Dirty* album because of "offensive" photographs on the cover (*MM* 15/8/92).

The sexual nature of many of the covers here meant that those retailers who sought a "family" clientele would not stock them for fear of offending customers, especially those with children. But the net result was censorship, however subsequently justified. Such censorship varies from retailer to retailer.

The "generalists"

Boots: Britain's biggest retail chain in 1992 (Blackhurst 1993)[1] definitely sees itself as a family orientated store. Music is a secondary concern, present only in some of its branches and, perhaps unsurprisingly therefore, it has tended to take a somewhat cavalier attitude towards music and has often censored product. It sold Hendrix's *Electric Ladyland,* but only in a brown paper bag (*M M* 9/11/68). In July 1972 it would not stock Nilsson's *Son of Schmilsson* album because one track, *You're Breaking My Heart,* contained the phrase "fuck you". Boots commented that: 'The situation will remain that way until the word on the record and booklet of lyrics is removed' (*M M* 29/7/72) and thus called for the direct censorship of a record.

Boots was among the stores that refused to stock Peter Cook and Dudley Moore's *Derek and Clive* album (*NME* 25/9/76) and during punk it joined other major retailers in banning The Sex Pistols' *God Save The Queen* (*NME* 4, 11, 18 and 25/6/77) and *Never Mind The Bollocks.*

In 1984 Boots stopped stocking The Smiths' eponymous debut album and the single *Heaven Knows I'm Miserable Now,* because both contained a track about the Moors Murders - *Suffer Little Children.* After complaints from one of the victim's family, Boots withdrew the single because its lyrics were 'offensive to the family' (*M M* 15/9/84). By 1991 this family store did not even consider stocking stickered albums, including Guns 'n' Roses' *Use Your Illusion* albums (*The Guardian* 30/10/92).

W. H. Smith: This chain's history of censorship goes back to its days as a newspaper and books outlet on railway stations (O'Higgins 1972, p.73). In 1991 it had a market share of 8.2% in UK music (*Music and Copyright* 12/9/92). Like Boots, it elected to sell Hendrix's *Electric Ladyland* in a brown paper bag (*NME* 9/11/68) and declined to sell the *Derek and Clive* album (*NME* 25/9/76). Its attitude to punk bordered on the paranoiac. Not only did it refuse to stock The Sex Pistols' *God Save The Queen* single and *Bollocks* album (*NME* 11/6/77 and 22/10/77), but some of its branches also left a blank space in some shop chart lists where *God Save The Queen* should have been (Coon 1982, p.90).

It also banned Guns 'n' Roses' *Appetite For Destruction* (*NME* 1/8/87), King Kurt's *Big Cock* (the cover featured a large cockerel) (*NME* 22/10/88) and NWA's *Just Don't Bite It* (*NME* 13/10/90). But whilst veering toward the censorial, double standards, not any principled stand, emerge: it has resisted attempts by the CAP to get it to remove soft porn from its top shelves. W. H. Smith sells porn, but not some pop.

The idea of the market as a censor was reflected in a letter I received from the company which said that it was unlikely to stock hardcore rap or metal records as they had 'an extremely low market potential' for the firm (W. H. Smith 1992). It thus contributes to the marginalization of such genres.

Woolworths: Owned by the Kingfisher group this chain held 18.9% of the British music market in 1992 (*Music and Copyright* 12/9/92) and aims its music sections at the teen market (ibid). It feels that it is impossible to monitor the vast amount of product that comes out each year but told me that:

> Woolworths is a family store and as such, our suppliers, in conjunction with our Entertainment Department, do attempt to identify before release any items which contain contentious lyrics. If we are able to do this we pressurise the record companies to sticker the product with warnings. In some cases, we may decide not to stock the item at all (Woolworths 1991).

The term "contentious lyrics" allows plenty of room for discretion, but Woolworths at least entertains the idea that, once informed of potential offence, customers can make their own minds up about whether or not to buy.

Woolworths were ambivalent in their attitude towards The Sex Pistols. Whilst they banned *God Save The Queen* and *Bollocks* (*NME* 22/10/77 and 4 and 11/11/77), in 1980 they cashed in on the band's notoriety. An advertisement in that year advertised their *Rock 'N' Roll Swindle* soundtrack for sale at a reduced price with the slogan "How Low Can The Sex Pistols Sink?" (*NME* 28/6/80). Once the initial fuss had faded Woolworths returned to letting the profit motive take precedence.

But not totally. Woolworths still reserve the right to censor. It exercised this right in 1984 with The Smiths' records referred to in the Boots section (*NME* 16/2/85) and The Ex Pistols record (*NME* 15/9/84). In 1990 it banned NWA's *Just Don't Bite It*, commenting that: 'It's certainly not the kind of thing we would dream of stocking in our family stores' (*NME* 20/10/90). So again the "family" appears as a censorial excuse. The next year Woolworths only stocked De La Soul's *Is Dead* album on the condition that it was stickered and it placed "Over 18" stickers on albums such as Anthrax's *Attack of The Killer Bees* and Skid Row's *Slave To The Grime* (Longrigg 1991).

The specialists

HMV: Owned by EMI, this chain had a market share of 11.2% in 1991 (Negus and du Gay 1994 p.401). In 1979 it advertised the Sex Pistols' *Bollocks* LP in its sale, modestly calling it *Never Mind* (*NME* 14/7/79), but this limited liberalism ended in 1980 when HMV became embroiled in controversy over the Poison Girls/Crass single *Persons Unknown/Bloody Revolutions*. The Poison Girls' Vi Subversa obtained a copy of a letter apparently from John Tyrell, HMV's MD, telling staff to either destroy copies of the record, or send them to head office for destruction (*Sounds* 7/6/80). HMV seemed to fear prosecution, although it admitted that the chances of this were "slight" (*NME* 14/6/80). The letter actually emanated from Brian McLaughlin, an executive under Tyrell, and stipulated that Crass records were not to be sold (*Sounds* 21/6/80). In 1982 when the Crass free flexi single *Sheep Farming In The Falklands* was covertly placed in shops across the country it was reported that 'at the HMV Shop in Oxford Street, any copies found on the premises are immediately destroyed' (19/6/82).

HMV stocked The Smiths' *Suffer Little Children* which other majors banned (*NME* 15/9/84), but in 1985 they refused to sanction The Ex Pistols' single (*NME* 16/2/85). In late 1986 the censorial wind really started to blow through HMV. In December they refused to issue the Fuck Facts newspaper that came free with the Dead Kennedy's *Bedtime For Democracy* album and, ironically, dealt with the band's censorship problems in America. The band responded by instructing their label, Alternative Tentacles, not to let HMV have any of their product.

It seems likely that the word "fuck" upset HMV, as they refused to stock Big Black's *Songs About Fucking* in September 1987 because of the title (*NME* 26/9/87). It was then revealed that HMV had compiled an Obscene Product list, which was dated 16 February 1987 and included all records on the Crass label, all Dead Kennedys records, Conflict's *Increase The Pressure*, Microdisney's *We Hate You White South African Bastards*, Ian Dury's *Four Thousand Week Holiday* and various punk and satanic metal records (*NME* 3/10/87).

HMV explained that it was bound by the Obscene Publications Act and that:

Whatever the artistic merit of this product, the fact that it could find its way into the hands of young children is something that should concern us all (ibid)(2).

So the slight risk of prosecution was mixed with moralizing over the welfare of children to excuse censorial action. This was shown to be somewhat hypocritical in autumn 1990 when HMV gave away an in-house copy of *Q* magazine which included a Bob Geldof interview containing various swear words. The fact that this could fall into the hands of children did **not** appear to be "something that should concern us all".

HMV also withdrew copies of Flux's *The Fucking Cunts Treat Us Like Pricks* from sale in October 1987 (*NME* 10/10/87) and did not stock Dead Kennedy's singer Jello Biafra's anti-censorship *No More Cocoons* album (*NME* 28/11/87). It also joined the boycott of NWA's *Just Don't Bite It* (*NME* 13/10/90).

HMV do not feel obliged to explain their policies to potential customers. I was advised that 'the stocking policy of HMV is confidential and we are unable to make comment on it' (HMV 1991) and told that:

> ... as retailers HMV are liable for prosecution under the Obscene Publications Act for selling product deemed to be obscene. Therefore to protect our staff from possible prosecution HMV reserve the right to withdraw certain product (ibid).

Our Price: This chain started in 1971 and became part of the W. H. Smith group in 1986. By 1992 it had 318 shops in Britain and the largest market share of any of the specialist chains - 10.5% (*Music and Copyright* 12/9/92). Its stocking policy has attracted little press attention, although it refused to stock Flux's *Fucking Cunts* in 1984 (*NME* 12/5/84) and only stocks singles that have already charted. It has also been accused by the chairman of the BPI of treating music like baked beans (Negus and du Guy 1994, p.395). Its position on censorship is that, whilst not wishing to act as censors:

> ... we would not wish to offend any of our customers and have issued guidelines in order to avoid such situations. These guidelines are based on freedom of expression under the law (Our Price 1992).

It sold NWA's *Efil4zaggin* album after it was cleared in its obscenity trial and generally leaves censorship to the market.

Virgin: This chain is unusual for a major retailer in having broken the law by selling bootlegs in its early days when owner Richard Branson let store managers decide whether to stock them (*MM* 20/11/71 and *NME* 9/5/92). But as Branson sought media respectability Virgin adopted a more censorial attitude. In 1982 it took the unusual step of distancing itself from the free Crass flexi-disk, *Sheep Farming In The Falklands* (*NME* 19/6/82). In August 1987 it dropped plans for window displays featuring the controversial cover of Guns 'n' Roses' *Appetite For Destruction* (*NME* 1/8/87). A month later it refused to stock Big Black's *Songs About Fucking*, not because of its title, but because on the inner sleeve group leader Steve Albini advocated using heroin (*NME* 26/9/87).

Virgin commented that:

> We have no blacklist, we don't want to dictate people's taste. If the word "fuck" is on the sleeve then there's a chance we won't stock it ... but there are no hard and fast rules (*NME* 3/10/87).

So the right to censor was upheld. Virgin shops were bought by W. H. Smith in 1988, who also bought a half share in their Megastore chain in 1991 (*The Guardian* 9/9/91). In 1992 that chain banned Cannibal Corpse's *Tomb of The Mutilated* (Heller 1992 p.4).

The independents and others

One result of the reluctance of many of the chain stores to stock punk records, and of major labels to sign punks, was a growth of both independent shops and labels. By 1992 such shops formed an alternative outlet for smaller labels that the majors could not or would not deal with. The independents have tended to have a more liberal stocking policy, not necessarily for ideological reasons, but for commercial ones - they can not afford **not** to sell records. For example, during punk the independents were of vital import in circumventing the majors' bans on *God Save The Queen* (*NME* 25/6/77).

The cost of this more liberal stocking policy has sometimes been an appearance in the censorial firing line. Mike Lloyd Music in

Newcastle Under Lyme received a phone call in 1977 threatening to fire bomb the shop if they continued to stock punk records (*NME* 3/9/77) and London's Small Wonder was raided by police for stocking The Sex Pistols' *Bollocks* album (Savage 1991, p.424). Because the censorial process often works backwards, from retailer to publisher, shops can find themselves at the forefront of censorship cases. In May 1980 it was reported that Birmingham police had been monitoring shops selling Crass records (*Sounds* 13/5/80), whilst in 1984 came the Spectrum/Crass, and in 1987/88 the Eastern Bloc/Flux, cases which are dealt with below.

Somewhat understandably, in October 1988 many retailers refused to stock the single *Eternal Nightmare* by US metal band Violence - because it came with a free bag of fake vomit (*NME* 29/10/80). Menzies refused to stock NWA's *Just Don't Bite It* (*NME* 13/10/90), as did the Midlands chain, Music Junction. The latter's owner, Bob Barnes, said they were 'not going to risk criminal charges' by stocking it (*NME* 10/11/90) and that as the law was too vague: 'We need some kind of censorship along the same lines as the video industry' (Halassa 1990b).

Many retailers were wary of a law that appeared too vague. The "tendency to deprave and corrupt" on which British obscenity law hinges has alarmed them, as was evidenced by a statement from the British Association Of Record Dealers (BARD) in December 1990 which called for a ratings systems for records - similar to that used for videos. This followed concerns over *Just Don't Bite It*[3]. Barnes said that 'for our own protection we've got to be seen to be making sure the things we consider obscene aren't sold' (*NME* 8/12/90).

Little has come of a ratings system so far and it seems unlikely in Britain. Too many problems connected with what criteria to use, who would do it and so on remain. Most importantly there may not be enough political capital to made out of introducing such a system. But the issue of what shops should do with records which could be deemed offensive carries on and there has already been an increase in the stickering of albums. Reactions to this are mixed. Some feel the "forbidden fruit" aspect of stickering records makes them more attractive to some customers[4]. Others argue that a chill factor may be involved and that stickered albums put off retailers who may decide not to take the (limited) risk of prosecution or the (greater) risk of offending customers (Gilliam 1991 and Wells 1987b).

Whatever the policy, stickering is a censorship issue. It is the equivalent of putting product on the top shelf or under the counter. It marks out certain records as "unclean" and thus liable to chain store boycotts. As a spin off of the PMRC's actions in America(5), it is also another instance of American censorship affecting Britain. The net effect of this is not only denial of consumer choice, but also a contribution to the ghettoizing of the music concerned. The customer who is denied the chance to buy, for example, Flux or rave records at Our Price has no effective complaint mechanism and the history of British record shop censorship is one centred upon a denial of choice.

The paternalism and professed concern for the welfare of staff and customers often masks an attitude which puts profit before artistic freedom(6). Whilst retailers cite the Obscene Publications Act in their censorial actions, few records are prosecuted and thus far, it has been independent retailers, who can least afford it, that have been hit when prosecutions for obscenity have been made. The paranoid might even feel that this apparent policy of picking on the smallest first is deliberate. Perhaps it is just the law's way ...

Notes

1. In 1991 Boots had 4% of the music marker, Negus and du Gay 1994, p.401.

2. See also Denselow 1989, p.272.

3. *M M* 15/6/91 claimed that '60 per cent' of retailers had refused to stock this record.

4. For example John Peel has spoken of swearing making records more attractive to adolescents. See also Longrigg 1991 and Holden 1993.

5. For the PMRC's stickering campaign see Denselow 1989, pp.265-9.

6. Negus and du Gay 1994, p.408 note the importance of not alienating customers. Denselow 1989, pp.211/2 notes shops refusing to stock Billy Bragg's *Brewing Up With* album because is was priced at £2.99.

5 'I fought the law' – pop into Court

The major piece of British legislation dealing with obscenity, and covering records, is the 1959 Obscene Publications Act. This defines an obscene article as one which, taken as a whole, tends to "deprave and corrupt" those who are likely to come into contact with it. Articles seized can be destroyed under Section 3 of the Act, which instigates proceedings at a Magistrates Court where a defendant has to show good reason why the material should not be forfeited. The proceedings apply only to those items seized. A prosecution under Section 2 is more serious, involving a High Court, jury, trial which can lead to an unlimited fine and imprisonment(1).

The Act's subjective nature has led to much criticism. One problem is that there is no way a retailer or publisher can find out in advance if an article is "obscene" - only the courts can decide that. The police's attitude to the law varies from force to force (again illustrating the way locality affects British censorship), but once a complaint has been made they are obliged to act. After raiding the police generally send material to the Director of Public Prosecutions (DPP) where decisions on whether or not to prosecute, and, if so, under which section, are made.

The complainant then becomes that almost mythical creature "a member of the public"(2) who contacts their local police and asks for action against an allegedly "obscene" article. The police are not obliged to reveal who complained, which means that their identity in particular cases is hard to ascertain. But evidence suggests that the pressure groups I discuss elsewhere often lie behind attempts to prosecute.

The first case of censorship to note concerns libel rather than the

1959 Act. In 1979 Roy Harper had to remove the track *Watford Gap* from his *Bullinamingvase* album. The song alleged that the Gap's service station served up 'crap' and 'grease and excrement' as food. Its owners, Blue Boar, sued EMI for this 'totally unjustified attack' (*NME* 3/2/79). EMI offered no contest, removed the track, made a donation to charity and paid the court costs. But more important than libel cases are attempts to prosecute pop for obscenity.

The Sex Pistols: "Never Mind The Bollocks"

The first prosecution of a record for obscenity came during punk and concerned The Sex Pistols. Their first album, *Never Mind The Bollocks Here's The Sex Pistols*, was released on Friday 28 October 1977. Ironically, it was neither "controversial" tracks such as *God Save The Queen*, nor the plethora of "fucks" in the track *Bodies*, but the word "bollocks" on the cover which brought the prosecution. However, bearing in mind Fabbri's comments on the importance of covers (see above) and the impression that the band were trying to create, the cover was undoubtedly part of their "message" and so the attempt to censor it was effectively an attempt to censor that message.

On Saturday, 5 November 1977 policewoman Julie Dawn Story saw a window display of the covers in Virgin Records' Nottingham branch and informed its manager Chris Searle that this was an offence under the Indecent Advertising Act of 1899. In London Virgin and Small Wonder record shops were also visited by plain clothes policemen (Savage 1991, p.425). When Searle returned the *Bollocks* covers to his window display on November 9 he was arrested and charged under the 1899 Act .

The case was heard at Nottingham Magistrates Court on 24 November 1977. Virgin's defence lawyer was John Mortimer QC, who had defended the *Oz* case. The prosecution unsuccessfully tried to make much of the fact that the word "fuck" appeared on the album (*NME* 3/12/77) - but this was irrelevant to the case. Expert witnesses who appeared included James Kingsley, Professor of English at Nottingham University. He testified that the word "bollocks" was a thousand year old Anglo-Saxon word which originally meant a small ball (ibid). In conclusion Kingsley said that he would 'take the title to mean: Never Mind the Nonsense here's the Sex Pistols' (Savage

1991, p.425).

This now seems so obvious that it is hard to see why the case was ever brought. Mortimer's summing up speech speculated that: 'It was because it was The Sex Pistols and not Donald Duck or Kathleen Ferrier that the prosecution was brought' (ibid. Emphasis mine).

This contentious point is supported by the evidence. The Sex Pistols were at this time under the media's spotlight. Records and gigs were censored and band members physically attacked. It appeared that, other censorial agencies having done their work on the Pistols, it was now the turn of the law.

But it failed. The case was dismissed by the magistrates. However, the senior magistrate said that:

> Much as my colleagues and I wholeheartedly deplore the vulgar exploitation of the worst instincts of human nature ... we must reluctantly find you not guilty on each of the four charges (*NME* 3/12/77. Emphasis mine).

With the cover cleared displays of it continued. Pop's next trip to court concerned the music itself, or at least the lyrical content. This time the prosecution was to be successful.

The Anti Nowhere League: "So What"

Punk band The Anti Nowhere League released their debut single, a cover of Ralph McTell's *Streets Of London* backed with their own composition *So What*, on the WXYZ label in December 1981. In late January 1982 it reached No. 1 in the *NME*'s Independent Chart. On 12 February, the Metropolitan Police raided a number of premises in London, including WXYZ's offices, the distributors, Faulty Products', offices and the pressing plant and seized copies of the single under the 1959 Act.

They acted after what Faulty Products believed were complaints by 'a number of public citizens' (*MM* 20/2/81). In this case there is evidence to identify the complainant. Whitehouse (1982) alludes to the record in her book, *A Most Dangerous Woman?* (pp.132-133), but neglects to mention the title. However a letter from NVALA confirmed that they instigated the case (Beyer 1992). Whitehouse pressed for a prosecution under Section 2 of the 1959 Act, her concern being 'children who buy such records' (Whitehouse 1982, p.132. Emphasis mine). But the police opted for a forfeiture under Section 3.

Bromley magistrates heard this first attempt to prosecute a record under the 1959 Act and found that it **did** fall within the ambit of that Act, in having the necessary "tendency to deprave and corrupt". Although WXYZ initially planned to appeal to the High Court it appears that no such appeal was ever launched - possibly due to the potential costs involved for a relatively small label. The seized copies were destroyed (*NME* 3/7/83).

But this was not the end of the story. In July 1983 the band tried to include *So What* on their *Live In Yugoslavia* album. Again police raided WXYZ and the distributors and seized 5,000 copies of the LP. Three months later a compromise was reached and it was released, with the five supposedly obscene words bleeped (*NME* 24/9/83). However it was further delayed when staff at the Damont pressing plant refused to handle it, although it was later pressed by Orlake and went on to top the *NME* Independent Charts. So why the fuss?

So What sets a young man's exploits to a punk back-beat. The singer asks "So fucking what?" as the song begins and then recites his exploits which include fellatio on an old man, bestiality, drinking urine, injecting heroin, getting pubic lice and VD, and under age sex with a schoolgirl. To all these admissions the singer retorts: "So what - you boring little cunt?". The general tone of the record could fairly be described as "over the top" and it verges on punk parody throughout.

The narrator's boasts are as much improbable as impressive. The tone is: "I've done all these things and I don't give a fuck, what have you done?" It is not a particularly articulate lyric, still less is it impressive musically, yet it is hard to see it as "depraving and corrupting". To do so the Bromley magistrates must have taken the lyrics at face value with no regard for context or the exaggerated bragging style of the singer. They clearly missed the parody here.

More pertinently *So What* does not appear to meet the criterion for obscenity laid down by the 1959 Act. This requires consideration of the effect on "persons who are likely, having regard to all relevant circumstances, to read, see or hear the matter contained or embodied in it". The band's audience would primarily have consisted of hard-core punks (not the children Whitehouse mentions) who were unlikely to be depraved and corrupted by swearing. In any case, swear words are **not** enough to make an article obscene under the terms of the Act, as was noted in the case discussed next. But this did not prevent the prosecution of a record which had already sold 36,000 copies (*NME* 25/9/82).

So What has the distinction of being the first record in Britain to be convicted under its obscenity laws. But the 1959 Act was also used against another relatively obscure band in the 1980s.

Spectrum Records and Crass

In August 1984 police raided the Spectrum Records shop in Northwich, Cheshire, and seized 19 records by artists such as Crass, the Dead Kennedys, Icons of Filth and Crucifix. This allegedly came 'after the father of a boy who had bought a record had complained to the police' (*Sounds* 8/9/84), but the fact that much of the material involved here was overtly anarchist was not lost on those subsequently involved in the case. Shop owner Graham Cheadle was charged under Section 3 of the 1959 Act and had to appear before magistrates to show good reason why the seized records should not be destroyed.

The case came before Northwich magistrates on 30 August, 1984. Cheadle was found guilty, had the seizure order against his stock upheld and was ordered to pay costs of £100. The magistrates opined that 'there is a lowering of standards and we feel we should do our best to halt such a fall ... It's in young people's interests that we do so' (*NME* 8/7/84) - an expression of ethical evangelism **not** required by the 1959 Act.

Crass, whose records were seized, were amongst those who believed that the case had political overtones. Band member Penny Rimbaud claimed that: 'we've been picked on because we are a small label and we've taken a stand about real obscenities like the Falklands war' (*Sounds* 8/9/84). Rimbaud's theory was given credence when the defence played parts of one of Peter Cook and Dudley Moore's swearing filled *Derek and Clive* albums to the magistrates, whose reasoning in deeming these legal and the seized albums illegal was hard to follow.

Crass set out to back an appeal and enlisted the support of the independent network. Their objectives were:

(a) to get the verdict reversed and (b) to defend the rights of retailers, labels and distributors to handle the material of their own choice, free from the risk of prosecution (*NME* 27/10/84)(3).

Labels, such as Abstract, Alternative Tentacles, Factory and Fast Forward donated money to the defence. The appeal was granted and heard at Chester Crown Court, before Judge Robin David, on 4 January 1985.

Crass' lawyers believed that they had good grounds for appealing because the magistrates had misdirected the original case by talking of the lowering of standards in society. They opined that 'the Court applied the wrong test and were concerned only to find four letter words without considering the underlying message' (Foskett, Marr, Gadsby and Head 1984).

The judge ruled that the magistrates **had** wrongly singled out the swearing without considering the context and likely audience. Cheadle had meanwhile withdrawn from his appeal without telling the court and so forfeiture orders against his stock were upheld. A policeman, acting as a DJ, played the records to Judge David and two magistrates. The judge concluded that only one was obscene. Records cleared included Crass' *Sheep Farming In The Falklands, Whodunnit* and *Bullshit Two*, Dirt's *Never Mind The Dirt, Here's The Bollocks* and the Icons Of Filth's *Used, Abused and Unamused*. The record found to be obscene was Crass' album, *Penis Envy*. In particular the judge said that the first track on the album, *Bata Motel*, was 'quite clearly obscene' (*Sounds* 19/1/85). Again this appears contrary to the 1959 Act which requires the work to be taken "as a whole".

The judge said the cleared records were 'crude, vulgar and they consist to a large extent of abusive rubbish but they don't tend to deprave and corrupt' and ruled that 'bad language does not satisfy the test of obscenity' (ibid). But he refused costs to Crass' distribution company, Exit Stencil Ltd., because they had 'been trading on the borders of obscenity' (ibid). As the case was brought under Section 3 it only applied to the seized stock.

Crass felt vindicated as their two aims, of overturning the original verdict and showing that the independent network could work together to defend artistic freedom, had largely been achieved. But the case proved expensive for them, costing in the region of £5,000 (Crass 1991). This caused a sense of weariness and demoralization in their ranks, which resulted in them abandoning their musical activities.

They were also left with the impression that the Court was reluctant to let them get away scot-free and so convicted a record that would not normally be found to be obscene. Certainly the singling out of *Bata Motel* which contains no swearing, unlike other tracks on the album, was strange. The album's tone is avowedly feminist and *Bata Motel* is a spoof of marriage and/or prostitution in which the female singer invites the listener to use and abuse her in various ways. It is hardly subtle, but again its parodic quality seemed to escape the Court. Once again the only way to find this track "obscene" would to be to take it purely at face value. Even given a misunderstanding of the genre such a mistake seems hard to make. Thus Crass' belief that *Bata Motel* was found guilty because the Court wanted to salvage **something** from the prosecution gains plausibility. It remains one of only two records successfully prosecuted under the Act - but there were other attempts to legally define pop as obscene.

Eastern Bloc and A Flux of Pink Indians

Punk band A Flux of Pink Indians released their album *The Fucking Cunts Treat Us Like Pricks* on the One Little Indian label in the spring of 1984. The band had a confrontational approach, and the title was the culmination of this, being inspired by the problems the band were having with violence at its gigs. Band member Derek Birkett (1991) later admitted that the title was somewhat heavy handed, but said that this was a deliberate, Dadaist style, ploy to get publicity and thus the album's feminist message into places it might not otherwise reach.

The album's title certainly attracted publicity. HMV and Our Price refused to stock it and an unsuccessful attempt was made to prosecute a shop in Scotland for selling it (*NME* 12/7/87). As major retailers refused to stock the album, it was mainly available through independent local record shops, including Manchester's Eastern Bloc, which specialized in independent music and also sold magazines, including anarchist ones. Its owners believed that it was this activity that first aroused the interest of Manchester police, whose Chief Constable was the renowned puritanical Christian James Anderton. His influence here again links religion and censorship and shows the

81

effect of locality on the censorial climate[4].

In September 1987[5], four years after the album's release, police raided Eastern Bloc, after an alleged complaint from "a member of the public". Although a large amount of stock was examined only the Flux album was seized. Martin Price, one of the shop's three joint-owners, was warned that he could face prosecution under the Obscene Publications Act or for indecent display - as the cover had been displayed in the shop's window. Again the independent network helped out. One Little Indian organized a Defence Fund and told companies who did not contribute that it would go through their catalogues looking for potentially obscene material and start to bring prosecutions against them.

The album was sent to the DPP, who decided that a case under the 1959 Act was not viable. Manchester police then decided to prosecute for "obscene display" and this case came to court in September 1988. Price conducted his own defence in the Magistrates Court, which soon led to an adjournment. The case suffered further adjournments and this led the police to drop it because it was costing too much. Price felt that this meant that morality could be bought, as he had been willing to go to court to defend his morality, but the police had put a price tag on theirs (Price 1991).

This was not Eastern Bloc's last encounter with Manchester police. In January 1990 it was charged, under the 1981 Local Government (Miscellaneous Provisions) Act, with selling tickets for illegal raves. This prosecution was brought privately by Anderton himself (*NME* 13/1/90), fuelling the shop's belief in a vendetta against it. Again censorship proved to be locally mediated. Certainly with Anderton as Chief Constable Manchester was often at the forefront of the battle against all things "obscene", with pop being one of those alleged obscenities.

Earache Records

The Nottingham based Earache Records label specializes in Death and Speed Metal and much of the material it releases takes Heavy Metal to its (il)logical extremes[6]. Its acts include Napalm Death, Lawnmower Deth and Sore Throat, makers of the 101 track CD *Disgrace To the Corpse Of Sid* album. Earache is a label whose tongue is firmly in its cheek.

On 27 March 1991 its offices were raided by police with a warrant to look for "obscene articles and associated documentation kept for gain". A large amount of stock was seized, including demo tapes sent in by unknown bands, covers of LPs by groups such as the Filthy Christians and Torture Garden and an Alice Cooper poster, complete with blu-tak! (see photocopies of warrant and schedule overleaf pp.82-84).

Most of this was soon returned but three covers were kept and sent on to the DPP for possible prosecution under the 1959 Act. These covers were from Carcass' *Reek of Putrification* (featuring a collage of dismembered and scarred body parts, knives, charred bodies, etc.), their *Symphonies of Sickness* (here a plain black cover opens up to reveal a collage of meat, eyes, maggot infested faces etc.) and Cadaver's *Hallucinating Anxiety* (here an animal's eye, maggots and parts of an animal's brain are spread on a sheet).

The covers are not exactly pleasant to look at, but it is hard to see how any of them could pass the legal criterion of having "a tendency to deprave and corrupt". Nausea is a more likely outcome than corruption. As such a prosecution under the 1959 Act always looked likely to fail, which raises the question of why Earache were raided. This time the ubiquitous "member of the public" was not mentioned Instead it seems that Nottingham Police were tipped off by Customs who earlier in the year had confiscated two photographs of autopsies, which were sent to Earache for consideration as album covers by American musician John Zorn. The threat of prosecuting the covers could be seen as a warning and certainly both Earache and Carcass subsequently adopted a more cautious approach to what they deemed as suitable material for their covers.

But the DPP could find no case for them to answer. The case fizzled out in November 1991 when the police telephoned Earache and told them to collect their stock. Carcass (1991) strongly argued that the covers were part of their overall statement and so attempts to censor the covers were effectively attempts to censor the band itself. Meanwhile, another form of confrontational music, rap, was rising. It was this music that led to what is arguably the most significant legal case surrounding allegedly "obscene" pop music thus far in Britain.

WARRANT TO ENTER AND SEARCH PREMISES

(P.A.C.E. Act 1984 s.15)

COUNTY OF NOTTINGHAM

PETTY SESSIONAL DIVISION OF...NOTTINGHAM...........................(CODE

On this day an application was made by: (specify name of applicant)

SHARON ELIZABETH BIDDULPH, WPC 89

for the issue of a warrant under (state enactment under which warrant is to be issued)

SECTION 3 OBSCENE PUBLICATIONS ACT 1959

to enter and search the premises situated at (specify premises)

EAR ACHE RECORDS, ROOM 19, WESTMINSTER BUILDINGS, THEATRE SQUARE, NOTTINGHAM.

and search for (identify, so far as possible the articles or persons to be sought)
OBSCENE ARTICLES AND ASSOCIATED DOCUMENTATION KEPT FOR GAIN.

Authority is hereby given for any constable, accompanied by such person or persons as are necessary for the purposes of the search, to enter the said premises on one occasion only within one month from the date of issue of this warrant and to search for the articles or persons in respect of which the above application is made. A copy of this warrant should be left with the occupier of the premises or, in his absence, a person who appears to be in charge of the premises or, if no such person is present, in a prominent place on the premises
Authority is also given to any such constable to enter the said premises if need be by force, and to search the premises and any person found therein.

Dated the 27.3.

Issued at 10 a.m./p.m.

Justice of the Peace.

See Over for Articles Found or Seized.

Certified a True Copy

84

VICE SQUAD PROPERTY SCHEDULE.

OFFICER IN CHARGE: PW 89 BIDDULPH OFFICER DEALING: PW 89 BIDDULPH

TIME AND DATE: 1025 HRS 27TH MARCH 1991

LOCATION: EARACHE RECORDS, RM 19, WESTMINSTER BAGS, NOT

O.T.F.P. No 49121 WHERE PROPERTY STORED: VICE SQUAD OFFICE

ITEMS	DESCRIPTION
1	12 × filthy Christians LP Sleeves
2	12 × filthy Christians LP records
3	5 × Torture garden LP Sleeves
4	5 × Torture garden LP records
5	6 × Hallucinating anxiety LP Sleeves
6	6 × Hallucinating anxiety LP records
7	16 × Carcass ~~Sleev~~ LP Sleeves
8	15 × Carcass LP records
9	24 × Symphonies of Sickness LP Sleeves
10	24 × Symphonies of Sickness LP records
11	1 × Meat Shits / Regurgitate Semen Cassette Case
12	1 × Reek of putrefaction Cassette Case
13	1 × Reek of putrefaction Cassette
14	16 × Torture garden Cassette Cases
15	16 × Torture garden Cassettes
16	1 × Necrotomy Cranial Dismemberment Cassette Case
17	1 × D46 TDK Cassette
18	4 × Hallucinating anxiety Cassette Cases
19	4 × Hallucinating anxiety Cassettes
20	9 × Symphonies of Sickness Cassette Cases
21	8 × Symphonies of Sickness Cassettes
22	33 × filthy Christians Cassette Cases
23	33 × filthy Christians Cassettes
24	1 × Naked City CD Case
25	1 × Naked City C.D.

O.T.F.P. No. 49.121.........

ITEM	DESCRIPTION
26	6 x Carcass CD cases
27	6 x Carcass CD's
28	6 x Filthy ~~Cities~~ Christians CD cases
29	6 x Filthy Christians CD's
30	Copies of newspaper comment (under Carcass file) (in cabinet)
31	Torture garden graphics
32	Photographs of animals? maggot infested
33	Decapitation graphic fudge tunnel
34	Alice Cooper poster (blue tak)
35	Fax copies of fender (scissors/foetus exposed) tx 18:40 Feb 18th 91
36	Address Book
37	Quantity of Naked City posters

86

Niggers With Attitude and *Efil4zaggin*

Niggers With Attitude (NWA) were a hardcore rap band from LA. By the time of the *Efil4zaggin* ("Niggaz for life" spelt backwards) case they had already been embroiled in controversy. Their first album, *Straight Outta Compton*, was critically acclaimed, but the FBI objected to one track, *Fuck Tha Police*, which, in an adapted causal argument, they claimed 'encourages violence against, and disrespect for, law enforcement officers' (Goffe 1989). When NWA played Birmingham in 1990 local councillor Alan Blumenthal tried to get the song cut from their show (Halassa 1990b). As already noted, in November 1990 many major retailers refused to stock their *100 Miles & Runnin'* single in 12 inch format, because of the track *Just Don't Bite It*.

Efil4zaggin was released in Britain, via the Island subsidiary 4th and Broadway, on Monday 3 June 1991. On Tuesday 4 June the Metropolitan Police raided the distributors, Polygram's, plant in Chadwell Heath and seized 12,000 copies of the album. This apparently followed 'a complaint to New Scotland Yard from a record dealer who had been sent an advance tape of the LP by Island Records' (*M M* 15/6/91)(7). The raid took place after a story about the record appeared in the *Daily Mail* (Marot 1991b).

It came despite the cover having two warning stickers on it, the original, PMRC derived, American warning of "Parental Advisory Explicit Lyrics" and a second from Island which read: "This record contains explicit language. It should not be played in the presence of minors!". Despite this Island was warned that it faced prosecution under the 1959 Act and copies of the record were sent to the DPP. The police expected a successful prosecution, as is shown by a letter from the Metropolitan Police to NCROPA which stated that the force had acted 'because it feels it is fully supported by existing legislation' (Metropolitan Police 1991). Article 19 and NCROPA protested against the raid, but CAP supported the police's action and described the album as: 'Open season on women' (Longrigg 1991).

The case was significant because it was the first time that a **major**, as opposed to independent, label had been involved in an obscenity case which centred on the music. Polygram, Island's owners, agreed with them on the need to defend the record. Unlike Crass, WXYZ, Eastern Bloc, and Earache, Island and Polygram could afford the finest legal representatives. They chose Geoffrey Robertson -

possibly the country's leading expert on obscenity law.

The case also got the sort of mainstream media attention that was notably absent in the Crass and Anti Nowhere League cases[8]. Island's MD, Marc Marot, determined to defend the album and attacked the BPI for adopting the "softly softly" approach of giving Island legal and media handling advice, but refusing to get publicly involved in defending the album, despite the fact that a number of BPI members such as Polygram (distributors) and MCA (publishers) had a stake in the outcome.

Marot defended the album by arguing that 'the potential to be offended is one of the prices that we pay for a free society' and favourably quoted *Music Week* editor Steve Redmond's point that, whilst the album might offend, 'it is a lot less offensive than the prospect of policemen building bonfires for pop records'. Marot summed up that: 'NWA is not great art; this is not a debate about aesthetic merit. It is about freedom of speech and your right to choose' (Marot 1991a). As noted earlier, it is interesting that the defence was couched in terms of ethics rather than aesthetics.

When, in a personal interview, I questioned Marot about the dubious morality of making money from a record that includes the killing of prostitutes and rape with a broomstick, he said that, whilst Island might make some money out of it, their prime reason for releasing the album was aesthetic. The company had a U2 LP coming out the following week and by comparison in Britain NWA were of no financial importance. Marot also pointed out that he was a well paid young man risking a possible jail term in order to stand by the album (Marot 1991b).

In the end such martyrdom was unnecessary. The case was taken down the judicial scale when the DPP decided to prosecute under Section 3 of the 1959 Act, rather than under Section 2. This meant that it was heard at a Magistrates Court and the issue was destruction of the albums, rather than involving a jury trial and a possible prison sentence. There is even evidence to suggest that the police would have dropped the case had Island agreed to the destruction of the seized copies[9]. The case was set for Redbridge Magistrates Court on 4 September, but adjourned to 7 November when magistrates ruled that the album was **not** obscene under the terms of the 1959 Act. They ordered that the confiscated stock be returned and that the Metropolitan Police pay costs of £1,000 to Island and £350 to Polygram.

During the case the record was played in court and Robertson, defending, said that rap was street journalism that sounded crude to the untrained ear, but was 'all part of the experience. It tells it like it is' (*The Guardian* 4/11/91) - a defence in line with the Millian idea of protecting free speech as part of a search for truth. Robertson compared the album to freely available pornographic magazines and said that, unlike them: 'This record arouses fear, concern and distaste. It does not arouse lust' (ibid). This proved to be the crux of the matter. The record might offend, but it did not "tend to deprave and corrupt". By law the potential audience has to be considered and the Home Office had opined that 'material which would tend to deprave and corrupt young people and was aimed at them might be caught even if it was harmless to adults' (Home Office 1991). Here Robertson successfully argued that: 'The people who are likely to hear it will be the people who are likely to seek it out' (*The Guardian* 8/11/91).

Island heralded their victory by issuing 2,000 posters defending the right to free speech (*NME* 23/11/91). However, as noted earlier, Island soon turned censor itself when it refused to issue Ice Cube's *Death Certificate* album in Britain until two tracks were taken off.

Meanwhile a spokesman for Liberty, the civil liberties group, said:

> We welcome this verdict. It was a small but important case for the industry ... NWA were lucky that Polygram were big enough to take on the Crown Prosecution Service, independent record producers couldn't possibly afford it (*NME* 16/11/91).

So again the amount of censorship artists are likely to suffer was linked to their commercial clout.

After the verdict Tory MP Sir Michael Neubert tabled a written question in the Commons asking the Home Secretary if 'in the light of the judgement in the NWA case ... he will bring forward proposals to amend the Obscene Publications Act 1959' (*Hansard* 12/11/91). Neubert wanted the law tightened as he believed that: 'This record crosses the boundary into extreme violence, and it is not something that society should condone' (*Select* January 1992). He was uncertain about how to change the law, but thought it should be via government, rather than the customary Private Member initiative (Neubert 1992).

Home Office Minister John Patten replied that he could not

comment on specific cases but that:

> The Government recognises that there is concern about the effectiveness of the Obscene Publications Act 1959. This is traditionally an area for Private members and the Government is prepared to support proposals for amendments which would make the law more effective and which appear likely to command sufficient public and parliamentary support (*Hansard* 12/11/91).

But tightening the law could hit pop and Marot has said that: 'If the law had been different at the time, we might not have put the album out at all' (*Select* January 1992).

The case was a landmark. It was the first time a major label had been forced to defend its musical output in court from charges brought under British obscenity laws. It may also mark the end of attempts to prosecute records under the 1959 Act. Certainly if *Efil4zaggin* is not "obscene", it is hard to think of a record that is. The album contains the killing of prostitutes and the portrayal of women as merely sexual pawns. Listeners are told how *To Kill A Hooker*, which will leave *One Less Bitch* to worry about. The narrator tells us of his joy when *She Swallowed It* and tells another woman *I'd Rather Fuck You*.

This is not easy listening, but neither is meant to be. It seeks to portray the reality of American low life, as it is, not as it might be. Rap is the ultimate confrontational music thus far and alienates both left and right. Whether its attempts to portray reality is the best grounds for its defence, however, remains a moot point.

Sampling: censorship via copyright?

In October 1991, as the NWA case continued, Customs seized 800 copies of Swedish death metal band Dismember's *Like An Ever Flowing Stream*. The case came before Yarmouth magistrates in August 1992. Here Stephen Harvey QC, prosecuting for Customs, used the causal argument that songs such as *Skin Her Alive* were 'liable to inspire a sense of violence in the listener' (Heller 1992, p.3). But magistrates were unconvinced and allowed the appeal by Plastic Head distributors. A Customs spokesman said: 'It's a worry for us that this sort of music can now be heard by teenagers in Britain' (ibid p.4) - again linking children with censorial intent. This case appears to have been the first example of Customs seizing a record since the Snivelling Shits' *Terminal Stupid*, which was pressed in France, was seized at Heathrow in 1977 before being allowed in (*NME* 5/11/77).

Whilst the Earache case was also linked to Customs, a more important development in censorship disputes was sampling, which rose with rap in the 1980s. Space does not permit entry into the complexity of copyright here, but Toop sums up the present (1995) legal situation, under the 1988 Copyright, Designs and Patents Act, thus:

> If the sample is qualitative a distinct sound is discernible to the average ear; or quantitative, the number of notes lifted from one track, and placed in another, or bearing a strong enough resemblance to the average ear, copyright is breached (Toop 1991(a), p.76)[10].

Frith (1988, p.72) has called the control of copyright 'a form of censorship' and it certainly has censorial implications, as being unable to sample means artists may not be able to create the music they want. A number of cases arose in the late 1980s including that of the JAMMS' album, *1987 What The Fuck's Going On*. A track here, *The Queen and I*, used large sections of ABBA's *Dancing Queen*. ABBA refused to allow this and ordered that all copies be returned and destroyed. When an attempt to meet ABBA failed the band burnt all the remaining copies they had - an event recaptured in their KLF incarnation as the track *Build A Fire* on *The White Room* album.

Most other cases so far have been settled out of court. Artists generally seem to accept being sampled as long as they are paid, although some consideration is given to whether the track is detrimental to the "original" version. Despite industry opinion that 'sampling is theft' (Andrew Jenkins, Polydor UK Legal Dept., Radio 1 22/1/91) the same sources admit that it is unlikely to stop (ibid). But *NME* has alleged that not being able to use a sample of Marc Cohn's *Walking In Memphis* stopped Shut Up and Dance's *Raving, I'm Raving* getting to No. 1 in 1992 after legal action by Cohn stopped further pressing of the record (*NME* 19-26/12/92)[11].

Sampling raises a number of issues about authorship, ownership of rights and so on[12], but the issue is also one of censorship. A common culture is being separated into ownership rights and then sold.

Ownership of rights, done in the name of protecting musicians' interests, is de facto limiting the creative potential of others. This is, at least, covert censorship by legal mechanisms, whilst more overt cases have occurred.

In August 1991 Central Television prevented Skin Up from releasing a single called *Blockbusters*, based on the television show where contestants ask the compere for clues beginning with certain letters. The record featured an acid house beat and the refrain: "I'll have an "E" please Bob" - a joke reference to ecstasy. After the *Daily Star* condemned it as 'a sick record about drugs', Central took steps to stop copies reaching the shops (*NME* 24/8/91). The same year the BBC got a court injunction preventing the release of a joke single by Verbal Vandalism. Called *Rhondda Rap*, it featured out takes of an BBC interview with then Labour leader Neil Kinnock in which he said 'I don't give a sod about politics' (*The Observer* 3/11/91). The BBC objected to breach of copyright, although Kinnock apparently had no objections.

Other legal cases

If, as I have argued, pop is about more than music, then legal attempts at stifling its non-musical aspects also need noting. In 1977 a girl in Liverpool was fined for wearing a badge advertising Wayne County's *Fuck Off* single (Savage 1991, p.577). Another fan was fined for wearing the Stiff Records T-shirt with the logo: "If It Ain't Stiff It Ain't Worth a Fuck" (Robertson 1991, p.91)(13). In 1980 Peter Shaw, a 19 year old Crass fan was sent to a detention centre for three months for singing a sacrilegious Crass song at a priest at York railway station (*Sounds* 7/5/80). In 1990 an Inspiral Carpets fan in Coventry was charged under the 1981 Indecent Displays Act for wearing the band's "Cool As Fuck" T-shirt (*NME* 28/7/90). Another in Bradford was conditionally discharged (*NME* 15/8/92). In 1992 the phrase "Let's Fuck" on a T-shirt saw an attempt to prosecute a Disposable Heroes of Hiphoprisy fan (*NME* 20/6/92).

More ominously anarchist band Chumbawamba reported that the Home Office had threatened to look closely at their political activities should they release, as planned, a single about Princess Diana called *Never Say Di/For The Love of a Princess* (*NME* 25/7/92).

Conclusion

I would be loathe to see *Efil4zaggin* banned and, whilst the case was going on, it seemed incongruous to me that a No. 1 album in America was effectively banned here for four months. I felt somewhat less free than my American counterparts and this worried me. NWA's is not a comforting voice, neither were any of the other records (or sleeves) that attempts were made to prosecute. But they were voices that should be heard. They were voices of scorn, anger, contempt and outrage, disgust and they provoked similar responses from those who sought their banning. Britain may not be a better place **artistically** for the likes of Crass and NWA, but it is certainly a much more vibrant place **politically**. These examples are on the extremes of the pop world, but it is here that much of what is new and interesting comes. There have been relatively few cases in Britain of attempts to legally stifle those extremes. Hopefully the evidence here has exposed both the arbitrariness and futility of such attempts(14).

Overall the acquittal of *Efil4zaggin* makes it unlikely that a successful prosecution of a record **can** now be brought under the 1959 Act. However, this is **not** the same as saying that the days of pop records, still less pop paraphernalia, being taken to court are over. Calls to tighten up the obscenity law are continually made by various interests, including The Obscene Publications Squad (*Gay Times*, July 1992) and Tory MPs such as Neubert and Michael Stephens(15). A moralistic future government, of whatever political shade, could heed those calls. The impact of this upon pop would not be liberating. The 1959 Act was not envisaged for use against pop, but it has been used that way. A more draconian law could well be more freely used.

Notes

1. For more on the Obscene Publications Act of 1959 see Robertson 1991, pp.182-199. Note that it only applies to England and Wales.

2. Palmer 1972, p.167 notes that such a person started the *Oz* case and p.217 notes their almost mythical status.

3. It should be noted that, in a personal interview, Rimbaud was an "absolutist" on free speech, Crass 1991.

4. In 1977 Anderton, newly appointed, launched 286 vice squad raids. In 1976 there had been 5, Sutherland 1982, p.163.

5. 1987 was a vintage year for censorship, see Wells 1987a.

6. For more on Earache see Spence 1988.

7. *NME* of 15/6/91 also reported the complaint as having come from a retailer. Marot 1991b said one theory was that a buyer at HMV may have approached the Obscene Publications Squad to see if it might face prosecution for selling the record. Another theory was that the complaint came from a trade union official at Polygram, the distributor. Cynics have suggested that Island themselves notified the authorities.

8. For example, see Toop 1991a and Longrigg 1991.

9. Confidential source.

10. For more on copyright see McFarlane 1989, Frith 1988 and Bagehot 1992.

11. For other cases see Bomb The Bass' *Beat Dis* in *NME* 27/2/88, Black Box's *Ride on Time* in *NME* 20/10/89 and The Orb's *Little Fluffy Clouds* in *NME* 25/7/92.

12. For more on sampling see Goodwin 1990a, Gray 1987 and Beadle 1993.

13. See *NME* 21-28/12/91, p.47 for the importance of T-shirts to bands.

14. Notably the only successful prosecutions of records centred upon their lyrics. Attempts at prosecuting covers have always been unsuccessful.

15. See *Hansard* 9/7/92 for Stephens on the need for new obscenity legislation.

Part Three
Broadcasting

6 Introductory note: British broadcasting and the law

British broadcasting is among the oldest in the world. The BBC formed in 1922 and became a public corporation by Royal Charter in 1927, changing from a (private) "company" to a (public) "corporation". It was immediately debarred from broadcasting "controversial material" (Briggs 1979, p.367). It was, and still is, governed by a Charter, the terms of which are periodically renewable by Parliament. The Charter obliges the BBC to 'not offend against good taste and decency' nor 'to encourage crime and disorder' or to transmit material 'offensive to public feeling' (Whitehouse 1982, p.86). The problem is that, as Tracey and Morrison (1979, p.119) have pointed out, this implies an orthodoxy about "decency" which simply does not exist. That being the case the BBC has been left to **interpret** this part of the Charter and has, as we shall see, frequently done so in a censorial way with regard to pop.

The BBC began television broadcasting in 1936 and had a monopoly in British broadcasting until the establishment of commercial television under the Television Act of 1954, which set up the Independent Television Association (ITA). A further Act in 1964 extended the life of this association. By then the BBC had agreed to follow taste and decency guidelines applicable to the commercial stations (Durham 1991, p.76).

In 1972 the Sound Broadcasting Act created the Independent Broadcasting Association (IBA) which replaced the ITA and covered both television and the newly created independent local radio (ILR) stations, the first of which, LBC and Capital, began broadcasting in October 1973. The 1980 Broadcasting Act extended the life of the IBA, but it was abolished under the terms of the 1990 Broadcasting Act(1).

This set up two bodies to regulate the commercial sector, the Radio Authority and the Independent Television Commission (ITC), both of whom are responsible for supervising licence renewals (subject to a bidding system) and programme content.

The Act extended the Obscene Publications Act to cover television and paved the way for more commercial radio stations, both local (e.g. Jazz FM and Kiss FM) and national (e.g. Classic FM and Virgin). The Radio Authority has the power to close down stations which broadcast offensive material. It has yet to do this, but it refused to intervene when Jazz FM sacked one of its directors and DJs, Giles Peterson, for playing a selection of "peace music" **before** the start of the Gulf war in 1991. Despite listeners' protests the Authority ruled that the matter was an internal one beyond their remit, although it upheld a complaint against Jazz FM for broadcasting Peterson's opinions, contrary to the requirements of political impartiality contained in the 1990 Act (*NME* 9/2/91)(2).

The ITC has yet to become embroiled in major controversies over pop, which partly reflects the fact that the 1990 Act also placed on a statutory footing the body which was set up in 1988 to oversee standards of decency in all radio and television networks - the Broadcasting Standards Council (BSC). This organization upheld complaints against the BBC for playing The Shamen's *Ebeneezer Goode* in 1992 (see below). It supplemented the Broadcasting Complaints Commission, which was set up in 1981 to monitor unfair treatment and invasions of privacy. The BSC is funded by the Home Office and in 1992 it was still under its first chair, William Rees-Mogg(3).

Pop was one of the BSC's immediate concerns. Its first Code of Practice warned that: 'The precise time of scheduling of all pop videos should be chosen with care' (BSC 1989, p.40). Comparatively few complaints to the BSC are upheld(4), but this might be because broadcasters have trodden warily, rather than because the BSC lacked censorial imperative. Its future is in doubt as the Labour Party is committed to its abolition and the Conservatives favour merging it with the BCC(5).

The 1990 Act also saw moves against subliminal messages in music, which are dealt with in greater depth below in the chapter on religion. Section 90(a) of the Act forbids the broadcasting of anything 'which offends against good taste' and part (c) requires the Radio Authority to ensure:

... that its programmes do not include any technique which exploits the possibility of conveying a message to, or otherwise influencing the minds of persons listening to the programmes without their being aware, or fully aware, of what has occurred (Broadcasting Act 1990).

This implicitly bans any recording containing backward messages, provided that it could be proved that these messages convey a message the listener is unaware of. Alex Maloney, of Face The Music Ministries (see below), has claimed the credit for getting this clause in the Act, after help from the Conservative MP Andrew Bowden. Section 6 of the Act places similar restrictions on the use of subliminal messages on television, although the British Psychological Society (1992) has doubted that such messages can affect audiences. Subliminals take us into the world of high tech, but censorship in British broadcasting has a much longer tradition, as the next two chapters illustrate.

Notes

1.   The IBA was allegedly abolished after its refusal to ban the Thames documentary *Death On The Rock* upset Margaret Thatcher. See *New Statesman* 26/8/88, p.12.

2.   For the Radio Authority's ruling see their *Complaints Bulletin* No.1, April 1991.

3.   In June 1993 Mogg was replaced by Lady Home see *The Guardian* 5/6/93.

4.   For example see *Viewer and Listener* Autumn 1992 and Spring 1993.

5.   See *IOC* Vol.21, No.5 May 1992, p.34.

7 'What's that sound?' – control and censorship of British pop radio

The influence, both historic and contemporary, of radio on the course of popular music is hard to over estimate. Despite the increasing significance of video, radio remains of vital import. For example, a March 1990 survey found that: 'More people buy records after hearing them on the radio than any other form of advertising or promotion' (*NME* 31/3/90). This fact brings with it a form of censorship, as Negus (1992, pp.108-10) has noted how artists' material will be deliberately altered, or censored, in order to make it "radio friendly". But more overt censorship is both more notable and forms a greater part of fans' consciousness[1].

This chapter outlines the history of radio in Britain, the progress of popular music within it, the "pirates" that have attempted to undermine official radio and various bans that have occurred during the period in question. It concentrates most heavily on the BBC and Radio 1 because, as Barnard (1989, p.1) notes, the BBC tradition has had enormous impact on the **whole** of British radio.

British radio - an overview

Marconi patented radio in 1896, but government interest in the medium really began in 1914 with the realization that it was a means by which an enemy could contact the British public and vice versa. Henceforth there was a movement toward bringing the airwaves under state control. In 1921 a licensing system was set up and government control of the airwaves was further entrenched by the setting up of the BBC in 1926. Like the Company which preceded it, the new Corporation had a monopoly on broadcasting. The British Broadcasting Company was, after reports by the Sykes Committee (1923) and the Crawford Committee (1925) allowed to continue until January 1 1927 when the British Broadcasting Corporation, under the director generalship of John Reith, took over.

Reith aimed to simultaneously "elevate and educate" the audience. One result was a policy where "culture" and "entertainment" were put into two diametrically opposed camps (ibid, p.8). This legacy proved long lasting. The BBC has always operated a dual form of censorship. The most obvious form of censorship, outright banning, has, paradoxically, been the least common. The second is, arguably, the more insidious. This is the ignoring, or marginalization, of certain genres.

Up until 1929 vocal choruses and the announcement of titles by dance bands was forbidden and "scat" singing was banned in 1936 (ibid, pp.10 and 13). The term "hot jazz" was forbidden in the 1930s (Chapman 1992, p.9). The war saw bans for such records as *Santa Claus Is Bringing You Home For Christmas* and *Deep In The Heart Of Texas*, the latter because listeners in munitions factories tended to stop work and start clapping at the appropriate time (Barnard 1989, pp.22 and 27).

The other form of censorship, ignoring or marginalizing genres, also prevailed. In the early 1930s, notes Chambers (1986, p.140), 'jazz was excluded from the BBC'. Briggs (1979, pp.761-762 and 1985, pp.249) reports that all pop was carefully vetted for offence in the 1940s and Barnard (1989, p.37) writes that in the 1950s: 'Rock 'n' roll was held at arm's length by the BBC'. In the early 1960s the BBC deemed American Rhythm and Blues 'unsuitable for British audiences' (Eliot 1987, p.131). This is what one might term a very British form of censorship. It is censorship not by banning(2), but by exclusion. Radio 1 carried on this tradition via the virtual exclusion of genres like folk, reggae and jazz from its daytime shows.

The war saw radio split into the Home Service and the Forces Network. In 1945 the Home Service continued, the Forces Network became the Light Programme and a new service, the Third Programme was introduced in 1946. This came to incorporate Network 3, which became the Music Programme in 1964. Up until the arrival of commercial television in 1954 the BBC faced only limited opposition in the form of Radio Luxembourg which began broadcasting to Britain in 1933 but, as it only broadcast in the evenings, was never a real threat to 1 in 1967(3).

The BBC's emphasis on high culture meant that it was ill prepared for both the arrival of rock and roll(4) and the rise of The Beatles, which both led to dramatic increases in interest in popular culture. It was thus prone to accusations of being out of touch with large parts of the listening public. The amount of records it could play was also limited by its "needletime" agreement, negotiated by the Phonographic Performance Limited (PPL) who collected royalty payments due for the playing of particular recordings.

"Needletime" was based on the idea that using recorded music meant a corresponding lack of work for "live" musicians. It was designed to protect musicians' employment and to ensure that royalties were paid for the use of recorded material and dated from the 1920s (Barnard 1989, pp.16 and 27). Whatever its intent, needletime **did** contribute to a lessening of pop on the BBC. Radio 1 initially had to share an allocation of seven hours a day for records with Radio 2, although 1 broadcast 24 hours a day from 1 May 1991. But by the mid-1960s the BBC had become detached from parts of its audience and thus vulnerable to attack from those who were more in touch. This attack came from pirates.

Pop radio fights the law - pirate radio

Although the main period of the pirates - 1964 to 1967 - falls outside the years covered here, some understanding of them is necessary in order to appraise the role of 1, which followed(5). Radio Caroline started broadcasting on Good Friday, 29 March, 1964 and the other main pirate, London, began on December 23. None of the 21 pirates active from 1964 to 1967 was national and most aimed at the lucrative south east market. Many sought legitimation, which meant, says Chapman (1992, p.51), that 'some pirates constructed for themselves codes of behaviour every bit as restrictive as those observed by the legal broadcasters'. John Peel noted that, in comparison to 1, 'there were more disciplines on London, they banned more records' (Barnard 1989, p.48). One example was Pink Floyd's *Arnold Layne*, banned by London for being "smutty" (*Record Hunter*, *Vox*, May 1991).

Criticism of the pirates centred on interference with emergency service wavelengths, not paying royalties (see *The Times* 17/3/65), lowering broadcasting standards and so on. *Tribune* attacked them as populist opportunists and Tory MP Robin Cooke as potential broadcasters of Communist and Fascist propaganda (Chapman 1992, pp.32-34). The press, fearing loss of advertising revenue was also hostile, as was, naturally, the BBC.

Calls for government action against the pirates soon came and grew in the wake of the publicity surrounding the death of Radio City owner Reg Calvert on 11 June 1966 in a shooting related to a dispute with another pirate company(6). This led the Government to move and a Bill outlawing broadcasting from offshore rigs and supplying them was published on 2 July 1966, gained Royal Assent on 14 July 1967 and became law at midnight on 14 August.

Before the Act became law the government had used the 1947 Wireless Telegraphy Act to harass pirates resident in sea forts. By the time it came into force only Caroline was putting up much resistance. Radio 1 began broadcasting six weeks later.

The question remains as to whether the banning of the pirates was **the** most significant censorial action that has taken place in the history of popular music in Britain thus far. At the time The Raver column in *M M* saw the demise of the pirates as part of a wider campaign against pop (see *M M* 14/10/67), but on balance it appears that, whilst one form of pop expression was outlawed, fans lost little that was innovative. The pirates' output was primarily mainstream and seekers after more jazz or folk, for example, would have been disappointed. The needs of advertisers, not fans, occupied the minds of most pirate operators. Payola was common and Caroline eventually became little more than an outlet for records on the Major Minor label, run by one of its executives, Phil Solomon (Chapman 1992, p.115). The last Radio London chart contained 18 records that had yet to be released (ibid, p.194).

But 1967 was not the end of the pirates. 1968 saw an all-night protest vigil outside GPO offices in London (Hind and Mosco, 1985 p.14) and a rally for free radio was held in Trafalgar Square in August 1969 (*M M* 14/6/69 and 9/8/69). The 1970s saw only sporadic pirate activity (see Harrigan 1975) - but included the jailing, under the 1967 Act, of John Jackson-Hunter, a Liverpool DJ who had displayed a Caroline sticker on his car windscreen. Refusing to pay a fine of £500 for advertising the station, he went to jail for 60 days (*NME* 31/1/76, 14/2/76 and 10/12/77).

By the early 1980s pirates were again being heard. The new pirates

106

operated on the mainland and were primarily based in London. They were also more fan orientated than the 1960s pirates and covered a wider range of musical genres. By 1983 they attracted favourable reports in the music press (see *NME* 13/3/82, 31/7/82 and 15/1/83). The 1984 Telecommunications Act ended many of them as the DTI stepped up raids and prosecutions.

But by the late 1980s pirates were again common in London (see *NME* 20/6/87, 9/4/88, 5/11/88 and 17/3/90) and, following the 1990 Broadcasting Act's provisions for more commercial radio stations, some made the step from piracy to legality. Kiss FM is a paradigmatic case. The censorial point about pirates is that many felt themselves forced into piracy by the legal stations ignoring their musical tastes, especially club based dance music. Radio 1's failings were often mentioned here and this leads us to Britain's most important pop radio station.

"The station of *which* nation?" - the role of Radio 1

Radio 1 was born as the monopoly station of British pop on 30 September 1967. By 1992 it had 22.4% of the British radio audience, with 16.5 million people listening for at least five minutes a week (*The Guardian* 30/1/93). Although welcomed by *MM* proclaiming that: 'Britain's music fans can't lose. They'll get music all day every day' (*MM* 30/9/67), complaints soon came from within the pop world about the state of 1. Problems centred around its lack of autonomy, as its seven hours a day "needletime" was shared with Radio 2 (Barnard 1989, p.53). At night it joined 2 at 7.30 pm until its close down at 2 am. Within three weeks of its launch this middle of the road approach attracted complaints in *MM* (see *MM* 21/10/67).

Despite sizable audiences 1 was continually accused of not being youth orientated enough (*MM* 5/10/68, 12 and 19/10/68) and of concentration on singles when the pop audience was moving towards albums. Crucially, its monopoly position was attacked. Lack of competition was cited as the reason for it being out of touch and *MM* advocated commercial radio (*MM* 21/6/69). Again the censorial point was often that 1 was ignoring certain genres.

In April 1970 1 got more autonomy from 2 during the week and was given a new progressive rock show. Again a Reithian divide was apparent. The *Sounds Of The Seventies* programme that followed was on in the evening - "rock" began to find its marginal niche, away from the daytime diet of "pop". But Chapman (1972, p.272) contends that:

> Progressive rock was a recognisable part of the BBC middle-class cultural and intellectual milieu in a way that, say, soul or reggae could never have been and enjoyed a monopoly on promotion that was denied most forms of black music.

If progressive rock was on the sidelines, reggae was denied all access to the game.

Meanwhile the battle was on for 1's continued existence. Conservative victory in the 1970 general election meant that free market arguments about broadcasting were again prominent. But the Government eventually opted for the introduction of local, rather than national, commercial radio. The BBC used Radio 2, not 1, to counter the ILRs, getting it 15 hours more a week needletime, whilst 1 got none. When cutbacks came 1 was always at the forefront. A subtle form of censorship via denial of resources was in play.

The 1977 Annan Report criticized 1 for being too chart orientated and recommended that it increase the range of its output. By this time punk was creating pop history - much of which went unrecorded by 1, which excluded it from daytime shows. It did not overtly ban many punk records: its censorship was again the more subtle one of ignoring and marginalizing.

But punk had made 1 look out of touch and afterwards Barnard (1989, p.124) reports that its staff 'wore their hipness on their sleeves'. It got greater autonomy in January 1979 when it was further separated from 2 - between 6 am and midnight. But in March 1980 1 cut its air time because BBC economics meant it could not afford PPL fees (*NME* 15/3/90). However by the end of the 1980s 1 was established as the most listened to popular music station in Britain. Various changes took place in its structure, but it continued to be chart orientated and face allegations of ignoring certain genres of music. In part this was due to the widely held orthodoxy at 1 ...

Radio 1's two audiences

Radio 1 upheld its Reithian heritage via a notion of two audiences, one which wishes to be "entertained" whilst they are at work and one which comes home from work (or, importantly, an educational institution) and seeks "cultural" experience via the less mainstream music which can be played at night. This divide has important ramifications. The two audiences, 1 argues, require different styles of programmes and music. Former Controller Derek Chinnery characterized the divide as being between programmes of background music and those with 'music that perhaps requires **more actual listening'** (Barnard 1989, pp.56-57. Emphasis mine).

Chinnery's successor as Controller, Johnny Beerling, shared this view, believing radio's value to be that 'it's a secondary activity' and that 'the majority of people who want new music and serious presentation aren't there during the day' (*NME* 16/11/88). So, Barnard (ibid, p.116) explains that:

Radio 1 categorises popular music as **either** easy listening background music **or** as a culturally valid, quasi classical music requiring isolation to the periphery of the schedules, both in deference to its assumed superiority to standard pop fare and to prevent it disrupting mainstream programming.

But the whole question of a passive daytime audience is a contentious one (especially as unemployed aesthetes listen in) that 1 will not take on board. Its philosophy is "Ratings by day, reputation by night" (Grundy 1991). The censorial problem is that this involves a denial of air time for certain genres during the day. For example, Beerling said that black funk records 'don't generally sound good on radio' (*NME* 16/11/85). Punk, hip hop, hardcore thrash and rap, most world music etc are all deemed unsuitable for daytime 1. It is **not** the case that it panders to the charts, but it **is** the case that such genres do not get the daytime coverage they may merit simply because they do not fit in with 1's idea of a "station sound". This subtle form of censorship helps perpetuate the myth of some popular music being pap and some culturally valid. One result is that when censorship of pop **does** occur it is not held to be as serious as if, for example, novels are censored.

But 1's demarcation strategy has not always met with audience approval. In May 1976 5,000 Teds marched to the station and demanded a greater representation of rock and roll. This led to a 13 week series called *It's Rock and Roll* (*NME* 22/5/76 and 14/8/76). In

August 1986 Gary Numan fans picketed 1 in protest at the lack of air play he was receiving (*NME* 16/8/86).

These two examples reflect a concern that 1 has continually censored by exclusion. Where it has not omitted genres, it has often put them into ghetto spots, partly because of its (mis)conception of having to cater for two audiences, rather than believing that pop is capable of being a valid cultural medium at any time of the day. It was never argued that Radio 3's audience was so divided, and should have classical music only at night, so it is reasonable to ask why this "fact" is accepted for 1. A tendency to promote "chart friendly" material over pop which is made for albums has been apparent. This tendency finds expression in the playlist.

Deciding who gets on - Radio 1's playlist

Street (1986, p.116) has commented that, whilst bans may be interesting: 'What is of greater concern are the records that disappear before they even reach the public'. The playlist is often where records "disappear" and getting on it has often been crucial to a record's success[7]. In 1992 Radio 1's playlist operated on its daytime shows during the week from 4 am to 7 pm and consisted of half of the music in those shows. It had three parts. The A list consisted of 20 records which got around 15 plays a week, the B list was 20 records to get around 10 plays and the C list up to 10 records which got a few plays a week.

It was first introduced in 1973 to combat the launch of the ILRs and a feeling that chart hits were being heard too infrequently (Barnard 1989, p.119). Since then it has undergone various modifications[8], during which 1 has continually sought to underplay its importance to a record's chance of commercial success. In 1992 it was drawn up once a week, with input from various producers, DJs, secretaries, etc., under the supervision of playlist committee chair, Paul Robinson. In this sense 1 is much more democratic than commercial stations where one person, the Controller, often draws up the list (Barnard 1989, pp.128-133). The defining parameters of what gets on are somewhat intangible - Robinson (1991) talked of a "gut feeling" - but even a No. 1 hit is not always enough to guarantee it, as Iron Maiden found in January 1991 when their *Bring Your Daughter To The Slaughter*, got to that position but was not playlisted.

The censorial importance of the playlist is that it restricts the daily fare of the pop audience and is overseen by people whose overriding criterion is to make the "station sound" as appealing as possible to the greatest number of people. This automatically excludes genres such as hardcore rap and punk whose artists often set out to aggravate by their sound[9]. The playlist is an agenda setting item in British pop and remains contentious more for what it excludes than for what it includes. But more publicity is garnered by overt censorship.

Banned on the 1[10]

I have delayed this section not because it is unimportant - on the contrary each banned record is a cultural landmark - but because I agree with Street (1986, p.115) and Barnard (1989, p.120) that the ignoring and marginalization of genres is more important on a day to day basis. Nevertheless, the most obvious public manifestation of disapproval is actual bans and detailed attention to them is therefore necessary. Whilst outright bans are comparatively rare, their net effect has often been to show what was worrying Britain at particular times, again linking censorship to contemporary events. Some concerns last for years, others seem quaint in retrospect. Thus the ban on The Beatles *A Day In The Life* seems absurd if taken out of the context of increasing concern about the recreational use of drugs in 1967, but the ban on Wings' *Give Ireland Back To The Irish* is more understandable, if no more defensible, in the context of continuing conflict in the north of that country.

The casual observer of censorship on 1 is struck by its apparent inconsistency. But this may be due more to changing social mores and borders of acceptability, rather than the mysteries of BBC bureaucracy. Bans on Judge Dread records may now appear laughable, but homophobia, for example, may be less tolerated than previously. It is within this context of changing social mores that the network has to work.

The simplest way of documenting bans is to group them under broad subject areas. The main areas concern sex, politics, advertising, drugs, general "offence" and children. Whilst they continually evoked concern, the degree to which each is prominent varies along with the social context within which they occur. Thus radio bans may be the paradigmatic case of censorship's link to contemporary mores and events. Here I shall treat records played only after the 9 pm "watershed" and ones that are carefully placed, as well as outright bans, as examples of censorship.

I *don't* want your sex

The first record banned by 1 was Scott Walker's cover of the Jacques Brel's *Jacky* in December 1967 (*M M* 9/12/67). Ironically it came a month after the BBC had claimed that: 'We never ban records. The question of plays is at the discretion of individual producers' (*M M* 11/11/67)(11). *Jacky* was banned because it was deemed "bawdy" in containing references to "authentic queers" and "phoney virgins" (*M M* 9 and 16/12/67). It led to a protest by Walker's fans outside Broadcasting House. The record was later deemed suitable only for night time scheduling (*M M* 16/12/67). In 1991 Marc Almond covered the song and received daytime plays without having any problems.

In 1969 Max Romeo's *Wet Dream*, which contains the chorus: "Lie down girl let me push it up, push it up, lie down", was banned. The BBC at first denied it had banned the record (*M M* 5/7/69), but later it became apparent that it had. The record's title was not even mentioned in chart rundowns (*M M* 16/8/69).

The same year 1 banned, retrospectively, the Peter Sarstedt song *Take Off Your Clothes*. A taped version of the song was broadcast on the lunchtime Radio 1 Club in July 1969. After several complaints a BBC spokesman said: 'It should never have been broadcast. We are very sorry ... It will not be played again' (*M M* 26/7/69).

The most infamous ban of 1969, that of Serge Gainsbourg and Jane Birkin's *Je T'Aime*, again concerned sex. The BBC was again coy about declaring the ban, initially saying that: 'There is no list of banned records, and producers make their own decisions about what to play.' Later the BBC said that: 'The record is not considered suitable for play' (*M M* 16/8/69). As it neared the top of the charts the BBC announced that it would not allow it on Top of the Pops, even if it got to No. 1, and would play the instrumental version by Sounds Nice should that happen (*M M* 4/10/69). This proved unnecessary as it peaked at No. 2.

In 1972 Judge Dread began releasing a series of amended nursery rhymes with a reggae back beat, which told seaside postcard style stories. He began with *Big Six* and went up to *Big Ten* and all were banned by the BBC. The records were risque, but seldom obscene (swearing was present only in double entendres). Radio 1's refusal to play them meant a veto on a very popular artist.

Sex was also the reason behind another ban in 1972 - that on Wings' *Hi Hi Hi* (see *Vo x* January 1993). Often seen as being a ban based on drug references (Carr and Tyler 1975, p.103 - the chorus talks of getting "High High High"), the lines the BBC objected were of a sexual nature and spoke of lying on a bed, with a "body gun"(12) and of "doing it" "like a rabbit". The possible consequences of "doing it like a rabbit" were also kept from 1's audience. In August 1973 Procol Harum's song about VD, *Souvenir of London*, was banned. To get round this the band promoted "B" side, *Toujours L'Amour*, to the "A" side (*M M* 18/8/73).

1975 saw heavy breathing return with Donna Summer's orgasmic cries on her *Love To Love You Baby* single - which Radio Luxembourg played, as it had *Je T'Aime* (*M M* 21/2/76). Again the BBC proved reluctant to use the word "ban". Radio 1 and 2 Controller Charles McClelland said that: 'We certainly never use the word "ban" anyway' and that: 'The official policy with records of this nature is that there is no policy - each record is treated purely and simply on its own merits' (ibid).

But at this time 1 played both The Who's suggestive *Squeeze Box* and R. & J. Stone's proclamation that *We Do It*. Summer's ban appeared to be purely on the grounds of explicitness. At the same time Capital banned 10cc's *Head Room*, because of its theme of masturbation and mention of 'a flick of the wrist' (ibid).

Punk lyrics were little concerned with sex and so caused few problems there, although there are claims that in May 1977 The Stranglers' *Peaches* was banned from 1's daytime shows because of "unsuitable" lyrics (*Sounds* 17/5/80). There was also no play for the Buzzcocks' *Orgasm Addict* (Savage 1991, p.407) or X-Ray Spex's *Oh Bondage! Up Yours!* (Laing 1985, p.67). Ivor Biggun's ode to onanism, *The Winkers Song*, also reached the charts in 1978 without the benefit of Radio 1 plays (*NME* 26/8/78). But the main censorship that punk suffered was being marginalized and played only on the "specialist" weekend and evening programmes(13).

Thus far problems with sex had concerned heterosexuality, but homosexuality caused still more problems. When The Tom Robinson Band released its live EP *Rising Free* in February 1978 1 gave prominence to the track *Don't Take No For An Answer* and so avoided playing the EP's pivotal track, *Glad To Be Gay*, which Capital freely played (*NME* 25/2/78). Again explicitness appeared to be the problem, as The Village People's more discrete gay celebration *YMCA* received 1's endorsement later in the year (*Sounds* 2/12/78).

In 1982 The Special AKA's *The Boiler*, which dealt with rape, was dropped by 1 after a few evening plays in the wake of a judge's remarks that a rape victim had been guilty of contributory negligence by hitch hiking alone at night (*NME* 16/1/82) - another example of contemporary events affecting the censorial climate.

But homosexuality was the subject of the most infamous ban of the 1980s - of Frankie Goes To Hollywood's *Relax*. The campaign against it was initiated by DJ Mike Read, but embarrassing for 1 because it had previously given the band sessions and played the record some 70 times prior to the ban. Radio 1 producer Stuart Grundy later described the ban as 'a **terrible** mistake' (Grundy 1991. Emphasis Grundy). It was sanctioned by Chinnery who took a personal dislike to the record after Read started the campaign (ibid)[14] and said that:

> ... when the performers themselves confirmed it was referring to these sexual aberrations then it didn't seem to me appropriate that we should play it all (Street 1986, p.115).

Perhaps Frankie should not say so much.

In June 1987 George Michael's *I Want Your Sex* was deemed suitable only for broadcasting after 9 pm. Beerling explained that 'we feel this goes too far for daytime radio' (Heslam 1990, p.431). A similar restriction was placed on The Tams' *There Ain't Nothing Like Shaggin'* - although the record was about a dance craze and the word objected to does not have the connotations in America that it does in Britain. After several complaints 1 explained that:

> If members of the public are offended by the lyric of a song ... we have to take a decision about whether we want to offend them. In this case we don't (*NME* 5/12/87).

The ILRs played it freely.

By 1991 the word "sex" at least was acceptable to 1. In that year Salt 'n' Pepa's *Let's Talk About Sex*, Billy Bragg's *Sexuality*, La Tour's

People Are Still Having Sex and Color Me Baad's *I Want To Sex You Up* all received their fair share of daytime plays.

Overall there **has** been a movement towards liberalization in sexual matters, as shown by the playing of *Jacky* in 1991 after its ban in 1967 and by *Relax* being freely played on its 1993 re-release. But this has by no means been a free for all. 1 is no longer as prudish as it was in 1967, but neither is it a sexual libertine. Apprehension still mixes with endorsement.

Left on the shelf - Radio 1's political bans

The BBC was always wary of political records, banning, for example, Barry McGuire's *Eve of Destruction* in 1965 (O'Higgins 1972 p.133). Radio 1's concern with political records began with Wings' *Give Ireland Back to The Irish* which was released, after Derry's Bloody Sunday, in February 1972. The way the censorial climate is linked to current affairs is shown by the fact that, as Ireland remained in the headlines, the record was as unlikely to get played in 1992 as it was in 1972(15). Indeed the likelihood of it staying banned increased with the Government's October 1988 ban on the broadcasting of statements from organizations supporting terrorism.

On its original release the title was vetoed during chart run downs (*M M* 11/3/72). Linda McCartney saw the ban as 'symptomatic of Britain **at this moment**, with the miners' strike, Ireland and Rhodesia' (*M M* 26/2/72. Emphasis mine). However there appears to have been a hierarchy of sensibilities, as the BBC did not ban a pro-miners record by John and The City Lights (*M M* 21/2/76).

But Ireland was more problematic and the same month as The Wings' ban 1 banned McGuinness Flint's anti-internment song, *Let The People Go*. Writer Tom McGuinness rightly described this as 'straight forward political censorship' (*M M* 26/2/71). But it seemed that as long as records refrained from overtly political points about Ireland they were acceptable, as the BBC did **not** ban *Belfast '71* by Allan Taylor, which was also released at this time. The BBC explained that: 'The McCartney and McGuinness Flint records take a definite political standpoint. *Belfast '71* merely comments on the sadness of the situation' (*M M* 11/3/72).

An air of political cowardice, presented as neutrality, surrounds these bans. *Give Ireland Back To The Irish* is, in its own way, a peace

115

anthem, reflecting a view that peace will only come once Ireland is united. *Let The People Go* is as much about freedom as it is politics. But whilst it was permitted to describe the "sadness" (which is presumably apolitical) of the Irish situation, it was apparently **not** permissible to apportion blame.

A more balanced approach might have been to play **all** the records and thus give as many views as possible. The BBC Charter's requirement of impartiality does **not** imply a duty to ban unpopular opinions, showing the importance of the way the BBC **interprets** its Charter. The vetoing of *Give Ireland Back To The Irish* meant that the BBC contributed to a stifling of debate on arguably the most important issue in British politics. The BBC chose to stifle dissent, something its Charter does **not** require.

The same argument about stifling dissent also applies to the next two bans. Both concern The Sex Pistols and again show censorial sensibilities attuned to contemporary events. The first came immediately after the Grundy interview in December 1976 (see below)(16), which left the Pistols with a high public profile. As the press bayed for blood, 1 announced that the band's single, *Anarchy In The UK*, would not be played on its daytime shows (*NME* 11/12/76). BBC Chairman Michael Swann said that:

> The BBC does not as a general rule place an outright ban on the broadcasting of any record ... (with *Anarchy*) the senior people responsible for the programmes on Radios 1 and 2 decided that it should not be broadcast during the daytime or early evening, when audiences are of extremely varied types of people and much listening is casual. We did not think it right that the content of this record should be suddenly thrust on these audiences. It was thought, however, that it might be played in a late-night programme which has a specialized audience and a serious and respected presenter in John Peel ... the members of his particular audience, on the whole a pretty sophisticated collection of listeners, would be capable of forming their own conclusions about it (Whitehouse 1977, p.39).

This is a splendid example of Reithian elitism. The "casual" listeners must not have this record "thrust on" them, but the "sophisticated" evening listeners can take it all in their stride and even form their **own** conclusions! The ban helped the BBC to form daytime listeners' opinions for them.

The next ban was more overtly political and concerned the band's *God Save The Queen* single. The BBC banned it on its release for being in "gross bad taste" and thus contrary to its Charter. Others followed this example and banned the single. The fact that it was released to tie in with the Jubilee celebrations is crucial in understanding the reaction to it (see Savage 1991, pp.347 and 351). This was highlighted by a BBC spokesman's comment that: 'If it had been at any other time of the year, we might have given it the occasional play' (*NME* 11/6/77).

There were strong rumours that sales figures were falsified to deny the record the No. 1 spot in Jubilee Week[17] - a highly censorial action - such was the reaction against it. Here again the BBC stifled voices of dissent. In order to present a (false) picture of a nation united in Royal celebration the single was banned.

Radio 1 remained wary in the political arena and in 1981 its legal department advised Heaven 17 that their hit *We Don't Need This Fascist Groove Thing* libelled American President Ronald Reagan by calling him a "fascist". So the BBC dropped it and IBA stations banned an advertisement for it. The band then recorded a special radio version of the song with the lyrics "Reagan, fascist guard" changed to "Stateside cowboy guard" (*NME* 4/4/81).

Two years later, and with the Falklands War over for a year, 1 showed that not only records got censored. The Icicle Works recorded a session for Peter Powell's show which included the song *Gun Boys*. But before its broadcast they had to change the line "Remember when the Argies" to "Do you remember when" and change "So Margaret sent the fleet in" to "And so they sent the fleet in" (*NME* 27/8/83). The BBC had also banned Julie Covington's *Don't Cry For Me Argentina* during the war itself and Alan Hull's anti-Falklands War single *Malvinas Melody* was also avoided by all radio stations in 1983 (McSmith 1983).

In the run up to the 1987 General Election 1 decided not to play The Blow Monkeys anti-Thatcher single *(Celebrate) The Day After You*. A spokesman said that 'we have to strike a balance in the run up to the general election' (*NME* 23/5/87). Later 1 said that: 'The BBC Charter obliges us to refrain from political bias ... All the records we are playing now have no political bias' (*NME* 30/5/87).

However, this was **not** the case as 1 continued playing Labi Sifre's anti-apartheid song *Something Inside (So Strong)* as well as That

Petrol Emotion's anti-plastic bullets record *Big Decision*. A somewhat narrow definition of "political bias" was being employed. RCA soon decided to withdraw *Celebrate*, effectively killing it (*NME* 13/6/87).

October 1987 saw 1 accused of political cowardice, when the band Baby A claimed that they had been told that it would not play their *No Respect* single as it was "politically extreme". The record criticized the Government's youth policy and institutions such as the CBI, MSC and SPG (*NME* 31/10/87). It got no air play and the band faded from sight. Other political records encountered similar ignorals. Steel Pulse's *KKK* 'was ignored by Radio 1' despite charting in 1978 (Street 1986, p.118) and Paul said of his 1984 single in aid of the miners' strike, *Soul Deep*: 'They ignored it ... which is a lot more effective than banning it' (Denselow 1989, p.214).

But by far the most publicized ban of the 1990s thus far was initiated not by 1, but by BBC Radio Training. This was the infamous list of records that were apparently banned during The Gulf War. It included such innocuous songs as Aha's *Hunting High and Low*, Queen's *Flash* and Donny Osmond's *Soldier of Love* (and is included overleaf). It led to a protest "sing-in" outside Broadcasting House on 9 February, organized by Musicians Against The War (*IOC* Vol.20, Nos.4-5, April/May 1991, p.54).

Radio Training's Tom Neale wrote to *The Independent* (2/2/91) denying any ban. This seems to be the case and it is worth noting that this was a time of great sensitivity. For example, the playing of one of the records on the list - Paper Lace's *Billy Don't Be A Hero* - immediately after a Gulf bulletin led to 110 complaints to the BBC (Grundy 1991)[18].

The Rolling Stones also found their *High Wire* single, which criticized governments who sold arms to Iraq, did not get the amount of air play they might usually expect. Beerling commented that if 1 played it: 'I can see the headlines now. It would be another case of the leftie BBC supporting the enemies of freedom' (*Sunday Times* 17/2/91) - an interesting revelation of the censorial pressure that 1 was under. There where also allegations that Carter The Unstoppable Sex Machine's *Bloodsports For All*, about racism in the army, was vetoed during the conflict (*NME* 2/2/91) and The Happy Mondays had to omit the lines "Gonna build an airforce base/Gonna blow up your race" from their *Loose fit* single because of the war (*NME* 16/2/91).

GERRY, JOHN K, MONTY, MAUREEN, UPFRONT, KENNY JOHNSON,
SPENCER, BILLY B., BILLY MAHER, ROGER LYON, ROGER SUMMERSKILL,
ROGER HILL, SPORT: ROGER, MARCUS, ROB, ALAN JACKSON, PHIL HILTON,

GULF DISCS:	Please think carefully before playing anything of this nature which might upset our listeners. This has been	
ABBA	Waterloo	sent to us by Training Unit
	Under Attack	inLondon.
AHA	Hunting High and low	Jenny
ALARM	68 Guns	
ANIMALS	We got to get out of this place	
ARRIVAL	I will survive	

JOAN BAEZ   The night they drove old Dixie down
BANGLES   Walk like an Eqyptian
BEATLES   Back in the USSR
PAT BENATAR   Love is a battlefield
BIG COUNTRY   Fields of fire
BLONDIE   Atomic
BOOMTOWN RATS Don't Like Mondays
BROOK BROS   Warpaint
CRAZY ..BROWN Fire
KATE BUSH   Army Dreamers

CHER   Bang Bang (My baby shot me down)
ERIC CLAPTON   I shot the Sheriff
PHIL COLLINS   In the air tonight
ELVIS COSTELLO Olivers army
CUTTING CREW   I just died in your arms tonight

SKEETER DAVIS End of the world
DESMOND DEKKER Israelites
DIRE STRAITS   Brothers in arms
DURAN DURAN   View to a kill

JOSE FELICIANO Light my fire
FIRST CHOICE   Armed and extremely dangerous
ROBERTA FLACK Killing me softly
FRANKIE ...   Two Tribes

EDDIE GRANT   Living on the frontline
               Give me hope Joanna

ELTON JOHN   Sat. nights alright for fighting
& MILLIE JACKSON Act of War
J HATES JAZZ   I don't want to be a hero

JOHN LENNON   Give peace a chance
               Imagine
JONA LEWIE   Stop the cavalry
LULU   Boom bang a bang

119

```
McGUINNESS FLINT      When I'm dead and gone
BOB MARLEY            Buffalo soldier
MARIA MULDAUR         Midnight at the Oasis
MASH                  Suicide is painless
MIKE / MECHANICS      Silent running

RICK NELSON           Fools rush in
NICOLE                A little peace

BILLY OCEAN           When the going gets tough
DONNY OSMOND          Soldier of love

PAPER LACE            Billy don't be a hero

QUEEN                 Killer queen
                      Flash

MARTHA REEVES         Forget Me not
B A ROBERTSON         Bang bang
TOM ROBINSON          War baby
KENNY ROGERS          Ruby (don't take your love to Town)

SPANDAU BALLET        I'll fly for you
SPECIALS              Ghost Town
BRUCE SPRINGSTEEN     I'm on fire
EDWIN STARR           War
STATUS QUO            In the army now
                      Burnin' bridgaes
CAT STEVENS           I'm goona get me a gun
ROD STEWART           Sailing
DONNA SUMMER          State of Independence

TEARS FOR FEARS       Everybody wants to RULE, the world
TEMPTATIONS           Ball of confusion
10 CC                 Rubber Bullets

STEVIE WONDER         Heaven help us all
```

Overall 1 has interpreted political impartiality as meaning whatever is favourable to the government of the day. Its political cowardice means it has contributed to a denial of air time to minority opinions. Pop often has a radical edge and it is this edge that 1, by overt censorship and covert marginalization, has undermined. Pop can be confrontational, but the politics of 1 are generally compliant.

Ad nauseam?

Radio 1's compliant politics does **not** mean that it has always eagerly oiled the wheels of capitalism, as the BBC has constantly distanced itself from records which promote products. In the 1950s this reached an almost illogical extreme. Johnny Bond's *Hot Road Lincoln* had to become *Hot Rod Jalopy* to get BBC plays and The Playmates' had to change the words of their *Beep Beep* hit from "Cadillac" and "Nash Rambler" to "limousine" and "bubble car" (Sounds 10/1/87). In the years 1967 to 1992 there were various changes to lyrics and bannings of product related records.

The first came in April 1968 when Pink Floyd had to change a lyric in *It Would Be So Nice* from "Evening Standard" to "Daily Standard" (*M M* 6/4/68). This seemed inconsistent as a few months previously the BBC had quite happily played The Scaffold's *Thank You Very Much* which contains a reference to the *Sunday Times*.

In 1970 The Kinks had to change the lyrics of *Lola* from "Coca Cola" to "Cherry Cola" to get on 1 (Heslam 1990, p.313). Ironically, The New Seekers' hit *I'd Like To Teach The World to Sing* which was used, with a slight lyric change, to advertise Coke in 1971/72 was freely played by 1, but banned by commercial stations (*M M* 28/2/76). Paul Simon fell foul of the "No ads" veto with *Kodachrome* (held to be an advert for Kodak), the "B" side of *Mother and Child Reunion* and February 1973 saw the banning of Dr. Hook's *Cover of The Rolling Stone* (*NME* 15/10/77). A subsequent version that substituted the words "Radio Times" for "Rolling Stone" was also banned - so enabling 1 to keep up its veneer of impartiality. Fifteen years later Pop Will Eat Itself had to re-record *Def Con One* and cut the numerous references to "Big Mac's" in order to get played (*NME* 23/7/88).

But the BBC's most embarrassing moments with advertising have come when it has given too much exposure to its own products and rendered itself liable to accusations of bias. So in 1975 a record on BBC Records by Gibraltar band Buddy called *Rock Around The Rock* was banned by the BBC after BBC Records had announced that it would get: 'Full support from BBC and local radio' (*NME* 17/5/75).

The problems 1 has had with records mentioning commercial products are those that a publicly funded corporation faced in dealing with commercial enterprises. By 1992 advertisers avoided potential bans by using pop "classics" in television adverts and thus linking product and song in the minds of listeners, a more insidious practice than mentioning product in songs. The increasing use of songs featured in films also formed a subtle form of advertising. But some products seldom got mentioned.

No ecstasy at the BBC

In 1967, prior to the start of 1, the BBC banned a Beatles track for the only time. This was *A Day In The Life,* from *Sergeant Pepper*. Again contemporary events are relevant, namely the year's moral panic over drugs. But BBC nervousness towards drugs related tracks characterized the late 1960s, with songs such as The Byrds' *Eight Miles High*, Canned Heat's *Amphetamine Annie* and The Rolling Stones' *Mother's Little Helper* all being banned (*MM* 28/2/75). In 1967 it also banned The Game's anti-drugs single *The Addicted Man* (O'Higgins 1972, p.133) and The Rolling Stones' *We Love You* (Street 1986, p.114). In July 1970 the station banned Daddy Longlegs' *High Again* for referring to stimulants - which the band's label, Warner Bros, denied (*MM* 18/7/70).

A year later Mungo Jerry's *Have A Whiff On Me*, part of a maxi-single on which *Lady Rose* was the lead track, was banned. Their label, Pye, later reissued the single without the offending track on, thus allowing *Lady Rose* to go on the airwaves untainted. Douglas Muggeridge, head of Radios 1 and 2, said:

> It's going to be our policy to be very tough on this sort of thing. The track *Have A Whiff On Me* is quite definitely banned ... We have a duty to the public to avoid in every possible way any action that would lead to the encouragement of drug taking (*MM* 29/5/71).

The quote attributes **causal** consequences to listening to a record, implying that playing it would make people take drugs - a proposition Muggeridge might find hard to prove. It is also an act of moral cowardice. John Peel states that the ban was 'to stop any feedback from the public in the form of letters' (ibid).

Radio 1's concern about drug related records waned at the start of the 1970s - a reflection both of the decline in releases of that nature and of the BBC's more subtle method of ignoring any that were released. But the rise of rave music in the late 1980s saw drugs return as a major issue. Radio 1's initial reaction was to keep the music at a distance. Certainly ravers heard little of their music on daytime 1 (see Cosgrove 1989). But as such records began to chart they became increasingly hard to ignore.

In October 1988 D-Mob reached No. 1 with their single *We Call It Acieed*. But 1's reaction to it was, at best, ambivalent. It was the only record going up the chart not playlisted in the week of 14 October. A spokesman explained that this was 'because we felt it wasn't right for the mood of some programmes such as the breakfast show' (*NME* 29/10/88). Although **this** record received numerous plays from individual producers, the reaction to acid in general recalled the days of punk, with most censorship coming **not** by overt bans, but by more covert ignorals and marginalization.

But the censorial pressure 1 is under was illustrated when it was censured by the BSC for **not** banning The Shamen's *Ebeneezer Goode* in November 1992. The record's chorus contains the line "Ezer's good" (= Es [ecstasy pills] are good), which 1 thought was "sufficiently ambiguous" to permit daytime plays. However the BSC upheld a complaint against the station, which was held to have broken recommendations that it should not broadcast material which encourages 'tolerance towards the taking of drugs ... (especially) in programmes expecting to attract large numbers of young people' (BSC *Complaints Bulletin* No. 22 November 1992, p.10).

The great offender?

BBC bans because of offence have included John's Children's *Desdemona*, for the line "lift up your skirt and fly" (Wale 1972, p.12), Napoleon XIV's *They're Coming To Take Me Away*, for being about insanity (*MM* 28/2/76), The Group's *Bovver Boys*, for mocking football violence (*M M* 16/12/72) and Al Stewart's *Love Chronicles*, for the word "fucking" (Laing 1985 p.75). Swearing remains the most complained about facet of British broadcasting (*The Guardian* 28/10/91) so 1 has kept a daytime veto on records containing it. But although the BBC **has** banned records specifically because of swearing, the boundaries of acceptability have constantly shifted.

In December 1971 Radio 1 claimed not to be banning Bob Dylan's *George Jackson* single, which contains the word "shit". A spokesman said that:

> There has only been about nine single records ever banned by the BBC and it has got to be pretty bad for us to ban it. We ban LP tracks more often, but not so many singles are banned (*M M* 18/12/71).

So the record was not banned, although it was vetoed by the Jimmy Young show and Junior Choice (*M M* 11/3/72). A BBC publicity officer explained that: 'We did not bleep the word "shit" - we would not tamper with a record' (ibid).

But by 1974 the word "shit" **was** unacceptable. In January that year had to re-record their single *The Worst Band In The World* to get plays on 1. The phrase "we don't give a shit" became "we don't give up" and the phrase "up yours, up mine, up everybody's" was changed to "I'm yours, I'm mine, I'm everybody's". The original lyrics remained on singles in the shops (*M M* 19/1/74). Radio 1 also banned The Goodies' ode to flatulence, *Blowing Off*, in 1976 (*Daily Mirror* 18/12/76). In 1991 the word "shit" was changed to "spit" on Monty Python's *Always Look On The Bright Side Of Life* hit, but the word "bugger" stayed in on a record that the network played at all times of the day.

In 1973 1 banned *Hello DJ* by American country singer Don Bowman, a one sided conversation of a listener phoning to request his favourite record. It contained several bleeped out words (*M M* 9/5/73). But swearing does not have a monopoly on "offence". Several records have failed to get air play on 1 because they have been deemed offensive to listeners, including many of those already noted. Punk epitomized this and in July 1978 1 vetoed The Sex Pistols/Ronnie Biggs single *No One Is Innocent* because it included lines in praise of, amongst others, Myra Hindley and Martin Boorman (*NME* 15/7/78).

124

Sometimes "offence" is a passing phenomenon related to contemporary events. For example, during The Gulf War some artists temporarily changed their names in order not to cause offence (and so get radio play). Massive Attack became Massive for their *Unfinished Symphony* single and Tim Simenon dropped his Bomb The Bass monicker for his own name on his *Love So True* single (*NME* 2/2/91). These cases came under the exceptional circumstances of war, but other areas are of perennial concern.

Child's (no) play

In March 1970 The Equals' *Soul Brother Clifford* was banned from plays on 1's children's show, Junior Choice, for containing the lines "Sister Virgin you're an old cow." Producer Harry Walters explained that:

> My thinking is this: A school kid goes to school on Monday and calls the teacher an old cow. The teacher blames the parents, then the youngster says he heard the expression on Junior Choice (*M M* 28/3/70).

Again, here pop was endowed with a causal ability - the record will **cause** children to swear.

In 1974 the BBC noted the 'heavy responsibility' on producers of children's programmes, saying that 'great care' was used in selecting records for Junior Choice. Topics generally examined were 'references to drugs or drug-taking, obscenities or explicit references to sex.' All 'doubtful' releases were checked and:

> ... the BBC does not hesitate to institute a ban, although such action is not necessarily made public, because experience has shown that this is a sure way of winning publicity for an undesirable record (BBC 1974, p.7).

In 1976, when discussing the ban on Donna Summer's *Love To Love You Baby*, Charles McClelland said that: 'If a record is basically offensive to a family audience, then it shouldn't be played to a family audience' (*M M* 21/2/76). This concern for childhood innocence was spelt out in June 1987 when Beerling gave his reasons for only playing

George Michael's *I Want Your Sex* after 9 pm. He said that:

> The lyric and nature of the record is too sexually explicit for the massive Radio One daytime air play which a George Michael single would normally receive.
> George's following includes many impressionable young girls and many of their parents would take exception to the broadcasting of the disc on Radio One (*NME* 6/6/87).

Again the comments are illuminating and the partial ban reflects a societal concern - here the sexuality of young girls. Radio 1's paternalism again led it to interpret the BBC Charter on its more censorial side.

But 1 still displays a somewhat inconsistent attitude. Whilst denying that Color Me Baad's *I Want To Sex You Up* was barred from the Breakfast Show, Paul Robinson said that, rather than being playlisted, La Tour's *People Are Still Having Sex*, was:

> ... carefully placed by producers at times when children weren't listening. So it wasn't ... played in school lunch hours, it was played after 2 O'Clock ... when they were back in the classroom (P. Robinson 1991).

Again the logic was hard to follow. A record expressing a commitment to "sexing you up" was played all day, one commenting upon the fact that people were doing just that had to be kept away from school children on their lunch breaks. This is less commonsense than nonsense.

Radio 1 operates a rough watershed time of 9 pm. After this time it is possible that more risqué records and swearing might be heard. The odd "fuck" is not unknown on programmes such as John Peel's, although not usually until after midnight. But words like "motherfucker" rarely get aired, which greatly reduces the amount of rap that 1 can play. Mentioning Peel brings up another area that needs attention - the role of various DJs in censoring records they found offensive.

Two particular incidents are worth noting here. The first is Mike Read's part in getting *Relax* banned in 1984. After playing the record several times Read refused to play it in the chart rundown on his show and began a campaign to get it banned by 1, feeling that 'the lyrics are overtly obscene' (*NME* 21/1/84). Read's status was a factor in the ban as *NME* reported that: 'Radio 1 press officer Nick Underwood admitted that had a DJ of lesser standing objected to the single it wouldn't have been banned' (ibid).

Read's successor on the Breakfast Show, Mike Smith, was also involved in censorial action, but less successfully. On a review programme in July 1986 Smith took off the Jesus and Mary Chain single, *Some Candy Talking*, mid-play because he believed that "candy" referred to cocaine (Cooper 1986). As noted earlier, the link with contemporary events here is Boy George's drug problems which were then featuring heavily in the tabloid press. Smith asked: "Why give any more publicity to a subject which is in danger of becoming acceptable' (*The Guardian* 29/7/86). After taking the unusual step of consulting Peel, Beerling decided **not** to ban the single (Barnard 1989, pp.120-121).

Getting away with it

Before finishing with 1's censorship it is worth noting a few of the "ones that got away". Here the inconsistencies are at their most apparent. In 1973 Lou Reed's *Walk on The Wild Side*, which discusses transvestites and "giving head" got played(19), as did Sylvia's *Pillow Talk*. In 1991 The Divinyls paen to female masturbation, *I Touch Myself* also passed unhindered.

Drug references in Hendrix's *Purple Haze*, The Plastic Ono Band's *Cold Turkey* and Eric Clapton's version of J. J. Cale's *Cocaine* also passed unhindered. Desmond Dekker's 1969 No. 1 contains the words "my wife and kids they fuck off and leave me", albeit in a heavy West Indian accent(20) - 1 played it without flinching. The Kinks's *Apeman* also contains a reference to the air "fucking up my eyes"(21) and The Pixies' *Planet of Sound* refers to "fucking around" (*NME* 15/2/93) - both got played by 1.

There are countless other records that **might** have caused offence, but which 1 either played in ignorance or positively decided to play. But 1 does not have a monopoly on radio censorship of pop.

Commercial censorship?

A Conservative Government ended the BBC's radio monopoly by passing the Sound Broadcasting Act of 1972 which set up the IBA and gave it authority to licence commercial Independent Local Radio (ILRs), the first of which, Capital and LBC, began broadcasting in October 1973. In 1992 there were 105 such stations in Britain. Although aimed at diversifying broadcasting, Capital essentially provided competition for 1 by aiming at being better at doing more or less the same thing. Since then a great many more ILRs have come along, also competing along similar lines, with more specialist stations such as Kiss FM and Jazz FM coming in the 1990s and the first national commercial pop station, Virgin, arriving in April 1993.

As they are overwhelmingly regionally based, the independents seldom make the headlines in the way that 1 does, as any bans make regional, not national, news(22). They target audiences and so censorship here is more by market than by overt bannings. But these have also occurred. Certainly the IBA showed that "commercial" did not have to equate with "liberal". In 1976 it banned both adverts for, and the playing of, Peter Tosh's pro-cannabis anthem, *Legalise It*. A spokesman said: 'We don't like to use the word banned. But we have told the stations that the record cannot be played because it promotes drug use' (*M M* 2/10/76).

During punk, Capital censored The Sex Pistols more than 1 did. It did not play *Anarchy In The UK* as Controller Aidan Day said 'I don't think it's very good' (*NME* 11/12/76). ILRs refused an advertisement for *God Save The Queen* featuring the song mixed with the national anthem (*NME* 4/6/77). The IBA then ruled that it contravened Section 41a of the Sound Broadcasting Act, which dealt with taste and decency, and instructed commercial stations not to play it (*NME* 11/6/77).

Capital was alone in banning the band's fourth single, *Holidays In The Sun*, in November 1977 for comparing Belsen to a holiday camp (*NME* 7/1/78). It later simply ignored The Pistols' single with Ronnie Biggs, *No One Is Innocent* because 'Biggs glorifies evil' (*NME* 15/7/78). The IBA also banned The Physicals' *All Sexed Up* EP in 1978 (*NME* 23/12/78).

Noticeably commercial stations have consistently differed with 1 on bans. This has resulted in two public bodies - the BBC and the (then) IBA and (now) Radio Authority holding different views over what constitutes indecent or offensive material. For example, in 1987 when 1 banned The Blow Monkeys *(Celebrate) The Day After You* Manchester's Radio Piccadilly also banned it, but Capital and some other ILRs carried on playing it - without complaint (*NME* 23 and 30/5/87).

However later in the year the IBA was accused of back door censorship by instructing the ILRs to seek legal advice before playing the Billy Bragg/Oyster Band single *Ballad of A Spycatcher* in the wake of former spy Peter Wright's memoirs (*NME* 31/10/87). The BBC had already played extracts of the record(23). But the commercial stations proved more liberal later in the same year when they carried on playing The Tams' *There Ain't Nothing Like Shaggin'* during the day (*NME* 5/12/87).

Generally the commercials have appeared more willing than 1 to take risks on records of a sexual nature, but less so on more political material - possibly fearful of government opposition to licence renewal. Thus in 1988 the IBA was quick to ban The Pogues *Birmingham Six*, which details the Six's innocence and the disadvantages suffered by Irish people in English courts, after the Government's ban on broadcasting material supporting "terrorist" organizations. The IBA commented that: 'We think these allegations might support, solicit or invite support for an organization provided (for) by the Home Secretary's notice' (*NME* 19/11/88).

LBC subsequently prevented the journalist Paul Foot playing his favourite song, the 1798 song, *Kelly the Boy from Killane* as all political songs by The Dubliners were forbidden. *The Ould Triangle* was substituted (*IOC* Vol.18 No.2 February 1989, p.8). That Petrol Emotion, who had previously commented on the Irish situation, had their *Cellophane* single banned by the IBA in December, despite it containing no direct references to Ireland (*IOC* Vol.19 No.9 October 1990, p.4).

But on commercial radio the market censors most. Former Radio 1 DJ Liz Kershaw (1994) wrote of how 'the advertisers ... exercise their financial muscle in dictating the editorial content of programmes'(24) when she moved to commercial radio. Greater emphasis on the market does not ensure greater diversity, but greater subordination to the needs of advertisers. This raises issues of future censorship.

Conclusion

The bannings, restrictions and marginalizations that I have noted in this chapter have one thing in common - they were all initiated without consulting those in whose name they were being done. Censorial decisions about popular music radio have taken place without the active participation of fans. Government initiatives have given listeners more bodies to complain to and more stations to listen to, but continued the denial of any participation in editorial and programme content decisions. Fans can complain about bans, but are denied participation in decisions over further ones.

At 1 decisions on what to play and what to ignore ultimately rest in the hands of the Controller, under the control of unelected BBC governors, who are in turn accountable to the Heritage Secretary and so to Parliament - a highly indirect form of democracy. The Government's proposals for the BBC of November 1992 included a chapter on 'Making The BBC Accountable' (National Heritage Department 1992, pp.36-41) and suggested new viewer and listener councils. It remains to be seen as to how this effects the output of 1. Unfortunately the centralization of media ownership that is now going on will not give audiences more say in what they hear. Censorship, direct and via marginalization or exclusion, will be exercised with profits, not musical criterion, in mind.

The history of 1's censorship, though limited, shows a number of things. First, an air of well intentioned paternalism is manifest. A **genuine** desire not to offend is ever present. Radio 1 prides itself on being professional and responsible, but this "responsibility" has sometimes led it to attribute causal effects to popular music which are, to say the least, contentious.

The second feature of 1's censorial policy has been to show the anti-democratic nature of censorship. It has seldom seen fit to debate its bannings and the BBC operates a thirty year rule on seeing documents relating to censorship, which **may** make sense in programmes which affect national security, but is ridiculous when dealing with pop. The actual banning process appears chaotic[25], but the pop audience which pays for 1 has a **right** to know who is making censorial decisions on its behalf.

Banned artists have never had the right of appeal, something which, despite the fact that a long drawn out process may kill the "buzz" surrounding a particular record, would be a step forward.

Listener representation could also contribute to a more diverse and less censorial Radio 1.

The last point about 1's censorial policy over the years has been that it underlines once again the relationship between censorial action and contemporary events. Banned records are in this sense a social barometer, reflecting what society is concerned about at a particular time. This can vary from moral panics over drugs to the problems of war, and from sex to politics. Here 1 has played a role in the stifling of unpopular or controversial voices, citing the need for "impartiality" as its reason.

But it would be churlish not to note the many good things 1 does. It has tried to meet demands of minorities within tight budgetary constraints and has given various genres like rap and indie-rock their own shows, an indulgence the commercials can rarely afford. Radio 1 may marginalize by catering for two audiences(26), but the commercials cater for only one - the advertiser. 1 plays a far wider range of music than the commercials and Grundy (1991) claims that:

> ... in any one week Radio 1 will play a minimum of two thousand different songs, but a commercial radio station ... (has) a job to make four hundred.

Thus if 1 marginalizes, commercials often exclude completely. The free market has **never** been a guarantee of musical, or any other, diversity(27). The way Capital sought the **same** audience as Radio 1 bears witness to this. The arrival of Virgin as the first national commercial station was hardly encouraging. Its AOR format seems destined to stifle rather than stimulate new pop. Nostalgia and the market seem set to censor via exclusion(28). Radio 1 at least demonstrates a sense of pop music's cultural worth: commercial stations see it as a means to the wealth of their shareholders.

But 1's future seems precarious. The BBC's Director General declined to give assurances about its future in November 1992 (*The Guardian* 27/11/92) and the organization said its future plans include: 'Little or no room for radio programmes which consist of non-stop Top 40 music' (ibid). The station was not even mentioned by name in the BBC's *Extending Choice* document which outlined the Corporation's future plans in 1992. The new head of BBC radio, Liz Forgan, has said that the BBC is 'committed to Radios 1 and 2 in their present form' (*The Guardian* 18/2/93), but as 1 is based primarily on singles - a format which appears in decline(29) - a change in orientation seems inevitable. In July 1993 Beerling departed and was replaced by Matthew Bannister. His shake up has resulted in a dramatic decline in audiences (see *NME* 26/11/94) and more questions about 1's future.

This chapter has outlined the history, censorial and otherwise, of popular music radio in Britain. That history passed a crucial milestone with the arrival of Virgin. In many ways 1992 is an appropriate place to end the story, as it was the last year of 1's almost unchallenged supremacy. The future seems to lie with the market and thus a different form of censorship.

Notes

1. See BSC 1991, p.29 for the ability of 1's listeners to recall bans by the station.

2. The BBC has become far too subtle for this and is as sensitive to accusations of censorship as it is to the need not to offend. My 1991 enquiries about the possibility of being able to confirm or deny any BBC "bans" in the period covered here was met with a reply that: 'internal papers of the BBC later than 1962 are not open for outside research' (BBC Written Archives Centre 1991). A thirty year rule appears to apply.

3. Briggs 1979, p.757 notes that Luxembourg played more pop records than the BBC at this time.

4. For early rock 'n' roll records banned by the BBC see Barnard 1989, pp.37/38 and Martin and Segrave 1986, pp.70 and 72.

5. Morrison 1992, p.104 notes there would have been no Radio 1 without the pirates.

6. See Chapman 1992, pp.168-174 for further details.

7. See Negus 1993, pp.63-67 for attempts to get on this list. *Q* editor Phil Sutcliffe has said that bands felt that not getting on the list was a form of censorship, Radio 1 1993c.

8. See *MM* 9 and 16/3/74, *NME* 16/3/80, Barnard 1989, p.119, *NME* 17/5/86 and *NME* 16/3/91 for changes to the playlist.

9. Gillett 1983, p.xi notes that radio can not play anything too interruptive. In October 1985 there were strong allegations that 1 was ignoring black music, see *NME* 26/10/85.

10. A methodological problem here is that of deciding what actually constitutes a "banned" record. Grundy 1991 warned me that 'a lot of the bans that you read about are not bans at all – they are the publicity people going out of their way to try and engineer a bit of interest'. See *NME* 26/9/92, p.62 for an

example of this.

I have tried to be as rigorous as possible when deeming a record to be banned and satisfied that any record I cited in depth was banned or, at a minimum, given only selective plays.

11.   For 1950s bans see Chapman 1992, p37.

12.   McCartney said that the lyric was "polygon", Radio 1 1993b.

13.   See Laing 1985, p.35. But 1 was better than commercials who, says Frith 1983, p.125, ignored punk because it was aimed at the under 20s who were not good advertising fodder.

14.   Radio 1 1993a presented the decision as a muddled one where the BBC were swept along by the pace of events.

15.   A snippet of the song was played on Radio 1 1993c.

16.   On 2/12/76, the day after the interview, the *Daily Telegraph* reported the banning of *Anarchy*.

17.   See Savage 1991, p.364. McLaren repeated the claim in Radio 1 1993b. Other victims of chart fixing include Crass whose album *Christ The Album* entered the Chart at 26 in the summer of 1982 and fell out of the Top 100 the following week - a 'statistical impossibility' according to *Music Master* 1990, p.28. The Dead Kennedys *Too Drunk To Fuck* was also a victim of chart fixing and kept out of the Top 30 to prevent embarrassment to *TOTP* presenters during chart run down, Radio 1 1993b and Gilliam 1991. For chart hyping see Street 1986, p.117, *M M* 1/4/67, *NME* 11/10/88, and *Vo x* August 1992, p.32 and October 1992, p.6. For shops distorting their own charts see Negus and du Guy 1994.

18.   Similarly, Portsmouth's Radio Victory banned Blondie's *Island of Lost Dreams* during the Falklands War, Radio 1 1993b.

19.   According to Radio 1 1993a *Walk on the Wild Side* was eventually vetoed some years later.

20. I am grateful to Spencer Leigh for this reference.

21. I am grateful to Robert Chapman for this reference.

22. An example was Radio Piccadilly 1981 ban on The Freshies' *I'm In Love With The Girl on The Virgin Megastore Check Out Desk*. Set in Manchester, it became popular locally, but broke IBA rules on advertising and was banned. It received plays again when Virgin was changed to "a certain", Radio 1 1993a.

23. See *NME* 17/10/87 for the BBC passing this song.

24. See the *Radio Authority Bulletins* No.6 p.10 and No.7 p.7 for upheld complaints against "obscene" records.

25. This is judging by Radio 1 1993a.

26. For marginalization see *The Guardian* of 3/12/76 where 1 talked of playing records only according to "music merit" but that some punk was 'arguably not in this category'. On Radio 1 1993c Beerling denied that not playing records amounted to censorship, but this is a simplification of the issue.

27. Former Home Secretary Kenneth Baker noted his fear of the market by saying that it should not be allowed total freedom in broadcasting as: 'You can't go on having more and more pop stations', *The Observer* 16/2/92.

28. On Radio 1 1993c *Music Week* editor Steve Redmond talked of 'musical censorship' resulting if opening up the market led to less choice.

29. See Cosgrove 1988a. For a contrary view see E. Bell 1993.

8 Ob-Seen? Pop and television

Television moves pop broadcasting from a purely aural form, to a mixture of aural and visual and provides the possibility of artists offending by their actions, as well as by their words. The fact that televised pop has often been used as "family" entertainment also creates a more censorious environment, with the BBC's long running *Top of The Pops (TOTP)* exemplifying this. But television has also been important in spreading pop's message and several moments of television have passed into pop legend such as Presley only being shown from the waist up on America's *Ed Sullivan Show* in 1956, The Sex Pistols/Grundy interview in 1976 and the *Live Aid* concert of 1985.

The rise of video has made pop's visual aspects increasingly important, but initially television was wary of showing pop at all. Early shows like *Ready Steady Go, The 6.5 Special* and *Oh Boy!* were often oases in a pop desert and carefully controlled by their elder patrons. For much of the period I am concerned with the **only** regular shows for popular music on BBC television were *TOTP* and *The Old Grey Whistle Test (OGWT)* - the latter of which occupied a marginal space at the end of the BBC 2 schedule. Television again brought forth various forms of censorship - including banning, exclusion and marginalization.

Lennon (1991) writes that 'British broadcasting has always had a Nanny relationship with its viewers' and this is apparent in televised pop. At best pop has been seen as cheap entertainment, at worst a potential source of harm. It has been consigned to either "family", "children's" and "specialist" spots and seldom been given prime time spots. But its potential for getting out of hand was soon noticed, as early *6.5 Special* performances by Wee Willie Harris led to questions being asked in Parliament, where the BBC was accused of promoting "teenage decadence" (B. Welch 1990, p.75).

When pop started to get more serious British television struggled to cope.   The late sixties music press often commented on the lamentable state of TV pop, which was typified by exclusion and/or sterile, patronizing, formats.   In 1970 letters to *M M* complained that BBC 2's only pop show, Disco 2, had a late night "ghetto" slot - often after midnight (*M M* 6 and 13/6/80).   Its successor, the *OGWT*, suffered similar problems.   A 1970 *M M* investigation (26/9/70) into the state of TV pop concluded that it was inadequate both in terms of quality and quantity.   By 1972 things were little better - the BBC's coverage of pop was limited to the chart orientated *TOTP*, the marginalized *OGWT* and *Sounds For Saturday*.   Independent viewers had only *The Dave Cash Radio Show* (sic).

Throughout the 1970s *TOTP* and the *OGWT* held sway.   The arrival of Channel 4 in 1982 and various regional initiatives on ITV gave limited competition, but the BBC continued to rule the pop roost.   By the late 1980s, as satellite television entered Britain, pop was again used to provide cheap entertainment.   Programmes that have tried to show pop's cultural worth have tended to be one offs such as *South Bank Show* and *Horizon* specials.   BBC 2's last excursion into pop in 1992, *The Late Show: Later*, was first broadcast on 8 October 1992 at 11.55 pm - the same "ghetto" slot the *OGWT* was often consigned to. Little appears to have changed.   Moreover, censorship problems have constantly plagued televised pop as will now be shown, starting with Britain's largest cultural organization.

Pop and the Beeb - licensed to kill?

The BBC launched Britain's first regular pop show, *Hit Parade*, in 1952, *Cool For Cats* followed in 1956, and the *6.5 Special*, in February 1957.   On 1 June 1959 *Juke Box Jury* began its initial twelve year run. This programme produced the first censorial action in televised pop during the years in question here.   Again the 1967 drug scare is relevant: it was against this backdrop that the panel on the programme first condemned and then withdrew The Game's *The Addicted Man*, which EMI subsequently withdrew (see above). Television here effectively "killed" a single before it had had a chance to start (*M M* 14/1/67). Juke Box Jury was a "family" show - thus again linking this concept with censorship.

TOTP began on 1 January 1964, but by the early 1970s it seemed unable to cover a market which was splintering into pop/chart and rock/art sections. This divide was mirrored by a Reithian low/high-brow divide within BBC television where the populist BBC 1 got the charts (*TOTP*) and the cultural BBC2 got the progressive scene (*Disco 2, OGWT* etc). Here again was censorship via ghettoization, as the late night spots given to the BBC2 shows in the pre-VCR age prevented much of the rock audience being able to see them. In 1971 *MM* noted that 'ITV provide relatively no pop opposition' (*M M* 26/6/71). So, if the BBC censored via marginalization, the independent stations used exclusion.

By September 1971 it was announced that *Disco 2* was to be replaced by the *OGWT*. Three years later letters were still appearing in *M M* asking why the *OGWT* had to go out at 11.55 pm (*MM* 18/5/74). The *OGWT* seems to have been free from any major disputes over censorship, but elsewhere in pop the BBC found itself embroiled in censorial controversy.

In the run up to the 1979 General Election it postponed a BBC 2 *Omnibus* documentary, *Dread Beat An' Blood*, on British reggae poet Linton Kwesi Johnson. This was dropped from its scheduled showing on 5 March "because of its political content" and eventually shown, after the election, on 7 June. In the programme Johnson alleged that elements in the Conservative Party, including Margaret Thatcher, were racist. Asked if they were being censorious, the BBC declined to comment (*NME* 14/4/79). Birmingham police forbade a showing of the film at the city's Gala cinema on March 17 on the grounds that it was 'liable to incite a riot' (ibid).

Punk was also kept at arm's length by the BBC, although its early evening *Nationwide* news programme did a report on the Sex Pistols on 12 November 1976 (Savage 1991, p.255), some three weeks before the Grundy debacle (see below). This period saw favouritism in pop by regularly featuring artists who had BBC 1 series, such as Vince Hill and Cliff Richard, on *TOTP* (Street 1986, p.125).

In January 1980 The Au Pairs recorded the usual two songs for BBC 2's early evening *Look Hear* youth programme. One, the pro-feminist *Come Again*, was banned from broadcast, because its lyrics dealt with female orgasm. Producer Roger Casstles commented:

... we go out at 6.50 on a Tuesday night, we've got a large audience between 11 and 16, and I thought the lyrics were unsuitable ... They're basically about faking orgasm ... I thought that 7 O'Clock in the evening was not the time for a band to be on television singing about their sexual hang ups ...

... my worry was that parents of the under-14s watching would've had **their** say and the programme might well have been taken off the air. The popular media just aren't ready for these kind of lyrics yet ... If we're gonna get this sort of hassle ... I'm gonna play safe and only book bands from big labels' (*NME* 2/2/80. Emphasis in original).

Casstles' remarks merit detailed comment because they reveal several of the implicit censorial borders that producers working with pop timed for the evening had (and still have) to contend with. First there is the watershed. The song is inappropriate because of the programme's transmission time. A teenage audience is to be denied songs about faked orgasms. Furthermore the song is deemed unsuitable because it might elicit an unfavourable response. "Parents" and "the media" might get upset. Note here that it is **not** that the song causes harm to children, but rather their **parents'** complaints, that is the worry. The fact that the lyrics would have probably passed the vast majority of the audience by was unimportant - the **potential** response was enough to get the song censored.

The final comment about only booking bands from major labels in future is also revealing. It incorporates the idea that major labels are able to bring bands into line (the behaviour of Madonna et al since then may well have disproved this). This involves an implicit bias against "left field" or more independently minded (both musically and ideologically) artists. If these artists are harder to control it appears that the BBC is less likely to televise them.

By 1991 the BBC was televising the BPI's annual Brits award, with Jonathan King running the event. The Gulf War was on when the Brits were shown in 1991 and artists appearing were told not to mention it (*NME* 16/2/91). Those who disobeyed this, including Lisa Stansfield and Sinead O'Connor, were subject to censure (*MM*, 16/2/91). The following year the KLF were cut from the televised highlights after a plan to cover the audience in offal (*NME* 22 and 29/2/92).

By then the BBC was considering its future. With the spectre of market forces haunting it the future for minority musics again appears to be one of censorship via exclusion. But overt censorship is also still on the agenda. In 1993 BBC2's *Late Show* cut the word "motherfucker" from Rage Against The Machine's *Bullet In The Head* (*NME* 6/3/93). But for years there was only one show ...

Top of The Pops - charting censorship?

From its inception on 1 January 1964 *TOTP* was always unashamedly chart orientated. What really mattered was **not** introducing new music, but who was No. 1 in the charts. Artists who did not chart were unlikely to appear on *TOTP*. This meant that to get prime time television exposure artists almost **had** to alter material in order to try and crack the charts and thus *TOTP*. Again this did not entail overt censorship, but marginalization. This was taken further by *TOTP*'s notion of itself as family entertainment and a broadcasting time of around 7 pm, which always militated against it featuring anything from the more extreme parts of popular music. But overt censorship was by no means unusual.

In 1967, after Mick Jagger and Keith Richards successfully appealed against initial custodial sentences for drug possession, the Stones released *We Love You* to thank fans for their support. Peter Whitehead made a film, featuring a court room scene, for the single. According to Bill Wyman (1991, p.541), *TOTP* rejected the film as, 'Producer Johnnie Stewart did not consider it suitable for the type of audience that watched the programme'. Whitehead commented that:

> Pop music today is a socially committed form and the BBC are being irresponsible to ignore what is happening in the whole of the pop business today ... Pop is not all sweetness and light, as the programme would like to see it (ibid).

Drugs again caused problems in September 1968. Sly and The Family Stone were in the charts with *Dance To The Music* and when they came over to tour *TOTP* decided to have them on. However, as the band went through Heathrow Airport bassist Larry Graham Jnr. was arrested and charged with possessing cannabis. *TOTP* then cancelled their booking. A BBC spokesman commented that:

In the light of the circumstances which occurred at London Airport the day before the show, Johnnie Stewart ... did not want to have them on the programme (*M M* 21/9/68).

TOTP banned The Kinks' *Plastic Man* because it contained the word "bum". It suggested the word "thumb" instead, despite the fact the song had already been played on both television's *Dee Time* and on 1 (*M M* 3/5/69). This is an example of the discrepancies between *TOTP* and 1's censorial policy over the years. These partly reflect BBC inconsistency, but also the different problems caused by aural and visual representations of pop. But *TOTP* joined 1's ban on Jane Birkin and Serge Gainsbourg's *Je T'Aime* (*M M* 4/10/69).

The early 1970s engendered sexual confusion as glam rock artists such as David Bowie toyed with "gender bending". Bowie's film for his *John I'm Only Dancing* single in October 1972 featured him "interpreting" the song in an "ethereal" way and his manager, Tony DeFries, claimed *TOTP* rejected it on the grounds of it 'not being to their taste'. This was denied by the BBC who said that: 'A film has to be acceptable. It is up to the producer whether or not he decides to feature it' (*M M* 7/10/72). By 1973 *TOTP* was the **only** prime time TV programme for pop (*M M* 30/6/73) - again an example of censorship by exclusion and marginalization.

In 1976 Rod Stewart's *Tonight's The Night*, a record criticized by Whitehouse (1977 pp.38/39), was vetoed by *TOTP* as unsuitable for its family audience because of its lyrics (*NME* 5/6/76). But it was played by 1 and in a BBC TV special broadcast at the same time in the evening as *TOTP*.

When it became clear that punk was not simply going to go away, *TOTP* began to have bands like The Jam and The Buzzcocks on. But it held the line against The Sex Pistols' *God Save The Queen* thus contributing to one of the few overt blanket broadcasting bans seen in British pop. *NME* (11/6/77) reported that:

A statement issued jointly by BBC Radio and Television says the Corporation "has no intention of playing the record because it is in gross bad taste."

TOTP producer Robin Nash said that the single was 'quite unsuitable' for the show (ibid).

The next punk influenced band to fall foul of *TOTP* censors were

The Gang of Four. In July 1979 they were due to appear playing their *At Home He's a Tourist* single, but this was vetoed at the last minute when the BBC objected to the words "rubbers" and "packets". The song is about sexual exploitation in discos and contains the lyrics: "Down on the disco floor/They make their profit/From the things they sell/To help you cop off/And the rubbers in your top left pocket." The band offered to change "rubbers" to "packets" but this was rejected. The BBC suggested it be changed to "rubbish", but the band refused and were dropped from the show. BBC press officer Ann Rosenburg said that:

> We felt that the line was not suitable for the young and family audience which is the Top of The Pops audience ... "rubbish" ... would have been an acceptable compromise for us ... What we wanted to do was change the meaning. People, particularly parents, could have taken offence ... Changing it to "packets" doesn't change the meaning of the song ... (*NME* 30/7/79).

These remarks project a stereotyped view of the family cozily sat around the television in perfect harmony and listening to every syllable. That contraception may be a suitable topic for "family" viewing is not even considered, despite the fact that it **could** be argued that the song **might** be educational or that few of the viewers would have dwelt on the lyrics.

Rosenburg had no compunction in saying that the BBC sought to change the meaning of the song - a highly censorial act. The band could only appear if they agreed to change their song's meaning. Here censorship did not have to entail a complete ban, but playing a somewhat vague game of chance over what *TOTP* producers would accept.

Although bans from *TOTP* on the grounds of unsuitable lyrics continued, the rise of video in the 1980s saw a corresponding increase in bannings because of unsuitable visual content. In 1981 The Police's video for their *Invisible Sun* single, featuring images of Belfast, was rejected by *TOTP*. The song was anti-violence, but the BBC contended that:

> ... while the lyrics make oblique references to the troubles in Northern Ireland ... The film is solely devoted to footage shot in the Province which could be misinterpreted and said to convey

meanings which are not present in the lyrics (*NME* 3/10/81).

The problem of "misinterpretation" is endemic to any artistic project and is, at best, a flimsy excuse for censorship. Police manager Miles Copeland condemned the BBC as 'petty bureaucrats who are attempting to stifle artistic expression' (ibid).

Violence caused problems with The Rolling Stones' video for their 1983 *Undercover of the Night* single. Set in South America, it featured Mick Jagger being kidnapped and then shot through the head inter-cut with scenes of an American teenager trying to seduce his girlfriend as they watched the television news. The aim was to show how television had turned the horrors of real violence in South America into entertainment. Only in Britain was the video banned (Martin and Segrave 1988, p.277). Protection of children was again the main factor behind this censorship, as was shown by *TOTP* producer Michael Hurll's remark that 'the violence in that video was not what I would let my kids see' (*NME* 7/4/84).

In 1984 *TOTP* eventually joined in the BBC's ban on Frankie Goes To Hollywood's *Relax*. Here Hurll commented that: 'When I see all the problems and suffering going on in the world, I find it difficult to get worked up about the banning of a record by the BBC' (ibid). This superficially reasonable view is also one with an air of moral cowardice. Censorship of a No. 1 record **is** an issue (although **obviously** one which pales against the fate of the starving in Africa). The country's leading cultural organization banning the country's most popular record is of some import.

David Bowie caused the BBC further problems in 1987. His *China Girl* video, featuring him making love on a beach, had been heavily edited by the BBC in 1983 and this time the video for his *Day In Day Out* featured a woman being assaulted in the back seat of a car and then chased down a dark alley. *TOTP* banned the film. The BBC commented that: 'This video, although not a "nasty" in the recognized sense, was considered unsuitable for screening anywhere in the BBC schedule' (*NME* 4/4/87).

Again contemporary events are relevant. The comment about it not being a "nasty" only makes sense in the context over the "nasties" scare and the subsequent Video Recordings Act of 1984. At this time Hurll warned video producers of a "new puritanism" at the BBC, from which these events cannot be divorced. *NME* reported that Hurll had warned: 'that certain graphic content in the past was likely

144

to be turned down this year' (ibid) - again illustrating that censorship involves ever changing parameters, not ever increasing liberalization.

Evidence of this "new puritanism" came around the same time as pop's bete noires of the time, The Beastie Boys, had their *Fight For Your Right To Party* video banned by *TOTP*. It was initially shown, but later banned after complaints (*Sounds* 4/4/87). George Michael's *I Want Your Sex* video was also banned by the show in the same year (*NME* 6/6/87).

When acid house came to prominence in 1988 *TOTP* showed its customary caution. It featured D-Mob's No 1, *We Call It Acieed*, but received a number of complaints, some because band members were wearing "smiley" T-shirts, which were then being associated with ecstasy (again linking censorship to contemporary events) and some because of the song itself (*NME* 29/10/88).

As the record subsequently went down the charts the issue of it being on again did not arise, but it appears that *TOTP* had learnt a lesson. A spokesman explained that it had:

> ... received numerous complaints from upset parents following the appearance of d.mob and have decided that the word acid is not now acceptable in either a lyric or a title (*RM* 5/11/88)(1).

Sex and violence remained perennial concerns. In January 1990 Public Enemy's *Welcome To The Terrordome*, which features the band brandishing machine guns, was vetoed by *TOTP* as 'unsuitable for family viewing' (*NME* 27/1/90). *TOTP* also used a cleaned up version of Madonna's *Justify My Love* video later in the year, rather than the original one which featured her kissing another woman and various inversions of conventional sex roles (*NME* 15/12/90).

In February 1992 the Jesus and Mary Chain's *Reverence* was banned because of its lyrics, an amended version of which were played on Radio 1. *TOTP* explained that:

> Our producer felt that the lyrics "I want to die like Jesus Christ/I want to die on a bed of spikes" were unsuitable for broadcast at 7 pm, when children are likely to be watching the programme (*NME* 22/2/92).

The same reasoning presumably lay behind *TOTP*'s decision not to play Genesis' *Jesus He Knows Me* later in the year (*Vo x* December 1992). But *TOTP* refused to ban The Shamen's *Ebeneezer Goode* video in September 1992 and the BSC then upheld a complaint against the show for playing it(2). So this history of the show ends with it defying censors.

By this time the BBC was debating its future and *TOTP*'s own future was in doubt, especially as it is based on the apparently declining singles market. Its chart orientated format and reliance on a "family audience" always limited its potential to explore pop's extremes. When this was combined with a notion of a "watershed" time for words like "rubbers" and "bum", as well as for the portrayal of certain acts and topics, a conservative approach was inevitable. It is still as notable for what it excludes as for what it includes. But overt and covert censorship are by no means the prerogative solely of the BBC.

The independent television companies - underselling pop?

Unlike the BBC, independent television has never had a major long running pop series. With stations now obliged to compete with for their franchises every few years, this situation seems unlikely to change as few programmes on the independent network are guaranteed an extended run. Commercial television's regional structure means that its coverage of pop has tended to involve a series of local initiatives, which were occasionally picked up by other regions. The type of service pop fans received from the independent network thus depended on where they lived - again a reflection of the locally mediated nature of British pop censorship. However several shows did get shown nationally on the independent network, which meant that censorial decisions made around them had a national impact.

Independent television's first pop programme was *Oh Boy!* which began on 15 June 1958. Under the guidance of Jack Good a respectable form of youth entertainment was nurtured. But the running was not always smooth. In December 1958 an appearance by Cliff Richard on the show was attacked by *NME*'s Alley Cat columnist as:

... some of the most crude exhibitionism ever seen on British TV ...

His violent hip-swinging ... was revolting - hardly the kind of performance any parent could wish their child to witness (*NME* 3/2/79).

The *Daily Sketch* newspaper picked up on these comments and put pressure on Good to make Richard tone down his act, which he subsequently did - again showing the censorial power of the press.

Ready Steady Go was the next independent television pop show of any import and it began on 9 August 1959. The series finished before the period of this book. Perhaps the first major television pop event in these twenty five years on the independent network was the refusal of the Rolling Stones to go on the revolving stage, as was expected of all guests, after their performance on the live *Sunday Night at The London Palladium* on 22 January 1967 (Wyman 1991, pp.478-479). However the band censored themselves by playing *She Smiled Sweetly* instead of the more risqué *Let's Spend The Night Together* on the *Eamon Andrews Show* a few days later (ibid, p.482).

In June 1971 *MM* reported that 'the BBC has an absolute monopoly on how pop music is transmitted to the masses' (*MM* 26/6/71), as ITV only used pop in the context of "family" entertainment shows and the ILRs did not then exist. But some independent stations did seek to rock the boat a little. In 1972 Thames Television denied that there was a total broadcasting ban on Wings' *Give Ireland Back To The Irish*, as they intended to feature it, if Paul McCartney gave their *Today* programme an interview. Some pointed out that EMI, distributors of the single, were major shareholders in Thames (*MM* 25/3/72)(3).

Children were often the target audience of any pop programmes that ITV **did** show and this caused problems in November 1976. The late afternoon *Pauline's Quirkes* show featured pop, Quirke and resident band Flintlock. Some sketches, involving slave auctions and requests for the band to strip, upset moralist press commentators. Alan Coren of *The Times* described it as 'calculated to rot the minds' of its viewers (*The Times* 7/12/76)(4). The show's producer defended it as an attempt to de-mystify pop idols (*Daily Express* 2/12/76). But Anglia subsequently dropped the show (*The Guardian* 7/12/76)(5), although Thames, its makers, kept it on, again illustrating the regional nature of censorship. It is important to realize that television was already under scrutiny before the next case came along.

On Friday 1 December 1976 The Sex Pistols appeared on Thames' Today programme as a last minute replacement for Queen. The interview was conducted, in less than professional manner, by Bill Grundy. Importantly, it was this interview more than any **musical** event which put punk into the public eye. During it Steve Jones said of the £40,000 that EMI had advanced the band: 'We've fucking spent it', and when Rotten said "shit", Grundy asked him to repeat it, which he did. When Grundy made a suggestive comment to Siouxsie Sioux Jones called him a 'dirty sod'. Grundy goaded him by saying: 'Say something outrageous' and Jones responded with: 'You dirty bastard', 'You dirty fucker' and, after Grundy had commented '**what** a clever boy', 'You fucking rotter' (Savage 1991, pp.258/9).

The press, already agitated by the Quirke show(6), reacted apoplectically and called for heads to roll. Grundy was suspended and The Pistols eventually sacked by EMI. Thus began a whole series of censorial moves against punk. The band's offence had been to break the conventions of television, to swear at **tea time**, 'with the Children and Nan around', as the *Daily Mirror* put it (*Daily Mirror* 3/12/76)(7). Ninety seconds of television, shown only in the London region, engendered censorial actions against pop on a scale which had not been seen previously and would not be seen again until raves in the late 1980s. The importance of Grundy is not that it was itself an example of pop censorship, but that it shows how television can act as a prompt for other censorial action.

When *God Save the Queen* was released in June 1977 *NME* reported that the IBA:

> ... have instructed all commercial radio stations not to play it, claiming it is in breach of Section 41a of the IBA Act (a paragraph concerning bad taste), and ITV will automatically follow suit (*NME* 11/6/77).

As already noted, adverts for the single were also banned and the IBA banned adverts for the band's *Never Mind the Bollocks* album in November 1977 (*NME* 12/11/77). Martin and Segrave (1988, p.228) note that:

> The ITCA's head of copy clearance, Stuart Ruttledge ... said he had no objection to the ad, "It was the record itself we objected to ... Some parts of the lyric are unspeakable".

However the band did get the chance to appear on ITV's *So It Goes* in the same month (*NME* 26/11/77)(8).

Even after their split The Sex Pistols were still censored by ITV. *Revolver*, a show generally sympathetic to punk, drew the line at the Pistols' record with Ronnie Biggs, *The Biggest Blow*. A film of this was due to be shown on the programme in August 1978. Presenter Peter Cook announced the film when, reported *NME*, viewers saw it 'censored in front of their very eyes' (*NME* 19/8/78)(9). The decision to cut it was taken by Associated Television's director of production, Francis Essex, who claimed that it failed to meet ATV's 'presentation and performance standards' (*NME* 19/8/78).

The IBA had refused to tell ATV to drop the film, despite pleas from Tory MP Jill Knight for them to do so. *Revolver* producer Mickie Most explained the ban by saying that:

ATV decided that it wasn't in the public interest to show film of a convicted criminal living it up with scantily-clad girls on some Rio de Janeiro beach. It didn't merit inclusion either artistically or politically for the company (ibid).

The latter comment may reflect the fact that there could have been objections to ATV's broadcasting licence being renewed if its output had upset powerful interests, which gives an insight into the day to day censorial constraints those in television pop work under.

Independent television's Saturday morning children's show, *Tiswas*, joined *TOTP* in banning the video of The Police's *Invisible Sun* (*NME* 30/10/81) and the IBA also cut The Stone's *Undercover* before allowing independent stations to use it (Martin and Segrave 1988, p.277). Children were the reason given when independent television's *Get Fresh* programme decided to ban the video of Kim Wilde's *Say You Really Want Me* in 1987. It featured her on a bed with 4 men who were wearing boxer shorts. *Get Fresh* producer Mike Forte described the video as "too naughty" for his show. Wilde's label, MCA, commented that: 'Kim's brother and sister, aged seven and eight, have seen it and they approve ... They don't think it's rude' (*NME* 15/8/87). But ITV did and banned the video from their children's shows.

1987 was also the year of the Beastie Boys' notoriety. Their bans included one on independent television's *The Roxy*, which rejected the video for the band's *She's Crafty* single, featuring footage of an

American tour. Producer Alistair Pirrie, explained that:

> ... the spectacle of a near-naked woman in a cage being prodded by a group of unpleasant looking youths with beer cans is not the sort of thing to put on the air when a lot of young children are watching (*NME* 17/10/87).

Again the protection of children was given as a reason for censorship.

The Pogues were victims of ITV censorship in April 1988 when a Ken Russell film featuring their version of *The Gentleman Soldier* and footage from Northern Ireland was cut from the *South Bank Show*, where it was going to be part of the Irish section of an A-Z of British Music. The reason presenter Melvyn Bragg gave for its exclusion yet again exemplifies how the censorial climate is shaped by contemporary events. The screening was due just after two British soldiers had been killed after driving into a Republican funeral cortege in Belfast and Bragg said the film was:

> ... about a soldier who takes a girl into a sentry box. Afterwards the girl goes away and the soldier is blown up ... I thought that we could not show it in its entirety **after recent events** (*NME* 2/4/88. Emphasis mine).

Contemporary events also shaped the next IBA ban. The 1988 minor moral panic surrounding raves and the use of Ecstasy was underway when Children of The Night recorded a single called *It's A Trip*, which some Tory MPs wanted removed from shops because of its drugs references. It was due to be played on the late night *Hit Man and Her* programme in November, but the IBA vetoed the song at the last minute. The show's producer explained that: 'It was felt that we'd be treading dangerous water if we used it' (*NME* 3/12/88). The IBA also banned an advertisement by De La Soul for their *Three Feet High and Rising* album in January 1990 because it used the CND symbol, which contravened regulations regarding political publicity (*NME* 6/1/90).

The ITC does not record the number of complaints it receives regarding pop videos, so small is the amount (ITC 1991), but when controversy has arisen independent television producers, like those at the BBC, have not been slow to pull the plug on pop. This has inevitably meant that popular music, parts of which often set out to provoke and outrage, has often been only cursorily covered by television. But one television channel was specifically set up to provide **non**-mainstream entertainment: how has it treated pop?

The same old story? Pop censorship on Channel 4

Channel 4 started in 1982 with the specific aim of catering for minority tastes which might not otherwise get television coverage. It has often had an adventurous programming policy and taken British television into uncharted territory, which has led to controversy. It has however also been involved in censorship(10), which has encompassed pop.

In December 1982 the station was caught up in a furore surrounding the Virgin Prunes. The band recorded a gig, for possible broadcast by 4 on its *Whatever You Want* programme, during which members of the band simulated intercourse and oral sex. A vicar who heard of this complained to Mary Whitehouse, who passed on the information to Home Secretary William Whitelaw. Although the film was not scheduled for broadcasting the station found itself at the centre of a censorship row with some Tory MPs signing a Commons motion telling 4 to clean up or get out (*NME* 11/12/82 and *IOC* Vol.12 No.2 April 1983, p.44).

The channel's excursion into pop programmes had started on 5 November 1982 with *The Tube*. This programme went out live on Friday evenings, was 105 minutes long and featured a chaotic mixture of live acts and filmed interviews, etc. It was dropped after presenter Jools Holland referred to the audience as "groovy fuckers" in an advertisement for the programme, just prior to its broadcast. Switch followed and since then 4 has had a number of pop programmes, including *The Word* and the original *Chart Show*.

The Saturday Night Live show featured alternative comedians and music. The Pogues appeared on it in April 1988 and were halfway through their *Birmingham Six* protest song when the producer cut to a commercial break. Whether this was direct censorship or merely the scheduled time for the break was a contested point. The show's producer, Geoff Posner, claimed he was merely running to schedule, but the band's manager, Frank Murray, claimed that it was censorship and that the programme had to have two minutes of ad libs at the end to fill in the time left by cutting the song (*NME* 30/4/88). Censorship here was hard to prove, but the song's contentious nature and its subsequent banning by the IBA aroused suspicions.

The Pogues also suffered more of 4's censorship in August of the same year when their *Fiesta* video was banned from the *Chart Show*. Again protecting children was given as the reason. The film included bullfighting, drinking and a wine bottle smashing. *Chart Show* press officer Frances McPaddern explained that:

> ... we have a set of guidelines we have to adhere to because there are children watching. Drinking is one of the things we're not allowed to show (*NME* 6/8/88).

In 1983 the IBA ordered 4 to cut parts of The Stones' *Undercover* video in 1983 before allowing *The Tube* to use it for its early evening slot (Martin and Segrave 1988, p.277), but generally 4 has had a more liberal attitude than its competitors. Its late night pop programme, *The Word*, was the only British television channel to show Madonna's *Justify My Love* video uncut (*NME* 15/12/90). It has also avoided major controversies over pop censorship, although James allege that 4 stopped them from performing *Live a Life of Love* on the *Jonathan Ross Show* in 1992 because it was blasphemous (*Vox* September 1992) - a favourite Whitehouse bogey.

Videos and satellite television

MTV and other satellite stations are making an increasing impact in Britain and seem likely to take up an ever greater percentage of viewing time. They will doubtlessly become embroiled in their own censorship debates. Meanwhile the possibility of a pan-EC broadcasting policy could complicate matters still further. Worries over the effects of videos can be seen in *TOTP*'s decision not to show the video for Wang Chung's 1987 hit *Everybody Have Fun Tonight* because the editing technique used in it was held to cause epilepsy (*NME* 28/2/87) and in the eighty complaints *TOTP* received for showing Michael Jackson grabbing his crotch in his 1991 *Black Or White* video (*The Observer* 17/11/91).

Thus far censorship rows on the satellites have been rare.

Billboard reported that in 1989 the Cable Authority had drawn up a code for pop videos, as they caused 'more regulatory problems than all other programmes put together' (Hunter 1989. See also *NME* 5/8/88). But few censorial problems have occurred. MTV in Europe has rarely been in censorship rows - most of which have occurred in the USA[11]. In-house censorship by labels undoubtedly contributes to the comparative rarity of notable cases[12]. Different videos of the same song may be used for different programmes, depending on their broadcasting time (Hunter 1989).

Pop videos are also used as home entertainment, but thus far have failed to cause any major censorial rows. All must be classified under the Video Recordings Act of 1984 and most record companies seem to have succeeded in getting their acts to at least ensure that their videos get a certificate. The only exception I found to this was a video by Nine Inch Nails for their *Happiness In Slavery* track. Featuring American performance artist Bob Flannagan being tortured and pierced by a robotic device, it was refused a certificate by the BBFC and now rests in Island's vaults (*NME* 28/4/92).

The smallness of MTV's audience thus far[13] has meant its censorial problems have not been picked up on by the media. The situation for other satellite and cable stations appears to be the same. But as they gather viewers more censorship seems inevitable[14].

The visual aspects of pop have alerted the censors and, once alerted, they have acted on behalf of the audience, but seldom consulted them[15]. Televised pop has been allowed, but only conditions which have worked against its appreciation as a cultural form. But conditions upon the way in which pop can be consumed are multiplied once pop leaves home and goes to the concert halls.

Notes

1. See also *The Sun* 26/10/88, where the band Perfectly Ordinary People claimed to have lost 5 television appearances in the wake of the *TOTP* ban.

2. See BSC *Complaints Bulletin* No.22 November 1992. Radio 1 1993b said that *TOTP* producer Stan Appel decided to carry on using the track and ride out the short term storm rather than banning it, giving it more publicity and prolonging its chart life.

3. It was also alleged the EMI dropped the Sex Pistols in 1977 because it owned half the shares in Thames, which broadcast their interview with Bill Grundy.

4. The original quote was a few days before.

5. See Ryle 1976 for an attack on the show.

6. See, for example, *Daily Express* 2/12/76 which reports Grundy and Quirke on the same page, thus linking the two to show that something was wrong with television.

7. The *Daily Express* of 2/12/76 also complained that the Quirke show was shown at "tea time".

8. *So It Goes* was dropped after Iggy Pop went on wearing a horse's tail and swore. *Vo x* January 1992.

9. *The Biggest Blow* is also known as *No One is Innocent*, Savage 1991, p.563.

10. For examples of 4 censoring see Lennon 1991, *The Observer* 3/3/91 (on being unable to show the film of penises, *Dick*, and cuts to *Sex in Our Time*) and *The Guardian* 11/5/91 (where the BSC dismissed a claim against 4 for using swearing in a show about rap lyrics).

11. For examples of MTV policy in the US see *NME* 9/7/83 and 2/6/84 and *Gay Times* November 1991.

12. See Negus, 1992 p.98. Negus also points out that videos are often made with a world audience in mind, further limiting the chances that can be taken.

13. *The Guardian* 23/11/92 put satellite television's share of the audience at 5.7% of the total.

14. Young 1993 noted that the larger the audience, the more likely the BBC was to censor.

15. This may, belatedly, be changing. See *The Guardian* and *The Independent* 28/5/93 for the BBC planning more audience consultation.

Part Four
Live music

9 'Keep yer ya yas in' – censorship of live music

Live music moves pop censorship from the private to the public. Problems with live music can begin with finding a venue. This is likely to be covered by various local bye laws on safety, fire, age of audiences etc., which can restrict live music's availability. Objections can be made to the choice of venue, noise, the behaviour of the crowd - before, during and after gigs; artists' stage antics and last, and possibly least, song content. Objectors can range from local residents (who are a major added censorial ingredient here), through to councils and the police. Bans can be imposed before a gig, so it never takes place, or after it - so that a venue will not book certain acts again if they or their fans "misbehave" during a gig. Much of this activity is not aimed directly at censoring pop, but still has censorial impact.

The next two chapters look at various bans on live shows and the censorial agencies behind them. This chapter deals with indoor venues and the next with outdoor events. Looking at bans by venues will again show that censorial actions are often determined by contemporary events and locally mediated. Two agencies which often contribute to bans - local authorities and the police - are also examined here.

Venues

Problems surrounding venues come into two main categories. Firstly there is the problem of setting up a venue that is suitable for live popular music. This involves various regulations, health, fire and safety directives which can be imposed by local councils and possibly having to overcome objections by local residents who might not welcome the disturbance in their neighbourhood. These problems can be characterized as being those of the venue owners.

Problems can continue once the venue is open. Local authorities monitor venues and can close those whose activities they disapprove of. For example, in May 1978 London's Roundhouse, home to many 60s' "happenings", stopped presenting gigs after a series of a run-ins over noise with the GLC (*NME* 6/5/78) and in April 1990 the Fulham Greyhound, a regular gig for new bands, closed because it was unable to renew its drinks licence (*NME* 21/4/90). These examples again show the importance of locality to censorship in Britain. The point is not that all regulations are censorship, but that some bye laws can further blur any strict demarcation line.

Marginalization can occur via the bookings policies some venues pursue. This brings forth the second set of problems - those faced mainly by the promoter, often concerning venues objecting to certain acts. For example, in July 1971 Slade found it hard to get gigs because they were skinheads (*MM* 14/7/71). London's The Town and Country II faced criticism over its bookings policy in 1989 when it appeared to go "up market" and excluded bands it had previously been happy to book, including the Guana Batz and The Swans (*NME* 10/12/88). In March 1989 the policy was confirmed and the Jesus and Mary Chain, Psychic TV, Fields of The Nephilium and My Bloody Valentine were added to the list of pariahs. The venue's manager argued that they wanted 'to get a decent image for this venue' (*NME* 18/3/89). Excluding acts because of their fans appeared to be an integral part of this "decent image".

More ominously, overtly political bands have been victims of venue censorship. After suffering venue bans Crass took matters into their own hands and invaded the closed Rainbow Theatre in London in December 1982, squatting for long enough to play a gig with other anarchist bands (*NME* 18/12/82 and *MM* 1/1/83). They did this because: 'We simply haven't been able to get any club work in London' (*NME* 18/12/82). Crass (1991) estimated that a third of their planned gigs were censored and never took place. In March 1987 the anarchist band Conflict claimed to be 'unofficially banned' (*NME* 7/3/87) from venues in London. But venues themselves have often had problems with the authorities.

Night clubbing?

Consumption of live pop in Britain often takes place in night clubs and their history is one of a struggle for the control of leisure and of censorship, which can arise via local authorities using bye-laws to crack down on activities which they disapprove of and which have pop as their epicentre. Again the thin dividing line between regulation and censorship becomes blurred.

The drugs scare of 1967 provoked a police clampdown on London clubs and resulted in the introduction of a Bill which became the Private Places of Entertainment Act. This introduced a licensing system for any private entertainment undertaken for financial gain (Redhead 1991, p.93). It aimed to crack down on drug usage in clubs, but the restrictions imposed on attendances in the name of safety led Peter Stringfellow, then running the Mojo Club in Sheffield, to say that he thought that 'this bill could mean the end of a lot of clubs' (*M M* 11/2/67). Further evidence of this came with the closure of one of London's most famous underground clubs, UFO, in October 1967. It was forced to move out of its original Tottenham Court Road premises after the *NOTW* ran an "orgy" story and the club's landlord evicted it. A subsequent move to The Roundhouse was killed off by high rents (*M M* 28/10/67).

Punk also witnessed its share of club closures. Manchester's Electric Circus, which twice played host to The Sex Pistols' *Anarchy* tour, had to close in August 1977 after attendance restrictions made gigs uneconomic (Morley 1977). It reopened at a new site, where it limited its punk promotions to one night a week (*NME* 12/11/77). In 1978 London's leading punk venue The Roxy in Covent Garden closed after its new owners were refused a music and dancing licence renewal (*NME* 29/4/78).

Erics, Liverpool's leading punk venue, ran into trouble with the police over the amount of non-members being signed in. Despite a protest march and the support of local MP David Alton, it was closed in April 1980 (*NME* 22 and 29/3/80). Police objections surfaced again with the most famous club of the 1990s - Manchester's Haçienda, which in the late 1980s became a centre for the acid house scene in the north. But in May 1990 the police planned to object to renewal of the Haçienda's licence because it was being used as a centre for drug taking. A publicity campaign followed, including support from the city's council leader and mayor, and resulted in the venue winning a six month reprieve in January 1991. By September it had won its battle to stay open, but with a much stricter admission policy (*NME* 12/10/91).

Venues battling with local authorities to stay open is one side of the censorial coin, the other is chains which own various clubs having their own censorial policies. In 1967 Top Rank banned The Move from its venues because their stage act included chopping up televisions and effigies of Hitler. Rank executives labelled the band's act 'obscene and destructive' (*M M* 4/2/67 and 9/3/68). The ban was lifted the following year. During punk Rank treated each case on its merits, although The Sex Pistols were banned (*NME* 16/7/77 and *The Guardian* 3/12/76).

Mecca seems to have been stricter than Rank. In 1969 it banned Max Romeo from its Tottenham Royal and Purley Orchid venues because of the lyrics to his *Wet Dream* hit (*M M* 21/6/69) and in 1972 it banned The Sweet after allegations of "obscenity" at a Portsmouth gig, but relented later in the year (*M M* 17/6/72). In 1977 Mecca announced that:

> There is no way in which we would allow punk groups to play in our venues. We want to avoid pitfalls and our attitude is that these bands are undesirable. We wouldn't even agree to them playing private functions at any of our halls (*NME* 16/7/77).

Even in 1978, as many venues began accepting punk, the Mecca owned Lyceum banned bookings by The Sex Pistols, The Adverts, The Stranglers and The Damned (*NME* 18/3/78). It also imposed, then repealed, a ban on Generation X at its Coventry Locarno venue (*NME* 25/3/78), whilst its Nottingham Tiffanys was one of the many venues to ban Sham 69 (*NME* 10/6/78). In the late 1980s its Birmingham Powerhouse venue banned acid house nights after sensationalist reports in the local press, saying that: 'We will not be connected in any way with events of this nature' (*NME* 17/9/88). So rave had to look beyond Mecca for its spiritual home.

Other chains also adopted censorial policies. In 1977 the Trust House Forte chain banned The Stranglers from its Manchester Belle Vue because 'it's now company policy to have no punk at any of our venues' (*NME* 24/9/77). Their Pavilion venue in Colwyn Bay also banned the Buzzcocks in the same year (*M M* 26/6/77). The following year The Moss Empire chain banned Magazine from appearing at their Drury Lane Theatre as, according to Moss' head office, they verged 'on the punk and we couldn't risk the reputation of the theatre' (*NME* 8/7/78).

These cases show that there has been continual negotiations about the circumstances under which live pop can be enjoyed. Authorities or venues have **not** continually sought to clamp down on pop, but their actions, whatever their intent, have often resulted in censorship via a lessening of the amount of available outlets for live pop to grow in.

Rock doesn't always go to college

By the late 1960s the college and university circuit was of established importance. But one problem that has constantly plagued it has been whether to allow the general public admission. Those colleges who chose exclusion effectively censored part of the pop audience, as the very people whose taxes paid for the colleges were often denied access to entertainments within them.

Some bands have vetoed colleges that refused admission to the general public. In February 1971 the Rolling Stones threatened to drop gigs at Manchester and Strathclyde Universities because of their students only policy (*MM* 20/2/71). The latter venue also saw the cancellation of a Clash gig in November 1978 after band-member Joe Strummer tried to buy an advance ticket for it and was refused (*NME* 25/11/78). In mitigation it was pointed out that Student Unions (SUs) often had their hands tied by college authorities or local bye-laws (*Sounds* 25/11/78). But other bands took a similar stance and The Stranglers refused an Exeter University gig for this reason in 1979 (*NME* 17/1/81). The Merton Parkas pulled out of a Chelsea College gig in October 1979 at the last moment after being told it was student only (*NME* 20/10/79).

Student Unions also have a history of moral objections to some acts. Along with Labour councils, they have been one of the few places in Britain where the the left has had a chance to implement its own censorial agenda. In March 1976 a Conference of College Social Secretaries voted:

... to urge unions to ban all performances by go-go dancers, strippers or any other artists who exploit sex, which has become a common feature of some rock band's performances (*NME* 3/4/76)

although I found no evidence of bans arising out of this policy.

The next attempted ban again concerned The Stranglers and came in October 1978 after the band walked off after 15 minutes of a gig at Surrey University which was being filmed for the BBC's *Rock Goes To College* series. The band claimed to have been confronted with a student only gig which they had not expected and were opposed to in principle (*NME* 21/10/78). Some Surrey students then tried to get the band banned from the college circuit, with some initial success (*NME* 4/11/77). However *NME* soon reported that 'several universities are willing and keen to book them' (*NME* 9/12/78).

Student anger provoked another attempted ban in October 1988. This concerned a gig by American hardcore band Rapeman at Leeds Polytechnic. Leeds was one of the the Yorkshire Ripper's haunts and the band's name aroused the understandable anger of many women at the Poly who lobbied its SU to call the gig off. The SU claimed that when the band was booked in the previous summer it was known merely to be Steve Albini's new, unnamed, band - an allegation the promoter refuted.

The band's name contravened the SU's anti-sexist policy and it tried to cancel the concert, whilst the Poly's director called for a boycott (*Yorkshire Evening Press* 14/10/88). But the promoters, Ice, threatened to sue for breach of contract and the gig had to proceed. The SU then implemented a policy of non-cooperation by, for example, shutting its bars(1). The gig went ahead, but was picketed by Leeds Rape Crisis Centre and the Socialist Worker Student Society.

Other students also sought to control the types of acts allowed to play their halls or the material they played. Birdland only got one college gig after signing a contract containing a clause stipulating that they would not play their version of Patti Smith's *Rock 'N' Roll Nigger* (*NME* 11/8/90). In November 1990 Blur's merchandise stall at Warwick University was attacked by feminists opposed to a promotional poster which featured a naked woman astride a hippopotamus - which the band claimed to be a joke. The SU had allegedly tried to prevent the band using the poster and barred those wearing hippo T-shirts from entry to the gig (*NME* 17/11/90).

The next case again centred on Leeds Polytechnic SU who banned the band First Offence in June 1991 after they had made racist and homophobic remarks in an *NME* interview (*NME* 15/6/91). A month later it was reported that the band:

> ... have been outlawed from 37 college venues following their suggestion ... that homosexuals should be forced to identify themselves with armbands (*NME* 6/7/91).

This is far removed from the first example of college censorship I found, when the Principal of Farnham School of Art in Surrey halted Redd Sullivan and Martin Windsor's rendition of *She Was Poor But She Was Honest* (*M M* 2/3/68). By 1989 colleges dealt with bands like Fugazi, whom the London School Of Oriental Studies, previously a centre for such hardcore gigs, banned in November 1989 (*NME* 25/11/89). By this time cutbacks in grants and SU funding meant that college gigs were under more threat from lack of finance than they were from direct censorship. Other venues have had a more direct history of censorship.

The Royal Albert Hall - classical censorship?

The RAH's first foray into pop was an *NME* Poll Winners Concert in February 1955. It also hosted a *Pop Proms* with Marty Wilde, Jim Dale and others in 1958. Their first ban came in June 1968 and was placed on Nice after they burnt an American flag during a version of Leonard Bernstein's *America* (*M M* 6/7/88). Keyboardist Keith Emerson subsequently found that his new band Emerson, Lake and Palmer were also covered by the ban (*M M* 27/3/71).

Audience problems began when the Hall staged a *Rock Proms* series in July 1969. The last night of this featured The Who and Chuck Berry. At the end of Berry's act the audience stormed the stage, leading to a ban on rock and roll gigs at the venue. Hall manager Frank Mundy explained that: 'It's not the artists we object to, but the hoodlums they attract' (*M M* 19/7/69)(2).

The RAH never instituted a blanket ban on pop, but it introduced a highly selective vetting process. So in February 1970, whilst the general feeling was that rock was banned following the Berry incident, a CBS backed *Sounds of The Seventies* package was allowed to play (*M M* 21/2/70). But in November 1970 Ten Years After were unable to book the Hall because their fans had caused trouble at a previous gig there. The RAH confirmed that: 'A ban does apply to some groups where we've had trouble' (*M M* 14/11/70). On 10 March 1971 James Brown performed at the Hall, and was subsequently banned after audience disturbances.

Mundy said that 'I've never seen such unpleasant people', as Brown's audience, and that:

> We have nothing against the artist ... but it would seem that some concerts attract a certain type of audience ... at this concert women's handbags were being snatched from them and stewards were threatened with violence (*M M* 22/3/71).

Isaac Hayes was subsequently prevented from playing the Hall in December as it was felt that his audience would be similar to Brown's (*M M* 25/12/71). Mott The Hoople were also banned from the Hall in July 1971 because of their fans' behaviour (*NME* 8/10/77). These decisions soon attracted attention. *M M* (22/4/72) asked: 'Is it all a Right Wing plot?' and linked the Hall's bans with another "attack" on live rock - the Night Assemblies Bill - which was then before Parliament (see below). Meanwhile Mundy said that Shirley Bassey did not fit the RAH's definition of pop, as 'she doesn't cause the sort of hooliganism we get from others' (*M M* 22/4/72). Aesthetic judgements also clouded the issue as Mundy said that the New Seekers were permissible as 'They're gifted artists, and attract a different sort of audience' (ibid). He did not even think the matter was one for public debate and told *M M*:

> It doesn't concern you ... It's not for you to say in your paper whether we will accept X and refuse Y. **It's nothing to do with you.** It's a confidential matter between us and the promoters who seek to book the hall' (ibid. Emphasis mine).

This is the arrogance of the censor who has been asked to account for his actions, although in many ways the RAH's decisions were understandable. Its helpers and staff were often middle aged volunteers who did not understand pop or its audience. Evidence suggests that what was common practice at other gigs, such as dancing and shouting, was seen as outrageous behaviour by the RAH. Staff **were** threatened and violence occurred, but rather than try to remedy this, the Hall closed its doors to certain artists.

The Hall also sought a more worrying form of censorship, vetoing acts whose repertoire it did not like. Indeed, it seems to be the one venue that has campaigned against the lyrical content of shows. In March 1971 it denied a booking to Funkadelic. To get the booking promoter John Sullivan played two tracks - *Free Your Mind and Your Ass Will Follow* and a funk version of *The Lord's Prayer* to booking manager, Marion Herrod, who took exception to them and refused the booking - a decision Mundy described as 'right and proper' (*M M* 20/3/71).

RAH President Sir Louis Gluckstein said 'commonsense'[3] guided its decisions and that:

> When you've got a group that's going to produce a pop version of the Lord's Prayer and a number like *Free Your Mind and Your Ass Will Follow* then we are in a situation where we think that this ... could lead to disturbances ... We are not applying an unreasonable censorship (*M M* 27/3/71).

Seeing its censorship as "reasonable", the RAH continued to implement it. In November 1972 it banned a charity performance of the rock opera *Tommy* featuring the London Symphony Orchestra on the grounds that the story was 'unsavoury' (*M M* 4/11/72). The gig moved to a less censorious Rainbow. In February 1974 Caravan were banned from performing with the New Symphonia Orchestra purely and simply for falling within RAH's definition of rock (*NME* 23/2/74). Captain Beefheart was rejected a month later for being 'heavy rock' - a decision again made after the Hall had been played some of the artist's material (*M M* 16/3/74).

The most infamous case of the RAH censoring content was the banning of a performance of Frank Zappa's *200 Motels* by Zappa, the Mothers Of Invention and the Royal Philharmonic Orchestra on 8 February 1971. The concert was vetoed on the day it was due to take place, when musicians arriving for an afternoon rehearsal of the show found notices saying the show had been cancelled.

The Hall justified its ban by saying that the script was "obscene" (*M M* 13/2/71). Again the decision to ban the concert was made by Marion Herrod (Zappa 1989, p.120). Amongst the words objected to were "brassiere" and "crap" (*M M* 13/2/71). The show contained material dealing with groupies and songs such as *Half a Dozen Provocative Squats* and *Penis Dimensions* and Gluckstein described it as "filth" (*M M* 27/3/71).

Zappa, who had already played the Hall twice, had to pay the Philharmonic musicians for their rehearsal time, which left him out of pocket. He therefore tried to sue the Crown, as owners of the Hall, for breach of contract. The case finally came to court in April 1975, where the Hall's lawyers tried to turn the case into an obscenity trial (Zappa 1989, p.119). But, whilst the judge ruled that the content of the show did not fall within the legal definition of "obscenity", Zappa's case fell as it was not legally possible to sue the Crown for breach of contract - despite the fact that this had obviously happened (ibid, p.137). Gluckstein cited the many letters and messages of support for his stance, including a Commons motion by six MPs (*MM* 13/2/71).

In 1992 my letter to the Hall about current censorial policy went unanswered, but its censorious past is undoubted. But at least no one suggested that it cease its musical activities, a security rock venues seldom enjoy.

No sleep at Hammersmith?

By 1992 the Rank-owned Hammersmith Odeon (renamed The Apollo in 1992) was one of the most prestigious London venues. But it also has a dichotomous censorial history, having both censored and endured attempts at being censored. Its own censorial actions again centred on audience behaviour. It banned a proposed concert by reggae acts U Roy and The Mighty Diamonds in June 1976, after trouble at a Bob Marley concert (*NME* 3/7/76). Later it was reported that the Odeon had 'banned all future reggae concerts' (*MM* 28/8/76), but the venue commented only that 'if one was offered to us we would take a long careful look at them before committing ourselves' (*MM* 30/10/76). It also cancelled the second night of a Stranglers gig in February 1983 after crowd disturbances on the first night (*NME* 26/2/83). Five years later it was reported that the venue had banned all rap acts, after gangs had caused trouble on the tube before and after a Public Enemy/LL Cool J gig in November 1987 (*NME* 26/3/88. See also *NME* 14/11/87).

It has also sought to influence show content and banned True Life from appearing there again after singer Helen April partially undressed whilst performing their *Sex Slave* song in December 1982 (*NME* 8/1/83). It also stopped Little Steven from erecting an anti-apartheid stall at his November 1987 gig until leaflets criticizing Tesco and Shell were removed (*NME* 16/11/87).

But the Odeon also illustrates the problems a venue in a highly populated area faces. It has fought various attempts by Hammersmith and Fulham Council and local residents to restrict its activities. In August 1978 the council's Works Executive Committee met to consider a residents' petition complaining about noise from fans leaving the venue. The leader of the Liberals on the council, Simon Knott, planned to make accepting objections to the licence a condition of his party's support for the minority Tory administration (*NME* 26/8/78). But this move failed when Knott lodged his objections too late at the GLC (*NME* 2/9/78).

But the residents' campaign continued and the venue's licence was only renewed in March 1983 after it agreed to look into their complaints (*NME* 26/3/83). The next year local magistrates told the Odeon not to let lorries unload there late at night - threatening the viability of concerts (*NME* 21/1/84). A compromise was reached when it agreed not to move equipment between the hours of 11.30 pm and 7.30 am (*NME* 11/2/84).

All this shows the vulnerability of popular music venues, especially those in built up areas, to regulation which effectively censors. The Odeon survived attempts to close it made by residents who had every right to a decent night's sleep. But residents acted as covert censors - however valid their objections.

The song not the singer - objections to song content

This is by far the rarest form of censorship of live music in Britain, illustrating the fact that British censors rarely mind what is said (or sung) but can often take offence to the **way** in which it is done. The Zappa, RAH and Max Romeo cases are exceptional, but there have been other examples.

In July 1970 Edinburgh's Usher Hall considered banning "underground" bands after complaints from the city's leading ticket agency and the police. The agency's Mr. W. Dickson explained that: 'This is violent music and it brings out the worst behaviour in some grown ups who should know better' (*MM* 4/7/70). This is a rare example of beat, rather than lyrics, being objected to. But it echoes comments by RAH President Gluckstein that at some gigs 'people seem to take leave of their senses' (*MM* 27/3/71) - because of the music itself, rather than the musicians' antics.

Kevin Coyne's *Babble* production at London's Stratford Theatre Royal was called off in July 1979, following sensationalist press reports over some of the songs which contained references to the Moors Murderers. This led Newham Council to withdraw its support (*NME* 21/7/79). The show later went ahead at the Oval House.

Other performers have found themselves in trouble after swearing on stage. Slade's Noddy Holder was 'charged with using obscene language' after a gig at Glasgow's Green Playhouse in May 1972 (*MM* 20/5/72). In September 1989 punk poetess Joolz was convicted of the same offence whilst performing at an anti-fascist rally in Leeds, although she later successfully appealed against the decision (*NME* 30/9/89 and 25/11/89). But such incidents are rare. What is more common are objections to artists' stage antics.

Caught in the act

The sexual element of many rock shows has always caused concern for moralists. P. J. Proby's trouser splitting shows got him banned from many venues in the early 1960s (Wale 1972, p.308) and when Jimi Hendrix toured with the Walker Brothers in 1967 the tour's operators told him to clean up his act, because it was "too suggestive" (*MM* 8/4/67). In December of the same year Move singer Carl Wayne toured with Hendrix and was warned by managers of Moss Empires in Blackpool and Manchester that his act was "obscene" and that they would bring down the curtain on him if his act became unacceptable (*MM* 9/12/67). In 1973 the London Palladium, did not even give American all-women band Fanny a chance, banning their show because it was heavy rock and their clothes were "too sexy" (*MM* 7/7/73)[4].

Alice Cooper claimed to have been banned by British venues because of his act, which featured mock executions (*NME* 12/8/89), but I found no record of this. However, he set a precedent for theatrical performances which was mimicked by the next victims of censorship - The Tubes whose act featured semi-nude women. There was speculation on their arrival in Britain in 1977 that many venues would ban them, but the only ban came in Portsmouth where councillors objected to a bondage sequence and swearing in the show. An offer to cut both was rejected, as councillors decided that the band was 'unsuitable for Portsmouth' (*NME* 19/11/77).

Splodgenessabounds' exploits included trouser dropping, egg throwing and dropping flour on people's heads, which got them banned from a number of venues, including Deptford Albany (*NME* 6/10/79 and 9/2/80). Their messy antics were mirrored in the early and mid-1980s by King Kurt whose gigs saw much egg and flour throwing. This saw a number of venues, including Birketts in Leeds and Blackpool, banning them (*NME* 5/5/84. See also *MM* 2/6/84).

In 1991 American band GWAR, a modern day Tubes, toured Britain. Their act included mock decapitations, torture and castration - all in an over the top manner. This led to the cancellation of gigs in Manchester, Bournemouth and London after sections of the press, again a censorial agent, alerted local councillors to the shows. A gig at London's Astoria was called off after Westminster Council wrote to the venue and warned 'that the stage show could break **local** licensing laws regarding obscenity' (*NME* 26/5/90. Emphasis mine).

Acts have also been banned on the grounds of safety. The Plasmatics, whose show included detonating a car on stage with rocket flares, were due to make their Hammersmith Odeon debut on Friday, 8 August 1980. But the GLC's Fire Department banned the show on the day it was due to take place (*NME* 16/8/80).

In March 1984 Whitesnake had to to give a demonstration of their firework show to Leeds councillors before getting permission to use them in their Queens Hall gig (*NME* 10/3/84). In October of the same year avant-garde band SPK, whose act included live welding, sparked a "riot" at the ICA when fire officers imposed restrictions on this, so forcing the band to leave the stage after two numbers (*NME* 13/10/84).

Councils are, naturally, very aware of safety regulations, but bands performing in Britain have been denied the chance to perform their usual shows. Popular music fans **have** been denied the chance to see artists whose acts have been deemed unsuitable by local censors. Of more concern to fans, however, is that far more often it has been they, rather than the acts, that have been cited as a reason to call off, or oppose, gigs.

Ain't misbehaving?

The behaviour of pop fans has continually worried the authorities. In 1952 Newcastle City Hall banned a Johnny Dankworth and Nat King Cole concert because: 'Jazz audiences are rowdy' (*M M* 10/2/68). Initial problems around rock concerned films like *Rock Around The Clock*, as there were no live gigs by American stars until the late 1950s (see Martin and Segrave 1988, pp.32-5). In the early 1960s Britain witnessed Beatlemania and disturbances at various Rolling Stones concerts.

Whilst thousands of gigs have taken place without trouble since 1967 there has been a continual, if intermittent, censoring of live gigs, often centring on concerns about audience behaviour. Some venues have become so embittered by their experiences that they have left the pop field. For example, in August 1971 Liverpool's Philharmonic Hall banned concerts by 'pop or beat groups' because of audience behaviour at previous gigs (*M M* 21/8/71).

The early 1970s saw a number of venues banning acts whose fans had been over enthusiastic, rather than malicious. In December 1970 Deep Purple were banned from booking Manchester's Free Trade Hall as their fans 'were not considered suitable for the Hall', after a Croydon Fairfields Hall gig at which the crowd's foot stomping had caused worries that the balcony might collapse (*M M* 12/12/70).

Mott The Hoople found themselves banned from Cheltenham Town Hall and Brighton Dome because fans' dancing had damaged seats (*M M* 7/8/71). Osibisa were also banned from the Brighton Dome for the excessive dancing of their fans in 1972 (*M M* 24/6/72). In June 1973 the Dome banned David Bowie and Led Zeppelin because fans had damaged the building during gigs (*M M* 23/6/73), whilst Slade were banned from Edinburgh Usher Hall because of fans' behaviour in 1974 (*M M* 11/5/74).

Other venues allowed the reputations of bands' fans to precede them. In May 1975 The Bay City Rollers were banned by Sunderland's Empire Theatre - because it feared uncontrollable fans following the death, from a heart attack, of a Manchester policeman as he tried to control a crowd of Rollers fans (*M M* 24/5/75). The Clash's June 1978 gig at London Edmonton's Picket Lock was cancelled after local residents' concern about 'a distasteful audience' (*NME* 10/6/78). Bristol Hippodrome called off a Rainbow gig in January 1980 because of fears of 'the crowd reaction' (*NME* 12/1/80) and Prince was apparently unable to book Earls Court in 1987 as local residents objected to the type of audience he might attract (*NME* 4/7/87). More understandably, in the same year Irish Republican band The Wolftones had a gig at Edinburgh Playhouse cancelled as it coincided with the day that Celtic's arch-rivals Rangers won the Scottish football championship and sectarian violence was feared (*NME* 16/5/87).

Fear of violence shows many venue bans arose from genuine concern, rather than any bloody-mindedness. In April 1975 *NME* ran a special report about damage that was being done at gigs (*NME* 12/4/75). There has always been, as at many public events, violent incidents at gigs, but as punk declined so did behaviour at gigs. Bob Geldof was attacked on stage at The Music Machine in June 1977 (*NME* 29/10/77), April 1978 saw bands refusing to play Newcastle again after violent incidents (*NME* 8/4/78) and the year also saw trouble at London gigs of bands such as The Lurkers and Clayson and The Argonauts (*NME* 3/6/78, 16/9/78 and 21/10/78).

Much of this violence had political overtones. The National Front tried to make overtures to punk (see Burchill 1977), but were generally rebuffed - as the rise of Rock Against Racism (RAR) showed. The Angelic Upstarts were targeted by far-right agitators and had gigs in Wolverhampton (*NME* 9/6/79) and London's Nashville (*Sounds* 27/10/79) disrupted. But Sham 69 suffered most, with numerous gigs disrupted. Their leader, Jimmy Pursey, played RAR gigs, but the band courted right wing sympathy by playing *Land of Hope and Glory* and *The Dambusters March* as a prelude to gigs. Even their "final" gig at London's Rainbow, (their first in the capital for some time as, according to Pursey, 'we couldn't get a gig in town' [*NME* 14/7/79]), ended in chaos as a stage invasion after twenty minutes stopped it (*NME* 4/8/79).

The most explosive gig of this era came in July 1981 and again had strong political overtones. It came at the Hamborough Tavern in the London Borough of Southall, which has a large Asian population, and featured Oi bands The Business, The Four Skins and Last Resort. Coach loads of skinheads were bussed in for the gig and apparently provoked local Asian youths. A riot ensued and the pub was burnt down. Not surprisingly a backlash against Oi followed(5). The Cockney Rejects, another Oi band, cancelled a tour, and the Angelic Upstarts cancelled a Middlesbrough gig (*NME* 18/7/81. See also *NME* 11/7/81).

There are numerous other examples of violence, often politically inspired, that could be mentioned. I have included details of it here simply to illustrate the problems that can sometimes confront live pop. Venue censorship often has to be seen in this context. Fans can, and have, caused trouble and acts who have developed reputations for attracting troublesome fans have suffered in consequence. But should such bands be excluded the voice of pop becomes muffled. Such muffling reached a peak in 1977.

Punk and disorderly?

Punk merits a special section as the most censored pop genre during the years considered here. Such censorship included exclusion from many venues. Punk gigs were subjected to a degree of censorship unparalleled in British popular music history. But punk was far from innocent. An early incident that was to make venues wary came on 21 September 1976 at London's 100 Club where Malcolm McLaren had organized a two day punk festival. The second night saw the smashing of a glass, during The Damned's set, which resulted in a young girl losing an eye. It also caused punk to be banned from the club(6). An aura of violence was present in punk from the off. The Sex Pistols courted and practised violence and early gigs saw scuffles with audiences (see Savage 1991 pp. 168 and 172).

In mid-November 1976 a punk package tour featuring America's Ramones and Talking Heads and The Sex Pistols was announced. The American acts soon withdrew, to be replaced by The Clash and The Damned. This tour was the ill fated *Anarchy In The UK* tour of which only four of the original eighteen dates were played. The reason for the cancellations was the Grundy interview. Marsh (1977, pp.112/3) writes that after this:

> ... something very close to a temporary nationwide hysteria set in at the prospect of the Sex Pistols spreading their influence around the country during their much publicised tour.

Post-Grundy punk was out of bounds for many venues. In August 1977 Robson (1977, p.145) wrote that Manchester's Electric Circus was 'one of the few places in the north west where live punk music is allowed at all'.

Unorthodox behaviour at punk gigs, such as swearing and pogoing, made many promoters nervous. Such feelings were sometimes further fuelled by outbreaks of violence at punk gigs - not always originating from the punks. In June 1977 a gig by The Adverts and The Damned at Lincoln Drill Hall was attacked by non-punks (*NME* 29/10/77. See also Savage 1991, pp.335-356). A clash of Teds and punks was widely reported by a press that did much to encourage the rivalry (see Savage 1991, pp.374-375 and *Sunday Mirror* 12/6/77). Track Records tried to organize a gig with Shakin' Stevens and The Sunsets (a rock 'n' roll band) and American punk band Johnny Thunders and The Heartbreakers in order to bring the sides together, but were unable to get a venue to stage it (*NME* 24/9/77).

Nevertheless the music business soon found that it could accommodate most punk. In December 1977 leading promoter Harvey Goldsmith promoted many gigs on a Buzzcocks tour (*NME* 17/12/77). Laing (1985, p.xiii) notes that: 'One of the most significant achievements of punk was its ability to lay bare the operations of power in the leisure apparatus'. In the live arena this involved the revelation that councils and venues had the power to deny a section of the pop audience the live experience of its music - a highly censorial act given Frith's comment (1983, p.16) that: 'At the centre of Afro-American music is performance'. For a period of almost nine months - from the Pistols' appearance on *Today* on 1 December 1976 to the couple of months following the Jubilee of June 1977 - the announcement of a major punk gig was followed by speculation as to whether it would actually take place. This affected many of punk's leading lights:

The Sex Pistols: By the time of Grundy this band's involvement in violence had already saw them banned from London venues like The Nashville, The Marquee, the 100 Club, the Rock Garden and Dingwalls (see Savage 1991, p.172 and Laing 1985, p.132). When Grundy was broadcast a date on the *Anarchy* tour at Lancaster University on 10 December had already been vetoed by the authorities there (*NME* 4/12/76). On 3 December the package went to the University of East Anglia, only to find that the gig had been vetoed by vice chancellor Frank Thistlewaite, who 'because of the recent publicity surrounding the Pistols ... could not be satisfied that the event would pass peacefully' (*NME* 11/12/76)[7]. Again the role of the press is notable. Gigs at six other venues were cancelled on the same day. The link between contemporary events (and press hysteria) was seldom more obvious.

On Saturday, 4 December the tour was due to play Derby Kings Hall. The council's leisure committee demanded that the Pistols turn up at 2 pm, perform the show, and let the committee decide whether to allow it for the general public - a notable act of elitism(8). But the councillors were denied their censorial opportunity when the band refused to play for them. McLaren exploited the situation by issuing a statement that the councillors were 'too old to judge' the band's performance (Savage 1991, p.268), thus adding the myth of generational conflict to the actuality of municipal censorship.

The first date played on the tour was on 6 December, at Leeds Poly. The following day it played the Electric Circus in Manchester and a week later they played Caerphilly Castle Cinema. Savage (ibid, p.273) writes that:

> The previous week, two Labour councillors had attempted to get an injunction stopping the concert: when that failed, they led a carol-singing protest in the cinema car-park whose participants outnumbered those at the concert inside.

Also at the protest was Pastor John Cooper of the Elim Pentecostal church - the organization which, via Alex Maloney, was later at the forefront of the religious opposition to rock, in 1992.

Gigs were played on the 19th (Manchester Electric Circus again), the 20th (Cleethorpes Winter Gardens) and the 22nd (Plymouth Woods Centre). Towns which would not countenance the Pistols' appearance included Newcastle, Bournemouth, Preston, Liverpool, Bristol, Cardiff, Glasgow, Dundee, Sheffield, Southend, Guildford, Birmingham, Torquay and London (see Wood 1988). This illustrates at least two recurring points; the first is pop's power to offend, the second is the often locally mediated nature of such offence.

The band **could** have played at London's Covent Garden Roxy on 1 January 1977, but McLaren would not allow it as he wanted to spread the false rumour that the Pistols were banned from performing in London by the GLC (Savage 1991, p.292). There were no reports of trouble at the gigs that were played.

The Pistols' problems in getting gigs continued throughout 1977. In March *NME* reported that they were 'banned from appearing in every major city in Britain' (*NME* 19/3/77). But they **did** play a London gig in April, at the Screen On The Green in Islington. On

Jubilee Day, 7 June, they played a gig on a boat on the Thames. This was broken up by the Metropolitan Police.

In the summer of 1977 the Pistols toured under the name of SPOTS (Sex Pistols On Tour Secretly). Under this name they were able to play Wolverhampton Lafayette on 19 August and on the 24th they played Doncaster Outlook Club as The Tax Exiles. They also played Middlesbrough and Scarborough on this tour. But these gigs only went ahead because the band did not reveal their identity until the last minute. A bizarre consequence of this secrecy came in Maidstone in September when unknown band Dirt had to play in front of the town's councillors to prove they were **not** The Pistols before permission was given for a gig (*NME* 17/9/77).

In December the Pistols played a series of semi-secret gigs, with venues only announced at the last minute. Towns who vetoed the band on this occasion included Wolverhampton, Birkenhead, Bristol and Rochdale (Savage 1991, p.429). Gigs played were in Keighly, Cromer, Newport and Huddersfield - none of them at mainstream venues. The last gig, on Christmas Day 1977, was a benefit for striking firemen and their children. It was the last gig they ever played in Britain.

Punk's ability to expose those behind censorial decisions peaked on this last tour. Virgin placed an advert in the music press of 17 December listing letters refusing the band permission to play venues. These included Rank's comment of 26 October 1977 that 'we are not able to allow the band to play in any of our venues' (*NME* 17/12/77). Other banning letters came from the GLC, Cambridge, Bath, North Wolds and Derby councils. In January 1978 *NME* carried a story outlining the Pistols' bans from Dundee and Aberdeen. By then the band were in America and falling apart. Their case was the most extreme, but unexceptional for the times.

The Clash: This band was also on the *Anarchy* tour and so suffered the most explicit example of censorship of live punk. They were involved in two other early incidents that tarnished punk's image. The first was at their gig at the ICA in October 1976 at which Shane O'Hooligan (later Shane MacGowan of The Pogues) allegedly had part of his earlobe bitten off by a female fan (*NME* 6/11/76). The second came at The Rainbow in May 1977 when punk had the riot of its own that The Clash had sung of in *White Riot* and over 200 seats were smashed - leading to further venue bans on punk and still more tabloid headlines (*NME* 21/5/77). Clash manager Bernie Rhodes said that:

> You talk about getting banned and if that actually happened it
> would make everything simple ... But in situations like this you
> don't even know what's going on. You're being allowed to play
> but you still get problems, you still get harassed (*M M* 4/6/77).

As many of the examples above show, this process of discouragement
and marginalization often characterizes British censorship.

By October it seemed more venues were willing to take The Clash,
but a proposed gig at Liverpool Stadium was called off after trouble
with insurance and Ipswich council forbade a gig at the town's Corn
Exchange venue after "unsatisfactory behaviour" at a Stranglers gig
a few days before the Clash were due to play (*NME* 22/10/77).
Trouble at a gig in Bournemouth was widely reported and threatened
a series of gigs at the Rainbow (*NME* 19/11/77) - but these went
ahead without trouble, after the venue added extra security.

In June 1978 Liverpool Empire banned The Clash and the gig had to
be switched to Blackburn (*NME* 8/7/78). In November Birmingham
Town Hall and Odeon turned down bookings by the band (*NME*
18/11/78). In April 1979 the failure of a Clash gig to take place in
Chelsea led to disturbances and some 70 arrests (Laing 1985, p.140).

The Stranglers: This band is probably second only to The Sex Pistols
in the number of venues from which it was banned, including the
already noted banning by Surrey University. They first came to
national censorial prominence in January 1977. Just after the Pistols'
abortive *Anarchy* tour, The Stranglers played a gig at The Rainbow,
supporting the Climax Blues Band. Here the band's Hugh Cornwell
wore a T-shirt with the word "Fuck" on it - in a spoof of the Ford
logo. This got their set curtailed early. The band blamed the GLC for
this, who in turn accused the venue's management (*NME* 5/2/77). A
M r. Saxby of the GLC later commented that: 'We supported EMI on
their stand against the Sex Pistols and now **we're** taking a stand
against The Stranglers' (ibid. Emphasis in original).

In May a date at Leeds Town Hall was cancelled because 'the
venue's management decided that they were undesirable' (*NME*
21/5/77) and June gigs in Torquay (where the council decided that:
'The entertainment associated with this type of group is not in
keeping with the council's policy at any of the venues under its
control'), Nottingham (where they were deemed "unsuitable"),

178

Blackburn King George's Hall (which did not want to be involved 'with the sort of uproar surrounding groups of this kind') and St. Albans (the police here objected after 'swearing and spitting at bar staff during a recent Clash concert') (*NME* 4/6/77) were vetoed. Again contemporary events are relevant. The Clash's "riot" show at The Rainbow had taken place just before this and many councils (over)reacted to this by banning punk.

In the early months of 1978 it was rumoured that the GLC was preventing Stranglers gigs throughout London (*NME* 20/5/78) - a situation remedied when the band played an open air gig in Battersea Park in September. But when bassist Jean Jacques Brunel tried to book Drury Lane Theatre for a solo gig he was turned down because he was a member of the Stranglers (*NME* 14/4/79) and in September 1979 it was reported that Newcastle City Hall would still not allow Stranglers' gigs (*NME* 22/9/79).

News of disturbances at a gig in Nice in 1979 scared off Aberdeen Capitol who wrote to the band's agent stating that 'they no longer wished to go ahead with the booking "due to the situation which has developed in Nice"' (*NME* 12/7/80).

This is the last ban on The Stranglers that was uncovered by this research. Longevity seems to have mellowed both the band and venue reaction to them. But they illustrated two things. First, the importance of contemporary events. Initial bans came at the time of a general backlash against punk, which was continued by the involvement of the band in stage walk offs and so on. Secondly, the censorship was never centred on the music as such - it was directed at the behaviour of fans and band alike. Punk as a movement, not as music, was the impetus behind many bans.

Other Bands: In the initial backlash against punk all its leading lights suffered. Even The Jam, who proclaimed Royalist sympathies and did free gigs for the Jubilee, found themselves banned from Leeds Town Hall as "unsuitable" (*MM* 4/6/77) and were then prevented from playing a gig at Chelsea Football Club's Stamford Bridge ground by the GLC (*NME* 18/6/77).

In May and June 1977 The Damned had gigs at Stafford Top of The World, Newcastle under Lyme Tiffanys, Cromer West Runton Pavilion and Cheltenham Town Hall cancelled (*MM* 4/6/77). The Vibrators had several gigs cancelled immediately after Grundy (*NME* 18/12/76) and were banned from London's New Victoria Theatre. A gig they planned there with the Ian Hunter Band was switched to the Hammersmith Odeon (*NME* 28/5/77). In March 1977 Lou Reed was prevented from playing the London Palladium because of his "punk image" (*NME* 19/10/77). The Buzzcocks were refused a Wigan gig in October and in December Newcastle City Hall refused a gig by the Boomtown Rats because the council, the hall's owners, had banned punk after "trouble" at punk gigs in the city (*NME* 3/12/77).

1978 saw a let up in the anti-punk hysteria, but bans were still prevalent. The Radiators From Space were banned in February from gigs at London's Nashville and St. Albans City Hall (*NME* 4/2/78) and in May Newcastle Guildhall decided to ban "certain types of acts" - a euphemism for punk (*NME* 20/5/78). Generation X had trouble getting venues in December (*NME* 2/12/78). By 1979 bans were lessening, but Iggy Pop was denied the use of Dunstable Civic Hall in April because he had ex-Sex Pistol Glen Matlock in his band and was banned from Warwick University in the same month because the SU 'encountered resistance to booking a new wave act' (*NME* 7/4/79). In December Surrey University banned punk gigs after trouble at a UK Subs gig (Laing 1985, p.141).

The last punk act to suffer venue censorship was the Dead Kennedys whose British debut tour in September 1980 was banned from Dundee. *NME* (20/9/80) reported that:

> Following complaints about the group's name the local council met and decided on the ban. Commented Tory leader Jock Watson "It's in extremely bad taste, and their appearance wouldn't do the city any good at all".

The band were also banned from Mecca's London Lyceum and Hammersmith Palais venues (*NME* 4/10/80). These bans were the last ones associated with the punk period, but punk's legacy was long lasting in some places. In April 1991 Siouxsie and The Banshees were banned from using Belfast's Mayfield Hall - despite an assurance from the RAH that their fans were **not** prone to rioting (*NME* 20/4/91). Their punk heritage appeared to be enough for the venue to veto the show.

The punk era illustrates that when it is deemed necessary various bodies are prepared to stamp on pop. Trouble at gigs was usually cited as the main reason for banning shows, but content was also vetoed. The Dundee case again showed that one of the main vetoing powers were local authorities.

"Get outta town" - the role of local authorities in controlling and censoring live popular music

During punk councils were at the forefront of banning gigs and some were accused of 'trying to censor punk rock out of existence' (Parsons 1977). Local authorities have a long history of controlling and/or censoring live popular music within their boundaries(9) and they are partly obliged to perform these tasks as it is often they and local magistrates who issue venues with licences for music, dancing and selling alcohol(10). They will also be the focus of resident anger should venues upset them. Many venues, such as Newcastle and St. Albans City Halls, are council owned, which further increases local authorities' censorial potential. Councils are also an obvious example of locality effecting the censorial climate.

In October 1967 Windsor Council debated plans to hold a follow up National Jazz and Blues Festival to the one at the town's racecourse in the previous summer. A Councillor Wells described that festival as 'a big excuse for young people to attend one big love in' (*M M* 10/6/67) and opposed another festival on those grounds. But in January 1968 the council agreed to another festival.

Impromptu free concerts were also banned. The Edgar Broughton Band announced free gigs for Redcar and Blackpool in July and August 1971 - which the relevant councils summarily banned (*M M* 10/7/71). When they attempted to play Redcar and Brighton Broughton was arrested on both occasions and charged with obstruction (*NME* 24/7/77).

But punk really brought councils to the fore as a censorial force. Guildford council banned the Sex Pistols on the grounds that its young people 'should not be subject to this type of behaviour' (*Daily Express* 3/12/76. See also *Daily Mail* of this date). Preston banned them as 'parents would be up in arms' (*Daily Mirror* 3/12/76) if they had allowed them, again showing the censorial use of concepts of the family.

The Blackburn and Torquay bans on The Stranglers were instituted by councils (*NME* 28/5/77, 4/6/77, 20/5/78 and 9/9/78), as were The Jam's from Leeds and The Damned's from Cheltenham (*NME* and *M M* 4/6/77). Other council backed bans included Glasgow's ban on all punk in its venues (*NME* 25/6/77), Ipswich's ban on The Clash (*NME* 19/11/77 and 21/2/78), Portsmouth's on The Tubes and Newcastle's on The Boomtown Rats (*NME* 17/12/77). Music papers headlined with: "Local censors out in force to ban punk rock" (*M M* 4/6/77) and "Big Brother Declares War On New Wave" (*NME* 4/6/77). Hindsight makes such claims appear exaggerated, but punks had ample evidence with which to fuel their paranoia. Councils **did** ban punk bands from their towns.

Councils also sought to control one-off events in their areas. In 1989 Hammersmith and Fulham Council refused to allow the annual reggae Sunsplash festival to take place on Wormwood Scrubs, because they had not received the required three months notice from the organizers (*NME* 5/8/89). In 1991 Liverpool City Council vetoed a plan by The Farm and Ian McCulloch to play a free gig outside of the city's St. George's Hall because inadequate notice had been given and the Dunkirk Veteran's Association complained that the proposed site was too close to the city's war memorial (*NME* 29/6/91).

One can sympathize with councils, who are often forced to adopt a censorial role by residents' complaints and other political considerations. Public order problems can arise at gigs and thus councils may veer on the side of caution in order to avoid trouble. But councils are also subject to change via the ballot box and this can radically effect the council's attitude toward pop. Nowhere is this more evident than in the history of the GLC(11).

The GLC - rocking the city?

During punk the GLC was amongst the most censorious of local authorities(12). But it is also a prime example of how a council can change from pop censor to saviour. In March 1976 *M M* headlined its front page with: "Now Pop's X Rated" - a reaction to the then Labour run GLC's Code of Practice For Pop Concerts - produced after the crushing to death of teenager Bernadette Whelan at a White City David Cassidy concert in 1974 (*M M* 13/3/76). Its suggestions included splitting large teenage crowds into pens and a steward for every 30 indoor fans, or 100 outdoor ones. It was attacked by promoters as unreasonable and was not fully taken up when the Tories captured the council in the May 1977 local elections.

Allegations of a GLC blacklist surfaced after the Stranglers "Fuck" T-shirt dispute and the calling off of the proposed Jam gig at Chelsea FC referred to above (*NME* 5/2/77 and 18/6/77). In June punk bands alleged that the Tory administration was now using the Labour produced Code as a means by which to veto bands - although such claims were dismissed as "unfounded" (*NME* 9/7/77). Certainly the Code gave them enough scope. One section forbade performers from encouraging 'any action which may over-excite the audience including any enticement by performers by word or deed to encourage people to leave their seats' (ibid). Had this been enforced virtually all pop concerts would have been halted.

Instead what occurred was a series of random bans. These included a Clash 1978 Harlesden Roxy gig and the Plasmatics' Hammersmith Odeon gig - both on the grounds of safety. The council also vetoed a proposed gig by The Specials and The Selecter on Clapham Common in June 1980 (*NME* 21/6/80). By November 1980 a number of London venues like The Nashville, The Red Cow and The Electric Ballroom had closed and the GLC was again obliged to deny that it had an anti-rock policy (*NME* 15/11/80).

The following May saw Labour regain control and adopt a more positive approach to popular music, viewing it as a vital source of popular entertainment. Its first pop promotion came in July 1981 when it organized a Rock 'n' Royal concert at Crystal Palace to "celebrate" Prince Charles' wedding. Its success encouraged the GLC to further pursue its role as pop promoter (*NME* 22/8/81).

But this did not entail the abandonment of all censorial roles. As part of its Anti-Racism Year in 1984 the GLC announced that it would ban from its halls any artist who had broken the ANC backed cultural boycott of South Africa. It encouraged Labour controlled councils in London to do the same (*NME* 7/1/84) - although no major event seems to have been affected by this[13].

Contrarily, even during the run up to its abolition, the council still sought to expand its promotional role. A series of farewell gigs were announced - including one on the last day of the council's existence - 31 March 1986. Its abolition arguably involved *de facto* censorship as loss of this important sponsor meant that fewer gigs occurred. Other examples of municipal backing for pop has come from councils' involvements in venues such as the Leadmill in Sheffield, The Picket in Liverpool and The Waterfront in Norwich. These examples show that councils' involvement in popular music is far from being all censorial. However their role often involves control which can lead into the censorial arena.

Noise annoys

Volume control at indoor gigs has periodically caused problems, particularly in the early to mid-1970s when loud heavy rock was popular. In November 1973 Labour run Leeds City Council debated a 93 decibel limit for gigs in the city. Bands at that time played at an average of 105 to 110 decibels (*M M* 24/11/73). The move came after Ronald Fearn, a lecturer at the city's Polytechnic, produced a report claiming that noise levels in the city's clubs were too high. Luton Council also considered following Leeds' example, although other councils felt the limit was too low (*M M* 1/12/73).

Leeds eventually set out to impose a limit of 96 decibels. Elton John soon said that he would not play Leeds until the limit went up to 110 decibels (*M M* 8/12/73). The anti-noise lobby was joined by Labour Lord Kennet who put an unsuccessful amendment in the Lords to an Environment Bill which would have given local authorities the power to enforce noise limits at gigs (ibid). Meanwhile the Musicians Union began studying a 1971 report from the British Medical Association which recommended a 100 decibel limit (*M M* 15/12/73).

In Leeds Refugee were forced to call off a planned gig at Leeds Poly because of the limit (*M M* 19/1/74). In February the managing director of Mecca wrote to *M M* deploring the limit and Young Conservative Roger Ivey led a protest march to the council. Slade cancelled a proposed gig because of the limit and *M M* (23/3/74) explained that the legal situation was that whilst the law did not allow the council to stop a concert, it could fine venues and take their licences away.

But such action proved unnecessary as the limit was lifted as "unreasonable" soon after it was introduced (*NME* 8/7/78). In 1976 *M M* reported that rock had been given the all clear by Dr. T. A. Henry of Manchester University who claimed that, whilst fans were being exposed to high levels of noise, there was no evidence that their hearing was being impaired. He suggested that noise levels in industry might cause greater problems (*M M* 18/9/76). Although the debate over noise levels at gigs did not disappear (see *NME* 13/1/90 for an example), no other council took the Leeds route. It should also be noted here that whilst safety was the prime concern the net result was censorial[14].

The police and live pop - the thin blue pencil line?

Whilst generally becoming involved in censorial actions on pop at the behest of others, Britain's police have a history of initiating censorial actions. Wyman (1991, p.290) reports Blackpool police telling its Winter Gardens venue not to book the Rolling Stones again in 1964. In 1967 Police threatened to 'put an end to the Roundhouse all and everything it stands for' (*Record Hunter, Vox* August 1992) and during punk police heavy handedness at Sex Pistols river boat gig on Jubilee Day attracted a lot of criticism(15).

The same month *M M* reported that 'many punk bands have found the police taking an unusually close and active interest in their activities' (*M M* 25/6/77). In July *NME* headlined: "Police ban hits Clash Punkfest" as a planned gig at Birmingham Rag Market was called off because, said promoter Dave Cork, 'the police didn't want the show to take place' and so magistrates denied it a licence (*NME* 16/7/77). It was also reported that Glasgow police were ready to raid any attempted new wave gig in council venues in the city (*NME* 13/8/77). Wigan Casino had to cancel its Thursday night punk series 'because the police will not allow them to hold punk shows of any description' (*NME* 29/10/77). A Sex Pistols concert planned for Birkenhead's Hamilton Club the following month was also cancelled because of 'police pressure on the promoter' (Wood 1988).

Such pressure on gigs did not end with punk. In October 1979 a Splodgenessabounds gig at Chislehurst Caves was called off because 'the local police have requested that the owner cancel out the band's performance' (*NME* 8/10/79). In 1980 it was reported that The Angelic Upstarts were banned by police from playing their native North East (*NME* 28/6/80) and in 1987 the organizers of a Hunt Saboteurs benefit gig at Bradford University, featuring several anarchist bands, cited police intervention as the reason for its cancellation (*NME* 31/10/87). In July 1989 York police stopped a gig by The Farm because The Phoenix venue found its licence did not cover a large enough audience and they had to move to an alternative venue. The police then followed the group's entourage to ensure that no gig took place (*NME* 5/8/89). April 1991 saw police objections cited as the reason why a proposed two day show by The Charlatans at Stafford's Bingley Hall would not take place (*NME* 13/4/91).

The police can also pressurize clubs on a more continuous basis, as raids on London's Middle Earth Club in 1968 showed (*M M* 9/3/68). Punk's leading venue, The Roxy in Covent Garden, was closed after objections from the police amongst others (*NME* 29/4/78) and the police were also an influential factor in the closing of Liverpool's Erics venue in 1980 (see *NME* 28/10/78, 22 and 29/3/80). Three years later Liverpool lost its popular Masonic pub venue, when police objected to licence renewal - because of alleged drug use at the venue (*NME* 30/4/83).

Police chiefs have sometimes attacked pop with apparent relish. Thames Valley Police Chief David Holdsworth was in charge of operations at the time of the battle at the Windsor Free Festival in 1974 (see below), which seems to have put him off all forms of pop. In 1977 he said that public apathy had helped bring a breakdown in societal values and that among the:

> ... dangerous creatures in our society are the pornographers, the drug addicts and **the pop groups** ... Society has got to pull itself together and say: "What are we putting up with this bloody rubbish for?" (*M M* 26/6/77. Emphasis mine).

Holdsworth's remarks anticipate the descriptions of some rock as "aural pornography" that the PMRC used a decade later. He also used aesthetics to justify society's right to censor pop which was, after all, just "bloody rubbish".

Police activity yet again shows how locality effects censorship. The actions of Manchester police, particularly after James Anderton took over as Chief Constable in 1977 (Sutherland, 1982 p.163), illustrates this general point. His religious convictions meant retail outlets which specialized in alternative merchandise had to beware of police raids. Knockabout Comics, who stocked drug related literature, were raided in 1982 and had to wait until June 1984 before being cleared of an obscenity charge(16). It is also worth reiterating that the January 1990 legal move against Eastern Bloc for selling rave tickets was Anderton's personally (*NME* 13/1/90). It was also reported that Manchester police questioned Morrisey over his track *Margaret On A Guillotine*, which advocated the murder of Margaret Thatcher (Holden 1993, p.12).

Conclusion

The last example has an element of farce about it, but the censoring of live pop raises serious issues, especially as Dunaway has noted that pop's live element is crucial to its meaning (Dunaway 1987, p.53). Local authorities have banned acts, police forces closed venues and objected to gigs and venues themselves have introduced their own censorial policies. The by now familiar censorial forces are here joined by venues and worried residents. Behaviour and safety add new dimensions to the censoring. Audiences rather than acts can be the censors' main target and indeed a continuous thread links concern over the behaviour of Music Hall audiences in the early part of the century (see T. Davis, 1991) to worries over stage diving in 1992[17].

Decisions to call off or, ban outright, gigs cannot be contested and have civil rights implications. Once a gig is vetoed fans have little power and are again recipients of decisions they have no say in. This unhappy situation is likely to continue. Under a government determined to exert control over local authority finances and unwilling to intervene in the market decisions of the entertainments industry (or any other) there seems little hope for more consumer input. The beat may go on, but its live manifestation is often interrupted and such interruptions show no sign of diminishing[18].

Notes

1. See *NME* 15 and 22/10/88 and *Yorkshire Evening Post* 15/10/88.

2. Martin and Segrave 1988, p.135 also report an RAH ban on the Rolling Stones in 1969.

3. "Commonsense" is a Whitehousean term (see below).

4. For more on the censoring of clothes at gigs see Wyman 1991, p.285 and *M M* 25/6/77.

5. See above and below and G. Marshall 1991 pp.105-114 for more on Oi.

6. See Wood, 1988 for a quote from the club's manager.

7. *The Guardian* of 4/12/76 reported safety as the motivation behind the ban and one UEA lecturer's objections to it. But see Bromberg, 1989, p.151 and 155 for a cynical view of "bans" on Pistols' gigs.

8. The *Daily Express* and *Guardian* of 4/12/76 passed comment on the fact that two of the councillors involved were women.

9. For example, in the early 1920s Leyton council banned jazz, see Hustwitt 1983.

10. See Street 1993 for more on this. Clarke and Critcher 1980, pp.124-125 note regulation as a means of censorship.

11. The GLC provided perhaps **the** most prominent anti-punk campaigner in Bernard Brook-Partridge, Tory deputy of its Recreation and Community Policy Committee. See *NME* 7/9/77, Vermorel 1978, pp.184, 185 and 188 and Savage 1991, p.365. More recently his mantle has been taken on by Alan Blumenthal, a Conservative councillor in Birmingham, who has objected to NWA and Public Enemy gigs in the city, see *NME* 9/6/90.

Interestingly both have used causal arguments. Brook-Partridge said punk was 'calculated to make people misbehave' Hebdige 1987, p.158 and Blumenthal spoke of NWA provoking race riots in Birmingham, *NME* 9/6/90.

12.   See *NME* 15/9/79 for a Members song, "GLC", attacking it and Savage 1991, p.336 for the GLC's role in punk censorship.

13.   See Levin 1985 a and b for bitter attacks on this policy.

14.   See *The Guardian* 4/12/76, Chambers 1986, p.136 and *NME* 8/5/93 for other occasions when safety led to censorship.

15.   See *NME* 18/6/77, 26/11/77 and 9/5/92 and Savage 1991 pp.363 and 394 for more details of this event.

16.   *NME* 4/9/82, 31/7/82 and *Sounds* 23/6/84. For venue hassles with the police in Birmingham see *The Guardian* 2/5/91.

17.   See Syal and Davidson 1992 and *NME* letters page April to June 1992.

18.   For possibilities for the future of rock venues via centralization see interviews with the Mean Fiddler's Vince Power in *The Independent* 12/3/93 and *The Guardian* 7/5/93.

10 Festivals and raves: community censorship?

The years from 1967 saw the emergence of festivals as a vital part of the pop calendar, both in Britain and abroad. But the history of festivals is one of struggle and of resistance, by various interests, to having them in their neighbourhood. Even more so than with indoor gigs, many censorial actions here concerned worries over audience behaviour, rather than over the music. The debate over festivals and raves is primarily one of social control and arguments about who gets what access to open space. Nevertheless, attempts to prevent or disrupt them **do** have censorial overtones. At a minimum their cancellation is a lessening of the amount of popular music that is available. It also involves a lost opportunity for parts of the rock and rave communities to gather and to experience itself **as** community(1). (For my purpose "festivals" will cover **all** large outdoor concerts, as they throw up similar problems and objections).

The first British festivals began in 1955 with an outdoor jazz festival at Lord Montagu's stately home at Beaulieu, Hampshire. This became an annual event up to 1961, when it was ended after violence between rival camps of trad and modern jazz followers (Hinton 1990, p.5). The next major festival series was organized by Harold Pendleton, owner of London's Marquee Club, who started the National Jazz Festival at Richmond, Surrey, in 1961. This eventually became the annual Reading Festival.

By the late 1960s a divide emerged between free and commercial festivals. The commercials were, primarily, simply an attempt to make money. The free festivals were somewhat different and often orientated more towards politics than music. This frequently brought them into conflict with the authorities, especially if they were held without the permission of site owners. Meanwhile the commercials, whilst by no means free from opposition, courted, and often got, respectability as a means of making money. But various festivals brought varied responses.

One day events

By the 1980s these were often merely part of a major artist's tour, but problems surrounding them remained as local residents were always concerned about noise and inconvenience. For example, by 1971 one day events had taken place at London's Crystal Palace Bowl, but in May 1973 *M M* reported that a proposed concert there had been cancelled because **'a handful of people** have objected to the granting of a licence' and the hearing would be heard too late to organize a concert (*M M* 19/5/73. Emphasis mine)(2), although gigs returned to the Bowl later.

From 1968 onwards a series of free concerts were held in London's Hyde Park, with official sanction and varying degrees of success. By far the most famous was The Rolling Stones concert on 5 July 1969. The previous July Jethro Tull, Roy Harper and Tyrannosaurus Rex had played. These bands were acceptable but apparently rock and roll was not. In September 1969 *M M* carried a letter from Bill Haley's manager apologizing for being unable to arrange him a concert in Hyde Park as 'I was refused permission, the excuse being that followers of rock and roll would create havoc during the concert' (*M M* 6/9/69).

In 1970 Blackhill Enterprises, pioneers of the Hyde Park gigs, got permission for two concerts in the summer. Disturbances marred the first, featuring Pink Floyd, in July, whilst the September one featured Eric Burdon and Canned Heat. 1971 saw only one gig allowed in Hyde Park, featuring Grand Funk (*M M* 8/5/71)(3). A Hyde Park concert planned for 10 June 1972 by Blackhill was ignominiously cancelled because it fell on the Duke of Edinburgh's birthday and the army wanted to carry out routines in the park (*M M* 10/6/72).

A temporary lull in Hyde Park gigs followed whilst the authorities reconsidered their attitudes towards them. The Government had initiated the Stevenson Report (see below) into pop festivals and Paul

Channon, Minister of Housing and Construction, refused Hyde Park gigs, despite calls from the Young Conservative newspaper, *Tomorrow*, and Eastern Area Young Tories for him to allow them (*MM* 16/6/73 and 21/7/73). By summer 1974 Labour was in power and allowed Hyde Park gigs. Capital Radio sponsored one featuring Don McLean in 1975 and Queen played in 1976. This was the last of these gigs on any major scale.

In 1973 The Rolling Stones were keen to play at a Welsh castle, but a planned gig at Caernarfon Castle never materialized. A gig at Cardiff Castle was announced, but *MM* reported that this 'was cancelled ... after certain influences in the town brought pressure to bear.' A protest march by the Local Rights Information Bureau and the White Panther Party failed to change the decision (*MM* 18/8/73).

The show was switched to Pembroke Castle, only to be vetoed again. Permission for it was initially given by the Clerk of the Borough Council, but then withdrawn after locals protested. Paul Martin of GWF, who planned the gig, said that 'the fanatics won' and that: 'There was nothing rational about the decision ... They had no other reason than it was the Rolling Stones' (*MM* 1/9/73). Cardiff Castle showed that it was not hostile to all rock by allowing a concert featuring 10cc and Steeleye Span in July 1975.

The 1977 punk bans included that on the previously noted Clash outdoor gig at Birmingham's Digbeth Market in July. Permission was initially granted, but local magistrates refused the show a licence and it never took place. A planned punk festival in Windsor was also vetoed after the landowner who originally gave permission for the festival withdrew it when the nature of the event became clear. The mayor of Windsor had threatened the gig with a High Court injunction (*NME* 25/6/77 and 2/7/77).

In December 1978 the Lawn Tennis Association vetoed a plan by Queen to play at Wimbledon's Centre Court (*NME* 16 and 23/12/78). Obviously some venues were more suitable than others, but pop still provoked prejudice and censorship via the denial of sites. The volatile political climate of the early 1980s affected major pop events. The annual Capital Jazz Festival had to move itself from its home on Clapham Common to Knebworth amid fears of violence after the inner city riots in 1981. The same year also saw perhaps the most pernicious censorial act thus far on the festival front.

Britain's biggest reggae festival was due to be held at Battersea Park in August 1981. However the promoter, Oscar Carroll, received a number of threatening phone calls from men claiming to be National Front members. Carroll was told that the concert would be bombed. After the security firm contracted for the concert withdrew, it was cancelled. This is the only time racist threats have lead to the cancelling of a concert(4), but these cases illustrate again the links of censorial action and current affairs, specifically the inner city riots.

Another overtly political action stopped a major outdoor concert in 1985 when Oxford City Council planned to hold a Festival For Peace, featuring Bo Diddley and Aztec Camera. But it was refused a licence by the County Council. The organizer of the concert said that: 'the only reason they've turned us down is that the Tories simply didn't approve of a peace festival' (NME 22/5/85).

Commercial one day events became commonplace by the 1990s, but safety returned as an issue with the rise of raves and the deaths of two fans at the Donnington festival in 1988 (Rowan 1992). Restrictions by Brent Council on concerts at Wembley Stadium, after complaints from local residents, also kept the issue of the suitability of venues alive. Madonna was denied a fourth gig there in 1987 because of this(5). In 1992 The Cure were refused a licence for an Oxfam charity gig at Eastnor Castle. Again contemporary events are important as Malvern Hills District Council refused a licence following an illegal week long rave at nearby Castlemorton. U2 were also denied a licence for a gig in Heaton Park in Manchester (NME 23/5/92). In a more direct act of censorship The Violent Femmes were taken off the bill for a James concert at Alton Towers because the venue considered itself 'a family attraction' and the band 'not conducive to the environment' (NME 18/4/92).

Pop on the pitch

The staging of gigs in football grounds took off in the early 1970s. In April 1970 Reading FC organized a concert, which was wiped out by storms and the Scene '70 concert planned for Glasgow's Hampden Park in May was cancelled after poor ticket sales. A plan to move it to Partick Thistle's Firhill ground was vetoed by the club's directors after opposition from residents (MM 6 and 13/6/70).

The arrival of stadium rock in Britain was symbolized by The Who's gig at The Valley, home of Charlton FC, in May 1974. Its success did not impress the directors of Queens Park FC who refused to let The

Who play their Hampden Park ground later in the year. Local councillor Gordon Gibb called their decision 'disgraceful' (*MM* 22/6/74). However the GLC gave Charlton permission for another gig and The Who again played there, along with Celtic and Swansea's grounds on their 1976 *Put The Boot In* tour. In 1978 Charlton were refused permission for another festival because Bernard Brook-Partridge (see above) of the GLC's licensing committee felt that the promoters were too inexperienced (*NME* 8/7/78).

Queens Park Rangers used their stadium for a Yes gig in May 1975, but later found themselves in trouble after the gig broke GLC's noise limits (*NME* 14 and 28/6/75). Hammersmith and Fulham Council were soon considering banning future concerts at the ground (*NME* 28/6/75). A planned event at Torquay in 1975 was vetoed by Torbay Council. No reason was given, but it seems that the council were judging the event by the standards of the trouble at Windsor in 1974, again showing links between contemporary events and censorial action (*NME* 24/5/75). In 1982 A CND gig featuring The Jam was announced for the ground, but this was called off after what *NME* called an 'outcry from local residents who submitted numerous objections' (*NME* 29/5/82).

Local residents remained an obstacle to many football ground gigs. In March 1982 Queen proposed a gig at Manchester United's Old Trafford and *NME* reported that: '350 local residents have signed a petition opposing the concert' (*NME* 6/3/82). Later Trafford Council refused the licensing application, 'entirely on the strength of objections from local residents' (*NME* 27/3/82). After attending the Council and residents' meeting, promoter Paul Loosby said: 'It was disgusting - a charade. They simply dismissed rock 'n' roll fans as animals' (ibid)[6]. A month later Queen were refused a licence for a proposed gig at Arsenal's Highbury ground (*NME* 3/4/82).

Since the early 1980s events at football grounds have suffered fewer censorial actions. By the early 1990s it was apparent that, whilst residents often regarded such events as a nuisance, they also realized that they were not the end of civilization. Regular concerts still take place at such venues as Aston Villa and Manchester City. But the larger, longer running, events still encounter resistance.

Longer festivals - rock and a hard place

The National Jazz Festival, which became the annual Reading Festival, provides perhaps the best example of problems surrounding longer festivals. After five years at Richmond, beginning in 1961, Pendleton's festival moved to Windsor racecourse in 1966, despite, says Clarke, 'efforts by residents and the council to ban it' (Clarke 1982, p.24). Here the police complained that Pendleton set up a mixed sex marquee for fans to sleep in. In late 1967 the council voted to ban future festivals after complaints about "immorality" at that sunmmer's event (*M M* 14 and 21/10/67)[7].

As noted earlier, in January 1968 the Council relented and allowed the festival, after appeals from various pop celebrities. Instead it moved to Sunbury On Thames, without incident. However Pendleton encountered opposition when he returned to a racecourse based festival in 1969. He put his festival on at Plumpton, to the annoyance of local residents, including MP Martin Madden[8]. Although the 1969 event passed off peacefully, in 1970 Madden and other residents organized against it. Clarke writes that 'a meeting of local villagers at Chailey ... was told that every legal method to ban the concerts was being explored' (Clarke 1982, p.37). The festival was held in August after a judge ruled that Madden had brought his injunction too late. But Madden eventually succeeded in driving the festival away from Plumpton by securing a promise from the racecourse's owners that it would not be used for festivals again (*M M* 12/12/70).

So Pendleton again found his festival harried away from its home. But he had better luck when it began an unbroken run of thirteen years at Reading in 1971 and this became an important part of the annual rock calendar. By 1982 the festival was essentially a heavy metal event. It was around this time that its troubles returned.

In 1983 there was debate about moving the festival to another site in the town. The Conservatives won control of the local council and gave permission to redevelop the festival site, meaning that it could not be used for the 1984 festival. No new site in the town was found and it was dropped after East Northants Council refused a licence for an attempt to stage it at Lilford (*NME* 18/8/84). A proposed new site was vetoed in 1985 when Reading Council rejected the promoter's rent offer (*NME* 6/7/85).

In 1986 the festival returned to Reading in a field next to its original site. By 1992 it was re-established at the new site. *The Guardian* (30/8/92) reported that a sophisticated audio system kept noise levels down and that a "mum monitor" provided a hot line for worried parents - an important development as many early concerns about festivals centred on their potentially corrupting influence on the young. In 1993 the Mean Fiddler organization won control of the festival and at the time of writing its future seems assured.

Another venue which was a festival site for a while was the Isle of Wight. Its first festival took place in 1968 and festivals, at different sites, took place in the following two years before local censors had their way and stopped festivals on the island for all time in 1971.

The 1968 festival took place near Godshill. It began on 31 August, continued and drew 8,000 people. The promoters, Fiery Creations, then announced a much bigger festival, featuring Bob Dylan, the following year. It lasted from 29 to 31 August and was held near Ryde. But *M M* reported that the Ratepayers Association at Wootton Bridge were opposing a proposed 1970 festival (*M M* 27/9/69).

This festival went on to encounter more opposition than the previous two had, but went ahead from 28 to 30 August, at East Afton, with Jimi Hendrix headlining. But ominous signs preceded this. The National Farmers Union (NFU) advised its members not to provide it with a site (Clarke 1982, p.37) and Fiery Creations' Pete Harrigan spoke of receiving 'threats of personal violence' and said that 'the rear-admirals and brigadiers have been whipping up hysteria against us' (*M M* 25/7/70).

Whilst the festival passed off peacefully many residents objected to "hippies" taking over the island. Clarke reports that local MP Mark Woodnutt, who went to the site in disguise (*Hansard* 18/3/71), 'objected to nude bathing and fornication' (Clarke 1982, p.39) by the audience and to the prevalence of pot smoking (*M M* 10/4/71)(9) - again showing pop's attendant features provoking censorial action. Woodnutt orchestrated opposition to any 1971 festival and effectively used a safety measure as censorship. He tried to limit the amount of people allowed to attend night events on the island to 5,000 - meaning that a commercial festival was subject to a *de facto* ban.

Woodnutt's method was one which is rare in efforts to control pop in Britain - a change in the law. This was the 1971 Isle of Wight County Council Act, Part II of which:

... imposed licensing for both assemblies in the open air "at which

197

during any period exceeding three hours during the six hours following midnight there are not less than 5,000 people present" (Clarke 1982, p.51).

Parliamentary debate on the Bill was characterized by Tory MP for Eastbourne, Sir Charles Taylor's, frequent interruption with cries of 'fornication' (see ibid, pp.51-61). Aesthetic critiques were present via Robert Boscawen, MP for Wells, who made sarcastic remarks about pop's performers 'screaming through a microphone' as part of their "high art" (*Hansard* 18/3/71). The spectre of faceless businessmen exploiting children also surfaced in the debate and Labour MP Tom Driberg pleaded:

Let us hear no more humbug about the wickedness of promoters ... seeking to make great profits ... they lost money last year (*Hansard* 19/5/71).

The Act was passed in July 1971, with only six MPs voting against it, but not effective until December. Meanwhile Fiery Creations tried to arrange a festival but, the council rejected suggested sites and time eventually ran out for the organizers (Clarke 1982, p.61). In 1990 the Isle Of Wight County Council published a booklet eulogizing the festivals (Hinton 1990), conveniently having forgotten its own role in getting them banned.

In general the fate of festivals was mixed. A 1971 festival at Weeley, Essex, organized by its Rotary Club for charity, saw problems with weather and overcrowding (Clarke 1982, p.64). It was against this background that GWF decided to hold a festival in 1972. After being refused sites in Kent, Essex and Sussex, all due to local opposition (ibid, p.65), they settled on a site at Bradney Lincolnshire. Lindsey County Council voted to ban the festival, which then became subject to a court hearing. It eventually went ahead in June, with the threat of jail hanging over the organizers if they failed to meet court stipulations over crowd behaviour, traffic congestion and noise. It passed peacefully, but is, like the examples above, illustrative of the struggles and censorial attitudes then surrounding festivals.

The early 1970s saw debate over the future, if any, of pop festivals. In 1971, under a headline of "Festivals - the great debate", *MM* (10/4/71) sought the views of Woodnutt, Driberg and Mick Farren, leader of the British White Panthers and of The Deviants band.

Driberg saw the issue as a clash of ages and classes and argued that Woodnutt and his allies wanted 'to kill' the Isle of Wight festivals. Farren mooted the idea of a permanent site - a measure still not granted over twenty years on. By this time the Night Assemblies Bill had fallen and the Government had announced the setting up of the Stevenson Committee on festivals (ibid).

In 1970 another festival which both enjoyed a chequered career and became a major part of the annual festival calender started - Glastonbury. 1971 saw the only free Glastonbury and also saw Boscawen continue the tradition of MPs opposing festivals in their constituencies by tabling questions in the Commons on the police being too lenient toward drugs at Glastonbury (Arnold 1971).

By the mid-1980s the festival's attendances had grown further and it became a victim of its own success as attendances rose. After the 1983 festival Mendip Council tried to prosecute site owner Peter Eavis for breaking some of the licence conditions (*NME* 4/2/84). In 1987 *NME* reported that the Tory controlled council was trying to get the event banned (*NME* 9/5/87), but it went ahead. However by October local residents had voted against the festival taking place in 1988, with the local press leading the campaign against it (*NME* 3/10/87).

Glastonbury returned in 1989, but was again in trouble in 1990 when Eavis was fined £14,000 for breaching his licence in 1989 (*NME* 10/3/90) and the 1990 festival saw disturbances when "travellers" who were reluctant to leave the site after the festival ended fought with security guards (*NME* 7/7/90). In January 1991 it was announced that the festival would not take place that year (*NME* 19/1/91). In 1992 it returned, but only after a decision not to allow it was overturned in a magistrates court. Meanwhile at least one local resident has waged a continuous campaign against it.

Anne Goode moved to the nearby village of Pilton in 1981. She believes that the festival has grown into a 'gigantic monster juggernaut where kids are force fed support the miners, get rid of Margaret Thatcher propaganda and drugs'. She added:

> ... the whole thing is geared to - anarchy, and if you add to that the **very loud pop music** then you're going to get a pretty heavy scene. I think this has all the potential for corruption of young people ... If you add to that the occult scene into which people get drawn without realising it ... (*NME* 27/6/92. Emphasis mine).

Note again the concern for children and religious motivation.

Eavis claims Goode, who erected a 30 foot giant cross in opposition to the festival, is not representative of Pilton, but she was at least vocal enough to merit the attentions of *The Independent* (26/10/92) and a Channel 4 documentary team, which showed local opposition also centred around the Friends of Pilton, a group Eavis accuses of being newcomers to the village. The documentary's overwhelming picture was of a clash between town and country, with a need on both sides for a little more give and take.

Meanwhile festivals like WOMAD continue, although this event turned censor in November 1992 when it dropped reggae singer Buju Banton from one of its bills because of his homophobic *Boom By By* single (*NME* 21/11/92). The ban was welcomed by the homosexual rights group Outrage! and marks a rare example of "political correctness" causing censorship in British pop.

Overall the history of censoring pop festivals is primarily one of attacking pop's attendant features, rather than the music itself. But the net effect has often been to cut down on the chance to experience pop in a particular way. By 1992 commercial festivals appeared to be in favour with at least some sections of the media - but their free counterparts have had much less favourable responses.

The free festivals - no direction home?

Free festivals move us still further away from any simple idea of censoring pop as music and further into areas of social control and of politics, as many of the festivals had political aims and used pop as a background to politicking and creating a temporary alternative society. Although many had musical origins and well known bands frequently played them, the music was often of diminishing importance (Clarke 1982, p.85).

Moreover the events were portrayed to the public as "pop festivals" and, as many of them **did** centre upon pop, attempts to stifle the free festivals affected the censorial climate around live pop. Furthermore the vivid portrayal of some aspects of the free festivals sullied the image of popular music in the public consciousness, as the Torquay FC case above showed.

A myriad of free festivals took place from 1969 onwards and continue up to this day, now often intertwining with raves. Early free festivals included 1970s Phun City which took place at Worthing and was organized by *IT*. A High Court injunction against the festival by local residents was only lifted three days before its start, which left little time to erect fences, turnstiles etc. So the organizers made it a free festival (ibid, p.89).

Clarke reports eight free festivals in existence by 1976. But their existence was always somewhat perilous as the Deeply Vale, Lancashire, festival shows. It began in 1976, attracting around 600 people and ran until 1979 by which time attendance was around 8,000. In 1980 police barred the way to the site and the local council got an injunction against the festival covering all the land in its jurisdiction. It then moved to another site and took place, police preferring to let the 4,000 crowd carry on rather than to risk a confrontation. A court injunction prevented the festival in 1981 (see ibid, pp.168-70) and killed it off.

But confrontation was most chillingly employed at the Windsor People's Free Festivals (PFFs) of the early 1970s. These always had a strong political current, often incorporating protests against rent and/or drug laws. They again showed how pop can destroy the thin demarcation line between regulation and censorship.

The first Windsor festival was set up by William Ubique Dwyer as a "Rent Strike People's Festival" for August Bank Holiday weekend, 1972. Dwyer sought no licence from the Crown Commissioners who run Windsor Great Park, thus making the festival illegal. Despite this, and lack of facilities, 700 attended and it passed off peacefully.

In 1973 Dwyer, who viewed the Park as common ground, again did not bother getting permission. About 8,000 attended the festival before the police pressurized those remaining to leave the site on the tenth day. Nevertheless this festival was contained rather than repressed. This was to change in 1974.

The 1974 PFF saw what were then the most violent scenes ever witnessed at any British festival claiming links with popular music (to be surpassed only by Stonehenge in 1985). Dwyer organized it again, this time with the help of Sid Rawle of North Wales' Tipi people. The Crown Commissioners and local council refused to negotiate and the police changed their tactics from containment to repression.

After five days and a peak attendance of 8,000 people the festival dwindled down to 2,000. It was then, on 30 August, that the police decided to clear the site - smashing equipment and numerous heads along the way(10). Many accounts of police violence followed. The

Sun headlined: "Were the police too tough?" and *The Times* commented that: 'A warning that the field would be cleared after five days might have changed everything' (ibid, pp.112-4). In total 220 arrests were made and many injured. Berkshire's Chief Constable Holdsworth commented merely that 'the police achieved what they set out to do: restore law and order' (ibid, p.114), but the police action appears to have been, at best, quasi-legal.

Some Windsor residents were determined that the festival would not return. The Windsor Citizens Action Group mounted a vigorous campaign against it. They united with local MP Alan Glyn, the police's Windsor Festival Intelligence and Discouragement Group and Windsor and Berkshire Councils to stop any 1975 festival. An injunction against it was successfully brought and Rawle and Dwyer were jailed after defying this by publicizing the festival. The County Council spent £10,000 on advertising that the festival would not take place (ibid, p.123).

Within PFF only Dwyer was determined to have the festival at Windsor. With this in mind, wary of a repetition of 1974's violence, and with the issue of pop festivals becoming a political hot potato, Labour Home Secretary Roy Jenkins instructed the Department of The Environment to look for a site for the 1975 festival.

One was eventually agreed upon at Watchfield, a disused Berkshire airfield. This was provided with government assistance, although it was stressed that this was strictly a one-off. Local residents, including MP Airey Neave, voiced opposition to the festival, but it went ahead. The police appear to have made a disproportionate amount of arrests - 95 in a crowd of 5,000 compared with 115 for a crowd of 40,000 at that year's Reading Festival (ibid, p.134). The *Law Journal* later accused Holdsworth of harming relations with young people via his tactics (*NME* 18/10/75).

Any future government assistance was ruled out in April 1976 when Environment Secretary Peter Shore announced that no money would be forthcoming as it could not be justified at a time of cuts in public expenditure elsewhere (*NME* 24/4/76). Organizers tried to find another site, but one at Tangmere in Sussex was vetoed after local MP Tony Nelson pressurized the MOD, its owners, into taking out a court injunction against the festival (*NME* 14/8/76). After a site near Canterbury was also vetoed, the festival went to different sites at Tangmere and Broad Oak (and hence to Seasalter) and ended in confusion and police surveillance (Clarke 1982, pp.144-50).

Although the PFF moved to Cobham, Surrey, in 1977 and on to Bracknell in 1978, by 1976 it was, writes Clarke (ibid, p.174), effectively 'harassed into decline'. Meanwhile Windsor saw off a proposed punk festival in 1977 and a High Court injunction brought by the Citizens Action Group prevented any festival there in 1978 (*NME* 26/8/78).

Windsor's place as the major free festival was succeeded by Stonehenge. Centred on the summer solstice, it began in 1974 and became associated with pop in 1978 (*NME* 1/7/78). It continued in 1979 with some 3-5,000 attending what appeared to be a model of cooperation (Clarke 1982, p.167). Despite trouble with bikers in 1980, the festival continued in 1981 and 1982 (see *NME* 16/5/81 and 3/7/82). Up to 50,000 attended the 1984 festival and it was its growth that prompted moves against it.

By 1985 music was peripheral to the festival, but it remained an important part of the annual festival calendar. A court injunction was taken out against 83 named individuals preventing them from going near to the stones. On this pretext illegal police roadblocks were set up around Stonehenge and, following attempts to reach the stones, the convoy of festival traffic was herded into a field. The ensuing melee became known as the Battle of the Beanfield. Police attacked festival goers, smashing up buses and arresting occupants. Henceforth the festival was banned. It was always illegal but would have become legal in 1985 via an ancient Charter which made a festival legal in its twelfth year (*NME* 18/5/85 and Mitchell 1985).

The history of the free festivals vividly illustrates both pop's potential to offend and, if only via its attendant features, to cause disruption. Whilst moving from being pop events to having a wider agenda their importance to pop should not be under estimated. With the emergence of raves repression has again become the norm. Where they once consulted, governments now move swiftly to legislation. Governments are the last vital player in the debate on festivals.

Festivals and the Government - stopping the rock?

In 1972 festivals were threatened by the Night Assemblies Bill which was introduced into the Commons by Tory MP Jerry Wiggin with the initial support of the Conservative Government. Its introduction followed disturbances at Weeley in 1971 (Clarke 1982, pp.62/3). It sought to forbid gatherings of over 1,000 people at night unless local authorities were given four months notice. A second clause gave authorities the power to stop assemblies on the grounds of the land's unsuitability. As White (1972) noted at the time:

> The consistent record of local authorities' opposition to pop festivals suggests that few, if any, proposed sites would be "suitable for the purpose".

The Bill imposed fines of £400 for those offending against it. Opposition to it mobilized after its second reading in the Commons in January 1972 and GWF produced an alternative set of measures called the Charter for Festival Administration. In March 1972 it was announced that gatherings of under 3,000 and eight hours' duration would be exempt (*M M* 25/3/72). Meanwhile the NCCL opposed the Bill because it had grave implications for the right to hold political demonstrations.

In April the Government withdrew support for the Bill after receiving a report which said that its vagueness made it potentially a tool of great repression (*M M* 29/4/77). By May 1972 it was dead when it was "talked out" of Parliamentary time by Labour MPs including Gerald Kaufman and Les Huckfield (see *Hansard* 5/5/72). But opponents of the Bill stressed its implications for civil liberties in general: festivals only escaped because their opponents had strayed too far into other areas.

Meanwhile the Government launched a series of inquiries and working parties on pop festivals. The first, the Stevenson Report, was commissioned in 1972 and published in 1973. It took an essentially pro-festival line, believing that problems had arisen primarily because the festivals had taken off quickly without time for the authorities to acquaint themselves with the problems involved (*M M* 20/5/72). The Code of Practice it recommended was published on 25 June 1973 and it noted the need for it to be circulated widely in order to diffuse 'what is at times the highly-charged atmosphere of pop festivals' (Advisory Committee on Pop Festivals 1973, p.vii).

The report was advisory rather than statutory and argued that 'pop festivals are a type of recreation which should take place' (ibid, p.5), although it noted that:

... many millions ... seem to feel that the fact that tens of thousands of young people want to gather together in one place for days at a time away from their parents is, in itself, corrupting and evil (ibid)

- again linking censorial acts with thoughts of moral welfare. The report rejected such notions and had particular scorn for the media who had behaved 'with great irresponsibility' (ibid, p.8) when reporting the festivals. It saw no need for new legislation. It also noted that attitudes had hardened after the 1970 Isle of Wight festival, since which: 'The mere announcement of a proposed pop festival is liable to create consternation, if not panic, in the local community' (ibid, p.37) - yet again linking censorial attitudes to contemporary events.

A muted national outcry subsequently greeted events at Windsor in 1974 and the next government inquiry into pop festivals, set up under Lord Melchett by the Labour Government, met against this backdrop. This Working Group was formed to succeed Stevenson's in the summer of 1975 and it included Stevenson. Its primary task was to look at the free festivals. Some people, it noted, wanted festivals 'banned altogether on the grounds that they are a nuisance and encourage law-breaking and anti-social behaviour' (Working Group on Pop Festivals 1976, p.19). Noticeably music itself was again absent from the list of complaints.

The *Free Festivals* report, published in May 1976, saw nothing inherently wrong with festivals and followed Stevenson in calling for give and take. It even thought that some public funding, under the right conditions, might be no bad thing. It was adamant that the PFF should **not** get any special government assistance, though it supported its call for a permanent site.

The next, more general, report, *Pop Festivals and Their Problems*, was produced by a Committee chaired by Baroness Stedman and published in January 1978. It contained little new, noting that the law, much of which pre-dated pop festivals, was often too cumbersome when dealing with them but concluding that new legislation could not be justified 'merely to deal with the relatively minor problem of pop festivals' (Working Group on Pop Festivals 1978, p.vii). It also noted that: 'many people associate pop festivals with drug taking, immorality and a general disrespect for the law and for authority', a view often 'strengthened by sensationalism in

205

the media', but which 'cannot be dismissed as irrelevant' (ibid, p.11).

The report saw two main problems with free festivals. First, many organizers lacked status as authority figures, which left them unable to control crowds and, secondly, they were prone to using sites without owners' permission (ibid, pp.12-13). It rejected making it an offence to visit an unauthorized festival and asked for more cooperation on all sides and government provision of a site 'which might be available for pop festivals ... from time to time' (ibid p.18). So the well meaning pragmatic approach continued.

Since Stedman the political climate has changed and the emphasis has shifted from consent to coercion. Although no legislation specifically relating to pop **festivals** has yet been passed, there has been a tightening up of licensing and public gatherings - as evidenced by the Entertainments (Increased Penalties) Act of 1990, the Public Order Act of 1984, the 1988 Licensing Act and the 1994 Criminal Justice Act, parts of which deal with **the** major controversy surrounding British pop and its consumption in the latter period covered by this book.

Raves

Attempts to control raves are treated as an example of pop censorship here because, at a minimum, they have entailed the denial of certain ways of consuming pop. Moreover DJs and other acts perform, or express themselves artistically, at raves. Thus restricting the events can involve restricting artistic expression, or censorship. Raves also see safety once again donning a censorial cloak.

Starting in their own right in 1987, after being preceded by the "warehouse" scene, raves first came to public prominence in the summer of 1988. Problems arose because of the practice of holding them on large open sites, with or without the owner's permission (the matter is more complicated if the land used is "common" land), often in rural areas, and so depriving the nearest residents of sleep. This was compounded by concerns over trespass, drugs (especially ecstasy) and safety. By 1992 ravers had latched on to free festivals and forced raves on to the political agenda in a way analogous to the events of Windsor in 1974 and Stonehenge in 1985.

At first the scene was confined to clubs and a few parties held in disused warehouses (with or without owners' permission and certainly in breach of most fire regulations) in inner city areas. But the issue really came to prominence with the rise, from 1988 onwards, of outdoor raves. Initially centring upon the area around London's M25 orbital road, they soon went nationwide. Their highly visible and audible nature, combined with an association in the minds of many commentators and authorities with drugs, led to both a minor moral panic and the backlash that usually accompanies it. This backlash can be seen as commencing towards the end of the summer of 1988. In November *NME* reported that:

> The warehouse bashes are now virtually extinct. Police have advised disco equipment suppliers that if they hire gear to warehouse organisers they will be fined (Wells 1988b).

It also reported a spate of police raids on clubs and venue managers banning acid nights in the wake of stories in the *Sun* which linked raves and ecstasy. (Note again the press' role). The link between contemporary events and attacks on raves is provided by the fact that the scare over acid coincided with ministerial outbursts over "lager louts"(11).

Moves against raves were soon compared to those against punk, with censors targeting pop in a way which had not been seen for some ten years. But punk never dominated the charts the way rave came too. Neither did it initiate a change in the law.

Raves' opponents used emotive language to back up their case. Wells (1988b) paraphrased a *Sun* description of raves thus:

> Kids don't dance they "twist and jerk" to the "mind numbing beat" and the "hypnotic" lights. This is the **exact** same language used by extreme fundamentalists to attack rock music in the States, the same terminology used by the Russian government when they described pop as "decadent" in the 50s and 60s (emphasis in original).

By 1989 the horror stories had died down, but pressure grew in political circles for action against raves and the law began to be used against them. In August 1989 the Joy rave in Rochdale was served with two injunctions - against the site owner and DJ Mike Pickering - who stayed away from the event. It finally went ahead in defiance of these injunctions but only 2,000 people, instead of an anticipated

30,000, attended. Here the police decided not to break up the event -
a decision later criticized by both local MP Cyril Smith and Rochdale
Council (*NME* 12/8/89).

A planned rave by the Biology organization in October 1989,
featuring Public Enemy, was even less fortunate. Police illegally
blocked the M3 motorway to stop ravers making their way to it. The
same weekend a 3,000 strong Back To The Future rave at the Santa
Pod race track was broken up by police and a planned rave at
Lichfield was cancelled after a High Court injunction was granted
against it (*NME* 18/10/89). Again the idea of unscrupulous
businessmen exploiting hapless kids raised its head. Cosgrove (1989)
suggested that whereas aficionados of the music had been behind
warehouse parties, the new breed of rave promoters, exemplified by
young Tory Tony Colston-Hayter were 'accountants with rotweilers'
mixing 'profit and rogue economics' with little concern for safety.

Meanwhile Graham Bright, Tory MP for Luton South, John
Major's Parliamentary Private Secretary and responsible for the
"video nasties" legislation, began another moral crusade. He
sponsored the Entertainments (Increased Penalties) Act, of which
more below.

But ravers showed resistance to such censorship. In February 1990
a Freedom To Party rally was held in Trafalgar Square with some
2,000 attending. Its organizers, the Freedom To Party Campaign,
aimed:

> To defend the right to freedom of association, publicise the threat
> to civil liberties posed by the proposed legislation ... and to
> advocate reasonable reform of the music and dancing system'
> (*NME* 10/2/90).

It was backed by such promoters as Biology and Colston-Hayter.

Another demonstration in Manchester's Albert Square protested at
police harassment of raves (Redhead 1991). However the authorities
approach was not a process only of oppression, but rather a
dichotomous one of mixing it with containment. This involved the
granting of more all night licences for clubs at weekends. So the
chance to dance all night in the city was reaffirmed at the same time
as the countryside's right to a good night's sleep. Others, however,
demanded suppression and wanted the music itself outlawed. *The
Post* newspaper headlined a story on 24 October 1988 with "Ban This

Killer Music" (Melechi and Redhead 1988)(12).

Bright sought to deter illegal raves by increasing the penalties for organizing them. His aim was that 'the young have their entertainment in a safe and sane environment' (*The Independent* 3/3/90). The penalties for those providing unsafe, and presumably insane, entertainments were draconian. The Act, which came into effect on 13 July 1990, imposed fines of up to £20,000 for each proven offence (justified by Bright because of massive profits made at raves) or imprisonment for up to six months, or both. Labour offered no opposition to this, with the party's Stuart Randall claiming that 'everyone's won' as the Act was passed (*Hansard* 27/4/90).

Despite Bright's Act becoming law in 1990 raves carried on in 1991 with few major incidents. But controversy surrounding them escalated in 1992 as ravers attached themselves to the free festivals. The catalyst for a moral panic centring on "travellers", but encompassing raves and thus pop, was an illegal week long festival at Castlemorton in the Malvern Hills which up to 25,000 attended.

Here press coverage mixed aesthetic criticisms with moral indignation. Ravers were shown to be not merely a nuisance, but as making themselves such in order to pursue a culturally worthless form of music. *The Observer* (24/5/92) commented upon the 'ear splitting music' at Castlemorton, which it wrongly called 'this summer's new music'. An *Independent* (26/5/92) editorial spoke of 'young people ... (with) a desire to gather in huge masses and be **assaulted by loud music**' (emphasis mine) and then, more sensibly, called for a licensing system to enable 'a popular form of pleasure' to continue without causing upset. *The Times* (1/6/92) reported that raves contained 'music that had the beat and volume of a pneumatic drill'. Often one was left feeling that ravers would be tolerated if only it was Beethoven and not dance music that they played at "ear splitting" volume.

Raves continued after Castlemorton, but publicity around that event engendered a new determination by local authorities and police to act. In June 1992 *The Municipal Journal* (5-11/6/92) reported that Environmental Health Officers were examining raves and the *Local Government Chronicle* (5/6/92) reported that Dyfed and Powys police were taking measures to counter raves. A July festival **was** held in mid-Wales and passed off peacefully (*The Guardian* 28/7/92) and a large rave at Romsey in August was contained by police using roadblocks, which resulted in another rave being held just outside Winchester. Local MP, Michael Colvin, visited one site and said that, whilst he thought that a festival site should be made available for travellers, 'there could be a case for police having powers to call in troops when needed' (*The Guardian* 10/8/92). Travellers eventually left after being served with notices issued under Section 39 of the 1986 Public Order Act.

By 1992 some were asking if Bright's Act had had the intended effect. Prosecutions under it were rare and the *Sunday Times* (21/6/92) speculated that, as half the fun of raves was chasing the site all over the countryside and as legal raves missed out on this fun, illegal raves would continue. The Government nevertheless determined to clamp down on travellers and in spring 1993 promised that 1994 would see legislation in place that would give the police power to stop any convoy of over six vehicles. This provision was included in the 1994 Criminal Justice Bill, sections 58-64 of which specifically dealt with raves. As I write the full effects of the Act have yet to be seen. They will not be liberating.

Conclusion

Overall a process of containment and outright banning of raves has been apparent. In many ways raves move us away from the censoring of pop per se and into issues of public order. But that music is central to raves is undeniable - live acts can appear - and moves to counter them are therefore censorious as such moves stifle pop's message. It is the fact that music **is** at raving's centre that makes attempts to curtail raves simultaneously a move to censor pop. Some music **only** gets heard publicly at raves. Raves might be noisy inconveniences for local inhabitants, but so are many public events. The banning of both festivals and raves has censorial implications because it limits the amount of pop available and, perhaps more importantly, limits the pop audience's chances of experiencing itself **as** an audience.

While raves shared with festivals a reputation for drugs, the police said that their main concerns with raves were about safety and nuisance (see ibid). But on occasions the police themselves went outside the law and used illegal roadblocks to stop raves (Starmer 1990). So restricting the events has implications for freedom of speech and, when roadblocks have been used, on freedom of movement.

In the early 1970s a Conservative Government set up inquiry teams to investigate free festivals, but in the 1990s anti-rave legislation was passed without consulting those involved. In 1982 Clarke described the history of pop festivals as a slow triumph by the liberal lobby within the establishment, that lobby never got a chance to get involved in raves. The Criminal Justice Act seems to show that The Beastie Boys were right all along, ravers will have to fight for their right to party.

Notes

1. For festivals as community see Advisory Committee On Pop Festivals 1973, p.8.

2. It is always a contested point as to how "representative" those who complain about events are.

3. Opposition to Hyde Park gigs again came from an MP, in this case Harold Soref, who linked them to pot usage (Clarke 1982, p.61).

4. Other racist attempts at hitting pop include a series of phone calls to Capital DJ Dave Cash telling him not to play "woggy" music, NME 18/2/78 and 1/4/78. The British Movement allegedly threatened to kill Jimmy Pursey, Sounds 9/12/78. See NME 12/12/92 for a "fascist" threat to a J gig at ULU.

5. For Madonna's Wembley problems see NME 18 and 25/7/87 and 1/8/87. For opposition to a Michael Jackson Wembley gig see NME 23/1/88. NME 11/1/92 claimed that a limit of 12 gigs a year at the stadium meant that many bands were not bothering to play it.

6. This came after the Advisory Committee on Pop Festivals 1973, p.9 favourably compared the behaviour of pop fans to that of football fans.

7. Note also Sir Charles Taylor's comments about "fornication" in the Isle of Wight debate above.

8. The censorial role of the local MP is notable and includes Woodnutt's opposition on the Isle of Wight, Neave's against Watchfield and Boscawen's against Glastonbury.

9. But Woodnutt insisted that his opposition to the festival was not morally motivated (Clarke 1982, p.52).

10. For a fuller account of the mayhem surrounding the 1974 Windsor Festival see Clarke 1982, pp.99-114.

11. For examples see *The Sun* 27/9/88 and *Yorkshire Evening Post* 10/10/88.

12. For *The Sun*'s calls to ban acid see editions of 26/10/88, 1/11/88 and 3/11/88.

Part Five
Censorial campaigners

11   Keeping up the pressure

The National Viewers and Listeners Association

Mary Whitehouse and the organization she led as President up until 1994, the National Viewers and Listeners Association (NVALA), are by far the best known censorial campaigners in Britain.   Some understanding of them and their attitude to pop is therefore necessary if the censorial climate within which pop operates in Britain is to be understood.   So this chapter begins with them before going on to look at other moralist pressure groups who sometimes seek to censor pop.

Whitehouse was heavily influenced by her involvement from 1932 onwards with the Moral Rearmament Army (MRA), a Christian evangelical movement launched by American Frank Buchman and previously known as the Oxford Group.   Whitehouse saw the 1960s as a watershed.   In 1963 she was a teacher and shocked when the BBC televised a programme called *A Kind of Loving*, which left her pupils with the idea that 'we shouldn't have intercourse until we're **engaged**' (Whitehouse 1982, p.7. Emphasis in original).   For Whitehouse this epitomized all that was wrong with broadcasting at that time, being yet another example of the BBC[1] giving full licence to the forces of the "New Morality" whilst totally ignoring those of traditional Christianity.   She believed this entailed deliberate attempts by some at the BBC to propagate non-Christian morality and to undermine the notion of childhood, a concept very dear to her[2].

The renewal of the BBC's charter in January 1964 provided the impetus for Whitehouuse.   Aiming to mobilize public opinion, she got support from public figures such as her local MP Jasper More, Enoch Powell (then Minister of Health), Dr. Mark Hudson (then Bishop of Hereford) and MP James Dance. Whitehouse launched the Clean Up TV Campaign (CUTV) on 27 January 1964. Its first major meeting was on 5 May 1964 in Birmingham Town Hall, where two thousand people attended. Out of this came a "Clean Up TV" Manifesto, which was included in a petition that was presented to Parliament by Sir Barrett Cocks in 1965. Containing 40,000 signatures, this affirmed Christian belief, demanded it for the country's children and called on the BBC to put God 'back into the heart of our family and national life' (Whitehouse 1982, p.15). But the CUTV had no formal organization and to rectify this Whitehouse launched NVALA on 29 November 1965.

Although initially motivated by television, Whitehouse (1971, p.118) believes that 'the media are indivisible'. Subsequently NVALA has, amongst other things, campaigned against pornography, taken an interest in the *Oz* and *Little Red Schoolbook* prosecutions (both 1971), prosecuted *Gay News* for blasphemy in publishing James Kirkup's *The Love That Dared To Speak Its Name* poem (1976-8), campaigned to keep the *Deep Throat* film out of Britain (1976) and *The Last Temptation of Christ* off television screens (1990). It was also a moving force behind the "video nasties" scare which resulted in Graham Bright's Video Recordings Act of 1984.

But Whitehouse's greatest legacy may be the setting up of the BSC, a long held NVALA aim. The BSC's first chairman, Lord Rees Mogg, praised Whitehouse for thinking of the idea *(Viewer and Listener* Summer 1992), but NVALA soon complained about the "soft" line adopted by the BSC[3]. To understand why it did so it is necessary to know what NVALA believes.

A question of faith - NVALA philosophy

Like many of the pressure groups examined here, NVALA has a deep religious commitment. So it proclaims that: 'Christian values are basic to the health and wellbeing of our nation' (Whitehouse 1985, p.158). NVALA's outlook is problematic inasmuch as it is out of step with much that has occurred in Britain since the late 1950s, where religious belief has declined and morality has increasingly been seen as a personal rather than governmental concern. For Whitehouse

God has decreed moral standards forever and there is no scope for changing social mores.

Her remedy for Britain's alleged moral malaise centres upon what she terms "responsibility". This would include the media considering much more carefully the likely effect of their output upon audiences. Whitehouse (1971, p.138) states that: 'Responsible social control on every level is the only answer'. When the beliefs of NVALA are considered, the implications of this "responsibility" become obvious. Certain subjects would become taboo within popular culture, including homosexuality, rebellion, premarital sex, drugs, etc.

On the relevance of empirical evidence NVALA rides two horses at once. It quotes and tallies various reports on the causal links between media portrayals and violence, crime, sex, etc. But Whitehouse also says that 'we have got to get away from this silly notion of having to prove everything' (Merck 1988, p.192) and aims to:

> ... break the domination of those sociologists who demand "proof" of the effect of broadcasting before conclusions can be drawn and acted upon (Whitehouse 1971, p.181).

Instead of "proof" Whitehouse calls for "commonsense"[4], saying that:

> If we could somehow get back to this business of commonsense instead of trying to computerise and interpret, we would make a good deal of progress' (Tracey and Morrison 1979, p.77).

Commonsense, she says, is 'the sumtotal of human experience' (ibid p.84), but that experience always needs interpretation and its diversity militates against the acceptance of any commonly held idea of "commonsense".

Another constant theme is patriotism (see for example Whitehouse 1985, p.96). Whitehouse talks of having 'a deep faith ... in Britain and what Britain could mean to the world' (Tracey and Morrison 1979, p.54). Occasionally this can edge into xenophobia, as exemplified by her concern that children are 'pressurised into alien patterns of behaviour' (Whitehouse 1985, p.48)[5].

But what particularly shocked Whitehouse about the 1960s Underground was that much of its propaganda was deliberately aimed at children. Whitehouse says that her work:

... springs directly from my experience as a teacher, working with the children whose own lives had been adversely affected by what they had seen on television (Clare 1989, p.11).

All the pressure groups examined here use children and the family as moral touchstones, tending to posit trans-historical views of both. The reality is of changing conceptions between time, place and class(6).

Overall NVALA can be seen the archetype of the moralist pressure groups. It is religiously motivated and uses children to justify its brand of censorship. It is also prone to causal claims which it is reluctant to subject to scientific analysis. This become more apparent when its actions against pop are considered.

Pop goes NVALA

NVALA informed me that: 'We have **not** done any substantive research on pop music' (Beyer 1991. Emphasis mine). Despite this admitted ignorance, it has commented freely on pop and its effects and interfered with its dissemination. Street (1986, p.17) is wrong to say that NVALA have 'paid little attention to pop' because, as Whitehouse sees the media as indivisible, they have had to confront pop and have tried both to censor and to smear it.

The spectre of the 1960s - which Whitehouse (1971, p.150) claims 'prepared the ground for anarchy' - haunts NVALA analysis. Whitehouse (1977, p.38) has written that:

The whole "pop" scene, with its emphasis on the "counter-culture", has done **more than anything** to destroy the manners upon which Western society has been based (emphasis mine).

Causal claims are seldom more blatant, nor more unsubstantiated. Correspondence with NVALA revealed that its main concerns with regard to pop focussed on two areas. First, 'pop has an influence on young people especially when considering the lyrics' (Beyer 1992). Thus there is a concentration on areas which, as we have seen, the audience often perceives as unimportant and may not even hear (see above). But lyrics' significance become apparent in the second area of concern. NVALA General Secretary, John Beyer (ibid), wrote that:

In the 1960s the pop culture played a key role in overturning traditional values and this **certainly** helped to bring about an environment of "DIY" morality. Pop artists, by their lifestyles and their advocacy, have also reinforced this way of life and, sadly, so many young lives have become tragedies as a consequence (emphasis mine).

Pop is thus seen as giving succour to the permissive 60s. Furthermore it is held to have encouraged the decade's excesses, with pop stars' advocacy of "alternative" lifestyles and morality having had tragic consequences for the young. This is a causal argument(7), based on assertion rather than research.

Pop caused Whitehouse concern from an early stage. A 1964 quote of hers bears repetition:

There are many things in the accepted fabric of children's life which need to be dealt with in a forthright way - "pop" records for one. "My love can't wait" says one pop song. "Tomorrow may be too late," says another. Children accept many of the words on their face value but nevertheless are being brainwashed with the pornographic ideas which lie behind many of them (Tracey and Morrison 1979, p.42).

This requires some comment. It is factually incorrect as it quotes the lyrics to one song (Elvis Presley's *It's Now or Never / O Sole Mio*) and claims them to be from two. This shows Whitehouse to be a sloppy researcher who is trying to double the impact of her material. Such songs are then given the ability to "brainwash" children - a causal assertion.

In 1967 pop got comparatively little airtime, but Whitehouse (1967, p.180) felt it was too much, complaining that: 'the amount of time they (pop groups) get you would imagine that young people today en masse see only as far as a strumming guitar'.

The information that Whitehouse has received on pop is not from the most objective of sources. The only book on pop she references in any of her works is David A. Noebel's *The Marxist Minstrels* (Whitehouse, 1977 p.216), which she uses to back up her claim that: 'Drugs, revolution, immorality, black magic, devil worship ... characterize the songs of the "heavy beat" groups' (ibid, p.38). Noebel is best known for his claim that: 'The Beatles' ability to make teenagers take off their clothes and riot is laboratory tested and approved' (Street 1986, p.55). He saw rock as a Communist 'multibillion dollar assault on the moral foundation of civilized society' (MacKenzie 1987, p.36). We shall meet Noebel[8] again when the religious anti-rock sects are examined, but the point here is that Whitehouse regards him as an expert, one whose opinion is valuable. Her critique of pop thus is both under researched and empirically implausible.

Whitehouse moved from condemning pop to trying to censor it in 1967 when pop combined with her other demon, television, in the showing of the Beatles' *Magical Mystery Tour* film in December 1967. Her action proved successful, not in getting the film stopped, but in contributing to major upheavals at the BBC.

Whitehouse (1982, p.64) says that she read about the film and 'the words of a song which ... contained the line "you been a naughty girl, you let your knickers down"'. She contacted the BBC Chairman Lord Hill and said she 'hoped he would agree that it was most unsuitable for children's viewing' (Whitehouse 1971, p.101). Hill talked to BBC Director General, Sir Hugh Greene, who stood by his decision, which was carried out, to broadcast the film at the originally scheduled time.

Whitehouse's objections to a harmless line in Lennon's *I Am The Walrus*, seem inane over twenty five years later, but the fixed moral stance of NVALA means that it continues to hold the same objections. They led to a row between Hill, who felt that his authority had been undermined, and Greene, who was to depart the BBC the following July, feeling his independence undermined. Whitehouse (1982, p.65) cites this case as the the final straw for Hill. Thus her first censorial action against pop proved successful not in silencing the pop, but in removing from office a BBC Director-General in whom NVALA had no trust. Their next move against pop was less successful.

Tony Palmer's documentary on the Underground scene, *All My Loving*, was first broadcast on BBC 1 in 1968. Whitehouse (1971, p.199) objected because in it: 'Jimi Hendrix made obscene gestures and simulated the sexual act by using his guitar as a woman'. She also noted that BBC audience research showed that some viewers 'were repelled by the antics of some of the artists (notably The Who and Jimmy [sic] Hendrix)' (ibid).

After it was shown NVALA considered prosecuting the BBC and Palmer for "conspiracy to corrupt morals and outrage public decency" (ibid, p.120). A warning letter was sent to the BBC, but it still repeated the programme on BBC2 on 18 May 1969. Whitehouse arranged for 'four to six **responsible** citizens to view it' (*M M* 24/5/69. Emphasis mine) on its broadcast to decide whether it was obscene. On May 21 Whitehouse, John Barrett, Chief Constable of Lincolnshire and NVALA President, and the Bishop of Hereford went to see the DPP to investigate the possibility of an obscenity prosecution. This proved fruitless as they were advised that the Obscene Publications Acts did not then apply to television.

Whitehouse's view of pop also raised the familiar bogey of older people exploiting the young. She saw pop being used by the young to question moral standards, which was healthy enough, but:

> ... alongside this you have got many people - not teenagers - who are much older, who are using the questioning attitude of youth to destroy completely the standards on which society has been built (*M M* 31/8/68).

One such destroyer was Alice Cooper whose *School's Out* single reached No. 1 in the BBC charts in September 1972. Whitehouse's concern was that it was aimed at children and encouraged rebellion against authority at school. She wrote to *TOTP* producer Johnnie Stewart asking that the film of the song be removed. Whitehouse objected to: 'the whole mood of the film. It was quite anarchic' (*M M* 2/9/72) and told Stewart:

> You will see that the lyrics contain the following chorus - "Got no principles, got no innocence; School's out for summer, school's out forever; school's been blown to pieces, Oh! No more books, no more teachers". In our view the record is subversive. I hope you will agree and take appropriate action. It could also be incitement to violence (Tracey and Morrison 1979, p.89).

Note again the concentration on lyrics and the misquoting of them.

Whitehouse also complained to the Controller of Radios 1 and 2 and the DPP about the BBC playing the record, which she wanted prosecuted for inciting subversion (ibid). In a causal argument, she also linked the record to an assault on a headmaster by schoolchildren (*M M* 2/9/72). The net result of all this was again a partial victory. The BBC stopped showing the original film on *To p of The Pops.* Whitehouse claimed this was because of her intervention; the BBC denied it (ibid).

1972 also saw Whitehouse's most infamous intervention in pop with her attacks on Chuck Berry's *My Ding A Ling*, a song full of sexual innuendo centring on masturbation. Whitehouse claimed that it was not the content of Berry's song that upset her, but his treatment of it in a concert film that was shown on *TOTP*. She said: 'It's the *accentuation* of the double meaning by the BBC that I object to' (*M M* 9/12/72 Emphasis in original). She protested about:

> ... the way in which Chuck Berry told the cameramen to pick out some obviously embarrassed young girls who were not joining in all the so-called fun and games. But at no time did we object to the song itself (Whitehouse 1982, p.88).

Again a partial victory was achieved as *TOTP* cut some of the offending scenes (ibid, pp.88/9). The case again showed Whitehouse's fixed morality. Thirteen years later she said that: 'I'm quite sure a complaint had to be made about the way Chuck Berry behaved' (Wells 1985).

NVALA also tried to censor The Rolling Stones. When the band released *Exile on Main Street* in 1972 Whitehouse wrote to Lord Hill, saying that:

> ... the new Rolling Stones record, Exit on Main Street (sic), is being played on Radio One. This record uses four-letter words. Although they are somewhat blurred, there's no question about what they are meant to be ... The very fact that this programme is transmitted primarily for young people would, one would have thought, demanded more and not less care about what is transmitted. I would grateful if you would look into this matter (Caulfield 1975, p.107).

There was little need to add "and ban it" - the intent was clear enough. Again Whitehouse mixed factual inaccuracy with lack of comprehension. The album title is misquoted and it also lacks the swear words Whitehouse claims. There are a few "shits" in *Sweet Virginia* which are clear enough, but the alleged "somewhat blurred" words are less easy to spot. The BBC could not find them at all. Hill replied that he had listened to the tracks that 1 had played and found

224

none of the alleged words. 1 continued to play tracks from the album (ibid). Whitehouse was on firmer ground when she complained that the lyrics to the Stones' 1973 track *Starfucker*, which does contain a lot of swearing, were being distributed to children (Whitehouse 1977, p.24).

In 1976 Whitehouse claimed that NVALA only looked into pop after complaints sent to it (*M M* 28/2/76), but she objected to the lyrics of Rod Stewart's *Tonight's The Night* saying that as it was played by the IBA and BBC 'one can only assume that the lyrics of songs like that are considered quite acceptable by someone' (Whitehouse 1977, p.39).

During punk, Whitehouse commented that 'I am not shocked by punk, I am ashamed by it' (*NME* 17/10/92). She quotes the Grundy interview as an instance of declining standards on television (Whitehouse 1977, p.11), complained about the BBC playing *Anarchy in The UK* (ibid, p.39) and about it buying a copy of Alberto Y Los Trios Paranoias' punk spoof *Fuck You* single (ibid, pp.39/40).

Whitehouse (1982, p.132) also wrote of a 1982 record on which:

> The words are foul, the action they so crudely and violently describe involves bestiality, sex with schoolgirls and obscene practices involving human excrement

and detailed how she asked for the DPP to prosecute it. She does not mention its title but, as noted above, the author got NVALA confirmation that it was the Anti Nowhere League's *So What* (Beyer 1992). I also noted earlier the importance of "a member of the public" complaining to the police about "obscenity". Whenever a record is under scrutiny in Britain NVALA is often suspected of providing a censorial impetus. In this case such suspicion is confirmed as NVALA instigated the first successful prosecution of a pop record in Britain.

NVALA also tried to intervene in the Beastie Boys' 1987 tour, supporting Run DMC, by unsuccessfully calling for armed police to be present at the gigs in order to quell any potential riots (*NME* 25/8/87). So NVALA interest in pop continued, although it denied involvement in the NWA prosecution of 1991 (Beyer 1992), despite NCROPA claims that it was (O'Hagan 1991).

Overall NVALA's view of pop recalls much of the American Christian fundamentalist literature on the subject. Pop is treated with constant suspicion, calls for censorship and occasional censorial actions, ultimately of a legal sort. Whitehouse (1985, p.99) has written that:

> We need ... to realize the significance of the "heavy metal" image with its studded belts, wrist-bands, rings, knuckle dusters, barb-wire necklaces, and the T-shirts with violent images and messages.

For her dismissing this as "fun" is to be dangerously naive. It may be similarly naive to dismiss NVALA's influence. It has achieved censorial victories in the past and it will doubtless continue to do so in all fields - including pop. It also has allies.

CARE (Christian Action and Research Education)

CARE is a Christian research and education organization which has its roots in the Festival of Light (FOL) group, which formed in 1971 and campaigned on a range of moral issues. CARE is seldom active in the censoring of pop *per se*, but it monitors other mass media which pop uses. CARE's leaflets include "Monitoring your local video supplier" and "TV Watchdog". It publishes the addresses of broadcasting organizations and encourages members to complain if they see or hear anything offensive, which reinforces the suspicion that when complaints are made to broadcasters or to the BSC, complainants may well come from CARE or its fellow travellers.

The Community Standards Association (CSA)

The CSA was founded by Anne Whittaker in Cornwall in the 1970s and it aims to promote:

> ... those attitudes of mind and standards which are part of our Christian Cultural Heritage (sic) and to fight by all lawful means against **everything** which would corrupt these attitudes of mind and lower these standards of conduct in our national life and in our local community' (CSA leaflet nd. Emphasis mine).

Pop has been seen as such a corrupting force. Among the myriad of concerns the CSA lists is, under the sub-clause "Addictions": 'Pop Sub-culture' and under the heading of "Media", it includes concern over: 'Standards on Radio and Television ... Swearing, Blasphemy, Vulgarity and Obscenity' (ibid).

Merseyside CSA achieved local notoriety in October 1991 when Liverpool's Radio City commercial radio station reported that it had called for a ban on Oceanic's *Insanity* single because of its references to ecstasy. Merseyside CSA Secretary Ruth Slater (1991) denied calling for a ban, although she admitted that she might have agreed to the idea in the heat of the moment. Although she had not even heard *Insanity* her general view was that if records "plug" drugs they should be banned (ibid). She wanted 'responsible' stations and DJs not to play records which promoted drugs, thus avoiding the censorship which might otherwise be necessary (ibid).

Slater invoked the "beatist" critique of rock (see below) and told me that the drums she heard in pop were 'not all that different' from the "pagan" drums she heard whilst in Nigeria. These drums, she implied, must have an effect on the listener and almost certainly a detrimental one. The CSA has close links to other moralist pressure groups such as CARE and Family and Youth Concern.

The Conservative Family Group

Formed in October 1985, this group is vehemently anti-homosexual and was one of the few groups to campaign for the homophobic Clause 28 of the Local Government Act of 1988. It also attacked Health Minister Virginia Bottomley for her: 'Praise (of) Mr Freddie Mercury as "heroic"' (*Family Matters* March 1992). It has done little in the arena of pop, but its anti-gay stance has obvious implication for freedom of expression.

Family and Youth Concern (FYC)

This group was previously known as The **Responsible** Society (emphasis mine), which began in 1971. It has support from prominent people such as *Times* columnist Ronald Butt, who was given a CBE by the Thatcher administration. It claims to be interested in "obscenity" in all areas and seeks to educate, research and publish relevant information (FYC leaflet *About Family and Youth Concern* nd). Some idea of its concerns and outlook can be gleaned from its publications list, which includes; *The Truth About AIDS*, *Feminism vs Mankind*; writings against the Family Planning Association; and the works of G. K. Chesterton.

FYC claims to be secular, but has often worked with religious activists, such as the CSA, the Salvation Army and Catholic anti-abortion campaigner Victoria Gillick. It is also against some aspects of pop.

The Responsible Society called for a government enquiry into The Sex Pistols' *Carri On* album in 1979 on the grounds that it was "sick" (*NME* 18/8/79). FYC's Bulletin of August 1980 reported the work of music therapist Frank Knight who made the causal claim that the 'aural drug' of pop could 'encourage and cause individually wrong and socially harmful conduct' (Knight 1977). Many pop songs, he claimed, were symptomatic of a 'morally sick society' and had 'a shocking materialism regarding love'. His aesthetic critique was to label pop "mewsick" (ibid). FYC's *Bulletin* (No.30, August 1980) commented that Knight's argument was 'convincing', but neglected its censorial implications.

In 1986 leading member Joanna Bogle researched youth magazines and warned that: 'A curious feature of the current pop scene is its obsession with black magic and the occult' (Bogle 1986, p.5). She attacked *NME* for its gay contact adverts and claimed that 'when a pop star screams obscenities at her from the stage ... This helps to remove a girl's natural protection' (ibid, p.11). She also attacked *NME*'s coverage of the censorship debate in America and, somewhat bizarrely, commented that in its photos 'scowling seems to be popular' (ibid, p.12).

Bogle's criticisms mirror those of many moralists. She is ill informed and takes texts at face value, whereas much pop is tongue in cheek. She laments that: 'There is much about today's pop scene that is worrying' (ibid, p.11), but obviously has little knowledge of her subject. Her concern for the welfare of children is admirable, but ill informed, under researched opinions is less so, especially from a group which claims to publish material: 'Based on the most up-to-date scientific information' (FYC *About Family and Youth Concern* leaflet nd). Bogle (1986, p.11) adds aesthetic critique, when she talks of videos where 'the music pounds home the message'. Presumably music which "pounds" is up to no good.

228

In 1992 Radio 4 reported that FYC had called for a ban on The Shamen's *Ebeneezer Goode* (Radio 4 news 2/10/92). Although FYC Director Valerie Riches denied this to the author, she did reveal that she had been on 4 talking about 'the pop and rock cult' (Riches 1992) and added that 'the pop cult .... is an area which needs to be investigated' (Riches 1991).

The word "cult" is frequently used by moralists in relation to pop and has significance. It is an attempt to portray pop as in being sinister, suspicious, even demonic. The press also often uses this term to denounce pop. *The Sun* (15/10/76) called punk 'the craziest pop cult of them all', whilst the *Sunday Mirror* (12/6/77) reported on 'the amazing new cult'. The *Daily Mirror* (14/5/87) referred to the 'cult' around the Beastie Boys, a term also used in Mullen's 1986 attack on the *NME*. Bright used the term in the parliamentary debate on raves (*Hansard* 9/3/90), perhaps picking it up from *The Sun*, which has headlined calls to 'ban acid cult' (*The Sun* 1/1/88. See also *The Sun* 3/7/89). The word joins "responsibility" and "commonsense" as a key censorial term.

It is also the sort of term rarely used about pop outside of American fundamentalist literature. As links are made between American rock censors and organizations like The International Congress for the Family (see below), of which Riches is also a leading member, it would not be unreasonable to assume that she is *au fait* with that literature.

In 1993 FYC protested about two women kissing on the cover of the first Suede album (*Pink Paper* 1/4/93) and about the computer game Night Trap (*The Guardian* 29/5/93). It seems set to maintain interest in all popular media.

The International Congress of The Family

This is the British arm of the World Organization for The Family and the International Alliance For The Family, both of whom specialize in anti-abortion campaigns in Latin America. It has links with FYC and NVALA and claims to be 'working to counter the current threats to family life' (Conference Brochure 1990). One of those threats, it believes, is pop.

The Congress has friends in high places. In 1992 it listed 15 MPs, from all three major parties, on its Council of Reference and its 1990

Brighton conference was addressed by the Princess of Wales and Mother Theresa. Details of this Conference's views were passed on to MP Angela Rumbold (a former junior education minister) and hence to Prof. Brian Griffith, who was part of the Prime Minister's policy unit within Downing Street (Coward 1990).

This Conference saw concern expressed over the impact of pop when American Michael Keating, director of the University Christian Outreach movement, spoke and ran a workshop on rock. Valerie Riches of FYC and also a Congress supporter told the author that: 'My views on the subject were well expressed by Michael Keating' (Riches 1992). So what are these views?

Keating (1991, p.139) said that:

I think we are witnessing an attempt to steal an entire generation ... from their parents and from their God and to rob them from their own happiness.

Keating saw the method of such stealing as youth culture, in particular rock which is, he says, 'founded upon animal sexuality, rebellion against every form of authority, drug and alcohol addiction, and profound hostility to God' (ibid, p.140). He also raised the familiar bogey of a hapless audience being manipulated by unscrupulous profiteers. He said that: 'It is important to see that youth culture is not devised by the young ... (who) are caught in a snare they did not make' (ibid, p.141).

So, if youth culture is the problem, what solutions does Keating suggest? First he calls for a strong family to counter its influence, secondly he wants children's access to various media controlled:

We need to help our children to steer clear of the great harm that can come to them through false education, or bad friends, or **perverse movies and music** (ibid p.144. Emphasis mine).

Thus anti-rock arguments were accepted by a group well within the political mainstream in Britain. Keating was more astute than to call for censorship, but he focussed attention to the supposedly harmful effects of rock and suggested that parents should do their own censoring. He also raised the idea of children being obsessed by pop, saying that:

It is hard to exaggerate the importance of music in the youth world ... music defines the boundaries of youth culture. It creates a world in which young people live and provides them with their most exciting and compelling models for life' (ibid, p.142)

If this were true then cause for concern about rock might be justified. However, evidence suggests that most children are influenced far more by their parents than by pop (see *NME* 19/10/91 and Roberts 1983, p.38). As noted earlier, only a small minority become obsessive about pop music - most can take it or leave it and use it only as a background noise to other activities[9]. Keating is indulging in scare-mongering in order to precipitate censorship.

Conclusion

There are various other organizations which could have been mentioned here which are suspicious of pop. For example, the Childwatch group has called for rock to be treated as seriously as pornography (*20/20* February 1991, p.49). The purpose of this chapter has been to give a taste of the arguments of popular culture's organized opponents. Determining how much influence these groups actually have is problematic. There is a certain amount of intangibility about this, but their censorial influence has been noted elsewhere (see Graef 1991, p.76). At the very least a formidable lobbying network has pop within its sights. Members of this network are encouraged to write to broadcasting networks to complain about programmes and there can be little doubt that often the "member of the public" who complains will have links with them. The existence of the network means that even organizations listed here who do not focus on pop may contact those that do if they spot anything "offensive", especially as there is a great deal of cross-membership.

The similarity in outlook of British moralist pressure groups to that of American fundamentalists and the PMRC[10] means that their fortunes may become linked. Whilst the American right suffered when the Democrats seized the presidency, a backlash has begun (including the Republican capture of Congress in 1993) and should the PMRC wish to extend its activities beyond America, in these times of media globalization it might find willing allies in the groups mentioned here.

Certainly those within the broadcasting and record industries know who will be on the case if their output becomes "offensive". What is not so widely recognized is that the NVALA is only part of a much wider network which seeks to control cultural output in Britain and claims successes such as the cancelling of the plan to show *The Last Temptation of Christ* on Channel 4 in 1990. The fact that these groups have done little or no research into the effects of pop does not stop them from pontificating about its impact, issuing proclamations against it and attempting to stifle it. If pop is to address issues that concern its audience then all attempts by these groups to increase their influence should be resisted.

Notes

1. Whitehouse 1967, p.79 sees ITV as better than the BBC. She centres on the BBC as it is publicly funded. A. Smith 1972.

2. For Whitehouse's concern with children see, for example, Newburn 1992, pp.27, 28, 47 and 127 and Durham 1991, p.95.

3. For example see *Viewer and Listener* Autumn 1992 and Spring 1993.

4. "Commonsense" is a problematic concept. Barker 1984a, p.75 notes how campaigners in the comics scare of the 1950s increasingly relied on the concept. Wistrich 1978, p.61 noted that 500 years ago "commonsense" led to the burning of witches. Overall the concept is embroiled in struggle with Garofolo 1987, p.89 and Hebdige 1987, p.136 warning of its dangers.

5. Whitehouse 1985, p.48. See Newburn 1992, p.123 for Whitehouse's xenophobia.

6. For changing conceptions of childhood see Aries 1973 and Humphries, Mack and Perks 1988. See Cliff 1979, p.132 and Newburn 1992 p.78 for the importance of the family to all the pressure groups examined here.

7. For more causal assertions by NVALA see *Viewer and Listener* Summer and Autumn 1992 and Whitehouse 1967, pp.217-21.

8. For more on Noebel see Denisoff and Peterson 1972, p.122 and 127, M. Sullivan 1987 and Street 1986, p.55.

9. See Frith 1983, p.216 for music as the context, not focus, of youth leisure and p.231 for pop as a background to other activity.

10. See M. Sullivan 1987, p.322 for links between the religious right and the PMRC.

12   Religious censors – combatting the Devil's music?

Pop's most vociferous opposition has often come from Christian religious sects. Since the early American days of rock and roll priests and preachers have warned against the dangers of becoming involved in "the devil's music". The alleged pagan roots of rock, supposedly from African and Haitian voodoo rituals, were often emphasized. The overtly racist nature of many of these critiques limited any intellectual credence they may have aspired to and today such analyses are relegated to the fringes of American fundamentalist[1] churches. This is not, however, to say that they do not surface in Britain. This chapter examines first the history and then, in more detail, the beliefs of clerical censors in Britain.

Although much of the material I draw upon here is American in origin and on the margins in Britain, as we have seen many British would-be censors draw upon such material to back up their claims[2] and some understanding of it is necessary in order to fully survey the British censorial climate.

Rock and the Church: an historical outline

Popular music has often been at the centre of the Church's concern about the moral welfare of the nation. The 1890s anti-Music Hall campaigner Ormston Chant was fired by her religious belief (Cheshire 1974, pp.38 and 40 and Pearsall 1973 p.52) and Leonard (1964, pp.2 and 83) notes church opposition to jazz[3]. In September 1956 the Bishop of Woolwich criticized the film *Rock Around The Clock* because 'the hypnotic rhythm in the picture had a maddening effect on a rhythm loving age group' (Martin and Segrave 1988, p.35). In 1958 Methodist preacher Dr. Donald Soper condemned much of contemporary pop. Noting that much of it was American, and that it had been necessary to ban American horror comics via the 1955 Children and Young Persons (Harmful Publications) Act, he warned that: 'It may be just as necessary to curb trashy songs' (*M M* 29/3/58).

As rock's popularity grew, so came more overt calls for censorship from British clergy. Martin and Segrave (1988, p.49) note that a Reverend J. H. Chamberlain of Smethwick saw music as either God's or the devil's and, as rock was the latter: 'His solution was to "ban evil music" with the censoring being done by a board of "distinguished musicians"'. A Nottingham Pentecostal vicar told his congregation in October 1956 that:

> The effect of rock and roll is to turn young people into devil worshippers; to stimulate self expression through sex, to impair nervous stability and destroy the sanctity of marriage (*M M* 10/2/68).

Two main elements featured in early criticisms - first, the accusation that rock was based on devil worship and secondly, presumably as a consequence, that the behaviour of the listener was altered. A causal relationship between rock as music (not just lyrics) and anti-social behaviour was postulated from the off.

To these criticisms the aesthetic was often added. For example, Soper talked of pop as "artistic suicide" and "trash" and raised the idea of a hapless audience by accusing the industry of 'foisting rubbish on the public' (Martin and Segrave, 1988 p.50). Martin and Segrave (ibid) note that 'Soper was adamant that **some form of censorship was needed**' (emphasis mine). However British clerics did not form any censorial agency and so the history of the (attempted) religious censoring of pop in Britain is one of intermittent outbursts and struggles, rather than any concerted censorial campaign - the religious motivations of more full time censors like Whitehouse notwithstanding.

The church has a tradition of providing alternatives to those entertainments it disapproves of (see Bailey 1987, pp.35-55). So when rock 'n' roll arrived in Britain many in the church welcomed and promoted skiffle as a more wholesome alternative. Skiffle, says

Bradley (1992, p.127), thus became 'the acceptable, even slightly "cissy," face of youth, patronized by teachers, vicars and youth club leaders'.

Others were more restrictive. Street (1987, p.71) reports that during Beatlemania: 'Rev Thumond Babbs threatened to excommunicate any of his flock who went to a Beatles concert'. Jehovah's Witnesses also warned of the dangers of rock(4). By 1967 the battle lines between pop and sections of organized religion had been drawn. They were further galvanized by the remarks of John Lennon in 1966 that the Beatles were "more popular than Jesus".

1968 saw controversy when Immediate used a parody of The Lord's Prayer to advertise The Small Faces' *Ogden's Nutgone Flake* album (*MM* 22/6/68) and in 1969 the reaction to the formation of Eric Clapton's Blind Faith "supergroup" upset the Reverend T. E. Winsor of Tickenot, Rutland, who wrote to *MM* complaining of the "imbecilic commotion" surrounding the band. He continued that it was:

> ... a distressing feature of today's youth that a large portion of them can be wrapped in adulation of a group of long haired louts whom they have yet to hear

and lamented that they didn't show a similar faith in Jesus (*MM* 7/6/69).

In the late 1960s many pop musicians sought religion (see Turner 1974 and Farren 1975), but upset some Christians by turning toward eastern mysticism. George Harrison's involvement with the Hare Krishna sect is a paradigmatic case here. American Christian writer Bob Larson (1988, p.46) called the combination of western rock and eastern mysticism "deadly" but perhaps undermined his own argument by claiming that Harrison's musical popularity 'faded in direct proportion with his mystical involvements'. Exactly how he measured this was not made clear.

In 1974 Britain's foremost Christian rocker, Cliff Richard, attacked Alice Cooper's live show, saying that:

> I feel that if there are 13 and 14 year olds hooked on Alice Cooper, and they see dolls mutilated on stage, then it's bound to have a bad effect. If there's the slightest possibility of that then I think **it's valid to ban it** (*NME* 23/2/74. Emphasis mine).

The idea that kids will get hooked on Cooper is analogous to fundamentalist claims that rock itself is a drug (see, for example, Pyle 1985). But Richard rejected the idea of censoring rock records as 'there's not much you can do just by banning it' - a view he developed whilst serving on the Longford Committee (*NME* 23/2/74).

Richard also provides rare documented evidence of self censorship. He asked fans not to buy his 1975 single *Honky Tonk Angel* after he had recorded it without realizing that it was about a prostitute (Jasper 1986, p.31 and Richard 1981, pp.109-110). Much later he also unsuccessfully asked for a section of Comic Relief's *Utterly Utterly Utterly Rude* video featuring him singing *Living Doll* to be cut as he objected to other parts of the video, despite the fact that he played the concert at which it was filmed (*NME* 13/12/86).

In October 1976 Dr. Thomas F. Torrance, Moderator of the Church of Scotland, claimed that rock led to violence, mayhem and homosexuality. *NME* (23/10/76) reported his belief that the:

> ... music plays on subconscious emotions of those who listen and when it's played back years later, those who got off on those things in the Sixties psyche back to their adolescence.

Whilst these were isolated outbursts, the message from some clerics was clear - rock was dangerous and, at a minimum, should be approached with extreme caution. But while some were content to issue proclamations, others took more direct action. Punk saw renewed clerical interest in rock. *NME* (9/7/77) reported that amongst the main opponents of a proposed punk festival in Birmingham's Digbeth market in July 1977 were local clergy who objected because it was due to take place on a Sunday near a local church. As noted above, when the Sex Pistols played Caerphilly in December 1976 opponents to it included Pastor John Cooper of the Elim Pentecostal Church (Robson 1977).

In September 1981 another cleric, Rev. Professor Moelwyn Merchant, then Emeritus Professor of English at Exeter University, raised the spectre of rock as corrupter. He told a meeting of public school headmasters in Oxford that:

> I think that explicit sex is much less dangerous than ... pop records which lower the tone of human relationships ... It is the Disc Jockeys and their plugging of debasing sensory material ... who

are the real pornographers and we should identify them as such (*NME* 3/10/81).

In 1986 Peter Mullen, a York vicar, used a TES article on *NME* to attack rock in general. He claimed that those involved in a vicarage rape 'may have been fans of a heavy metal group' (Mullen 1986)(5) and that whilst he could not prove a causal link between the 'pop-cult' (see above) and violence 'it would be foolish to imagine there is never a link' (Mullen 1986). He also invoked aesthetics, feeling pop to be 'trivia, its melodies are bland, if non-existent, its rhythms tedious' (ibid). He showed his own ignorance by calling The Mekons *The Mekes* and describing *NME* as a fanzine, which it is not.

Other Christian opposition to pop came in the live arena. In April 1988 The Shamen were asked not to use filmed images of the Pope at a gig in Leicester Square's Notre Dame Hall as the venue's owners were a religious order (*NME* 16/4/88). Meanwhile Manchester's Haçienda club faced religious opposition in July 1988 when 40 members of the Victory Chapel in Salford blocked the club's Saturday night disco and had to be moved on by the police. The influence of American evangelists was evident here: the chapel is an offshoot of LA's New Harvest Christian Fellowship (*NME* 16/7/88).

Bands who used sacrilegious images have, unsurprisingly, encountered clerical opposition. In November 1988 Christian Death were banned from a gig at Deptford's St. Mark's Church 'following objections from a local archdeacon' (*NME* 12/11/88). A replacement gig at the Boston Arms in Tufnell Park was also called off after the venue saw one of the band's promotional posters which featured Christ masturbating. The gig eventually took place at the Pied Bull in Islington (*NME* 3/12/88).

Clergy in Brighton tried to get a Creaming Jesus gig in the town called off in March 1990. Canon Michael Butler of the Sussex Board of Social Responsibility labelled the band "blasphemous" and "disgusting". The promoter of the gig at the town's Richmond Club told the churches that it had been called off to avoid any demonstrations, but then went ahead with it (*NME* 24/3/90).

Others felt the need to move against the music in general. In September 1987 Alex Maloney, a lay minister with the Elim Pentecostal church, held a public meeting in Burton on Trent in which he warned of the dangers of "Satanic Rock"(6). In Liverpool in December 1990 the Praise Chapel, again part of an American church, the Christian Fellowship, held two public meetings entitled "Hells Bells: The Dangers of Rock and Roll"(7) - the title coming from an American anti-rock video produced by Reel To Reel Ministries of Florida, which was played at the meetings.

Around the same time the Truth Temple of The Bibleway Church in London's Woodford Green produced a leaflet called *The Truth About Rock*. It attacked Satanism in rock and ended: 'Friend if you are in any way involved in this evil music, I urge you please to turn away from this great DECEPTION' (Skynner nd. Emphasis in original).

Morrisey's *Ouija Board Ouija Board* single was criticized by the Christian Response To The Occult in November 1989 for 'encouraging youngsters to take an interest in the occult' (*NME* 25/11/89). Diane Core of the Christian Childwatch group called the single 'totally irresponsible' and added that:

> ... society wouldn't suffer if much of this stuff were banned... What we would like to see is a committee of some kind set up. It should involve a balance of parents, government representatives and young people (*20/20* February 1991).

WEA refusing to release the Jesus and Mary Chain's *Jesus Suck* (*NME* 20/27/12/86) also showed the power of passive Christian censorship. This was also evident in August 1989 when the *Aberdeen Evening News* and *Nottingham Evening Press* refused to take adverts for Depeche Mode's *Personal Jesus* single, saying that they did not want to cause offence (*NME* 26/8/89).

Christianity is not the only censorious religion in Britain. In the wake of the Rushdie affair the censorial potential of Islam has been much commented upon(8). This debate entered the pop world in June 1992 when Muslims objected to the use of snippets of the Koran in live performances by The Orb. After complaints by two Muslim bouncers at a Brighton gig the band dropped the section from their act. One member of the unofficial Muslim parliament had spoken of taking "appropriate action" if the recordings were not taken from the show (*The Independent* 28/6/92). However Christianity still exerts the greatest religious censorial influence in Britain, as the catalogue of cases below and above shows.

"Beatists" and "golden agers"

Christian opponents of rock can be crudely divided into two groups. The first, the "beatists", oppose rock's beat and tend towards causalist arguments[9]. The second, the "golden agers", argue that rock became corrupted and make favourable comparisons of 1950s music to that of recent years[10]. "Beatists" tend to be less affected by contemporary events than the "golden agers".

Perhaps the most extreme "beatist" tracts are those of the Chick organization, whose British outlet is the Penfold Book and Bible House, in Bicester, Oxon. Their *Battle Cry* newspaper regularly features teenagers telling of their addiction to rock before being saved with the aid of a Chick tract (see, for example, *Battle Cry* July/August 1991).

Chick's publications slightly update 1950s arguments about the pagan origins of rock. For example, Chick's Jeff Godwin (1985, pp.8-9) writes that: 'The rhythms of Rock music are directly opposed to the natural rhythms of the human body, especially the human heart beat'. Blanchard, a British evangelist, agrees and warns that 'excessive beat has real dangers' as:

> ... the element of relentless beat in rock music increases the danger of a shallow, emotional, unthinking response, made at the wrong level and for the wrong reason (Blanchard 1983 p.17).

The beatists argue that the main effect of this pagan derived beat is hypnotic. Hart (1981, p.95) quotes a psychologist as saying that rock's beat is:

> ... the same beat that people in primitive cultures use in their demonic rites and dances. If the beat is monotonous enough it can induce a state of hypnosis.

Godwin (1985, p.9) agrees that: 'The typical rock song can be summed up in one word: hypnotic'. MacKenzie, who repeatedly quotes Noebel, argues (1987, p.47) that a combination of drum beat and volume at live gigs often leads to 'a hypnotic trance like state in the listener'. His book was recommended to me by the Kings Church in Newport, Gwent.

A racist notion of "pagan" and "primitive" drumming and rhythms is often mooted and much of the "beatist" material originates from, and is aimed at, America's "Bible belt", where such sentiments appear to find a ready audience. When debating whether rock can be used for Christian purposes Hart (1981, p.142) asserts that: 'The music that came over from the slave-trade boats doesn't fit our theme'.

Pyle (1985, p.10) writes of being told by missionaries in Haiti and Africa that 'the beat and movement of their pagan and sensual dances ... are exactly the same as the beat and movements of the rock 'n' roll dances'. He talks of the 'jungle beat' of rock, a 'savage and dirty music' (ibid, p.24) and refers to Michael Jackson as a 'girlish little black boy' (ibid, p.30).

But the argument that rock consists of pagan jungle rhythms transferred from Africa into the heart of Christian American is at best questionable. As Palmer (1976, p.23) notes, it presumes that most of the slaves who were transported to America came from the coastal regions of Africa where the drum was the dominant instrument, whereas the majority actually came from the centre of the continent where stringed instruments dominated. It also omits the significant country and western roots of rock.

Britain has not been immune from racist theories about rock. In 1970 Charles Cleall wrote for the *Methodist Recorder* that rock may engender bad habits in church as its rhythm might hamper the ability to think. Martin and Segrave (1988, p.178) write that:

> In a subtly racist statement, Cleall concluded that rock and roll was a form of music not indigenous to Europe nor was it an accident that: "(1) the communities in which it is have never built a city nor a form of handwriting, and (2) that those young people who permit pops (sic) to reign over them are remarkable chiefly for their tendency to worsen themselves.

Another part of the beatist critique centres on repetition, which Blanchard (1983, pp.14-15) sees as dangerous. Mackenzie (1987, p.89) is concerned about the daily repetition of the same song. As an example he cites Blue Oyster Cult's *Don't Fear The Reaper*, which is about a suicide pact, and says: 'The effect of such a song can be devastating when heard at high volume repeatedly'. He also takes up a common theme by claiming that children are obsessed with pop (ibid, p.219).

Hart (1981, p.78) claims that what separates rock out from many other forms of music is dissonance, which, he says, is sparingly used in classical music, but over used in rock. If not resolved into consonance it causes tension - the result, he says, of rock. Rock, says Hart, 'appeals to the body's glands and sensuous nature' (ibid, p.45), so that a rise in promiscuity has accompanied its rise. It is one step from this to the next fundamentalist claim - that rock is physically harmful. Pyle (1985, p.45) is amongst those who tell the story of different plants being played classical and rock music, with the former thriving and the latter dying.

Yet McIver (1988, p.10) notes that:

> Fundamentalists never really devised a plausible theory to explain how the beat affected listeners, beyond linking it vaguely to hypnotism and pointing to its "savage," jungle origins. Recently the emphasis has shifted back to the words[11].

This brings in the "golden agers"[12]. For example, the PMRC backed Senate "Porn Wars" hearing of 19 September 1985 focussed on lyrics, not beat. Although the PMRC has distanced itself from the fundamentalists, it uses them as a research resource and they, in turn, urge participation in the PMRC (see, for example, Godwin 1985, p.330).

Maloney (1991) is also keen to draw distinctions between pop and the extremes he sees in heavy metal. Essentially a "golden-ager", he posits a cleaner era of pop which has been eroded by the emergence of heavy metal. His "golden ager" credentials are shown by his nostalgic lament that 'the values that were upheld 15 years ago are no longer precious' (Face The Music Ministries 1989, p.1). Golden agers also tend to focus on lyrics, which, as we have seen, are often unimportant to fans.

But even amongst "beatists" there is a feeling that, whilst rock may have been far from perfect before, it has now got worse. MacKenzie (1987, p.98) comments that: 'Today ... the messages portrayed by many artists are much more disgusting than they were twenty years ago' and Pyle (1985, pp.42-43) countenances the view that country and western music was good and wholesome until it discovered sex in recent years.

Nostalgia is a crucial motivation of censorial action (see Pearson 1983) and the beatist Godwin (1985, p.294) favourably compares Elvis to 'the rampaging, satanic, sex-stuffed Rock rapists around today!', while Maloney believes that: 'Never before has rock music plummeted to these depths' (*NME* 19/9/87). The feeling of reaching a new low develops into a view that something must be done and here that something means campaigning against rock. Such campaigns are underpinned by several objections to rock's non-musical characteristics.

Common aspects of Christian non-musical objections to rock

(1) *Lifestyle and sex*

The tendency for pop's attendant features, rather than the music itself, to attract censorship will already be clear and a notable feature of many fundamentalist critiques is that almost as much space is given to criticisms of lifestyle as to those of the music. The sex and drugs attract as much vitriol as the rock and roll. Often no distinction is drawn between them. Godwin (1988, p.77) argues that: 'The lifestyle of the performers cannot be separated from the music they make'. So, if musicians take drugs and have premarital sex, then the music they make has to countenance and promote such activity.

Blanchard (1983, p.42) lists 'rock musicians whose lifestyles or music show occultic influence' and even the more liberal Church of England expressed concern in 1992 that children's heroes might be:

> ... the latest rock star whose lyrics may be full of aggression, whose life style may hint at drugs and who makes no secret of life with his latest live-in girl friend (National *Society* 1992, p.31).

Presumably secret sin was preferable.

Sex is a major area of concern. For Godwin (1985, p.14) it is part of Satan's plan to use rock for diabolical purposes. He writes that:

> All the smutty and degenerate emphasis on sexual lust in rock music is designed to fire up teenage imagination and hormones, leading to active fornication. Why is Satan so interested in getting the kids sexually active? Because immoral sex serves a specific purpose - to spread demons.

Aranza (1983, p.25) cites Olivia Newton John's *Physical* as one reason for teenagers experimenting with sex and Mackenzie (1987, p.137) says abortion is 'one of the fruits of ... promiscuity, which is aided and abetted by Rock 'n' Roll'.

Fundamentalists also have vehement homophobia in common and the spread of homosexuality is often blamed on David Bowie (see, for example, Larson 1988, p.150). MacKenzie devotes a chapter of his book to the topic, but reassures his readers that, fortunately: 'Not all rock stars are gay' (1987, p.137). Jones (1988, p.117) says that 'homosexuality ... is a cruel and heartless weapon used by Satan to gain control of the minds, bodies and souls of its victims'.

The relationship of this to pop censorship is that if, as the fundamentalists claim, the "growth" of homosexuality is due almost entirely to the example of degenerate rock stars (Larson 1988, p.29), then one way to prevent it is by suppressing the music. This is the logic of the fundamentalists' arguments, although it is seldom so boldly stated.

Rock is also accused of causing drug abuse. Pyle (1985, p.9) lists rock stars who have died in connection with drug abuse and asks mockingly: 'Is there a relationship between rock and drugs ... You know the answer!' In Britain former Church of England General Synod member and Cabinet minister John Selwyn Gummer (1971, p.137) wrote that cannabis taking has been: 'Encouraged by the (pop) groups'. Godwin (1985, p.191) even asserts that increases in record prices can be directly linked to rises in the price of cocaine, as the stars need more money to feed their habit.

Fundamentalists argue that drugs are part of the pop lifestyle and, as the lifestyle is inseparable from the music, only by hitting the music can one deter drug use. The implications of this are obvious - any song mentioning drugs would be vetoed. The fact that numerous rock songs warn against drugs is either ignored or seen as equally dangerous because any mention of drugs is equated with advocacy.

(2) *Rebellion*

A once popular fundamentalist allegation against rock was that of it being a Communist conspiracy (Street 1986, p.55 and MacKenzie 1987, p.105), but this has declined in the post-cold war era. Meanwhile the claim that rock encourages rebellion amongst the young, and inter-generational strife, is frequently made. Pyle (1985, p.5) lists a set of Biblical quotes against rebellion and Godwin (1985, p.280) uses the fundamentalists' favourite quote, from Samuel, that 'rebellion is as the sin of witchcraft'. That Christianity itself was born out of rebellion is conveniently ignored.

Jones (1988, p.49) is amongst the many fundamentalists who use the Twisted Sister video of *We're Not Going To Take It* (which features a rebellious son blasting his father out of his bedroom window in a suitably over the top way) as the definitive example of rock as rebellion. This po-faced attitude characterizes many of the criticisms. As in other cases noted above, the one thing lacking in all of the more extreme critiques is any sense of humour or irony. Everything is taken at face value, nothing is taken as an act. This is especially true of satanism.

(3) *Satanic and occult references in rock*

There are various accounts of Satan having been a musician (see, for example, S. Davis 1985, p.73 and Larson 1988, p.118) and many band pop artists, especially within heavy metal, use satanic and occult references both in their songs and images. Some also claim to be satanists and some fundamentalists, including British ones, use this evidence to suggest that the music itself is the work of the devil and that the musicians are his dupes - willing or not.

Maloney's Face The Music Ministries claims that: 'Satan's desire is to rule the world' and that heavy metal 'is one of his methods of attack' (Face The Music *The Truth About Rock* leaflet, nd). Skynner (nd), another British evangelist, agrees that rock is 'a carefully masterminded plan instigated by Satan himself'. For Jones (1988, p.79): 'The purpose of rock is to get demons inside you to destroy you and drive you to hell'. Again Godwin (1988, p.16) goes furthest and suggests that rock is: 'Piped in from Hell'. As evidence of he cites Motley Crue, who were not commercially successful until they embraced satanism with the *Shout At The Devil* album (Godwin 1985, p.127). He neglects to mention unsuccessful satanic bands.

Fundamentalists reserve particular ire for Ozzy Osbourne and Jones (1988, p.77) claims that: 'A few thousand demons already live in his body' and calls his live show 'a satanic service' (ibid, p.78). Partly because of fundamentalist campaigners, Osbourne's song *Suicide Solution* was indicted in an American court in 1990 for playing a part in the suicide of a young fan (see Walser 1993, pp.147-151). Although acquitted, Osbourne has since sought to distance himself from the satanic image (*NME* 2/7/88).

A man often cited as proof of rock's satanic links is Anton Le Vey, head of the American Church of Satan and allegedly the man pictured in the middle cover of The Eagles' *Hotel California* album (MacKenzie 1987, p.184). But Le Vey sees rock as Christian and has said that:

> Heavy metal has succeeded because its symbology is more appealing than that of Christianity, which is why Christianity created it (Lyons 1988, pp.170-171).

He has called heavy metal 'the last big burp of Christianity' (Baddeley 1992).

These remarks are, of course, by no means conclusive evidence and so some cling to their view of rock as satanic tool. Jones (1988, p.80) claims Mercyful Fate's *The Oath* is 'the actual oath of allegiance to Satan recited when a person becomes a satanist'. MacKenzie (1987, p.32) attacks MOR singer Barry Manilow by asking if the "I" in his *I Write The Songs* might be Satan. Jones (1988, p.94) even has an explanation for those who doubt his word, telling his readers that:

> If thoughts like "he's crazy" or "he doesn't know what he's talking about" are flooding into your mind right now be careful. Those thoughts are coming straight from your enemy the devil.

A contrary point of view to the fundamentalists is provided by occult historian Russell who writes that:

> The Devil no doubt has some interest in cultural despair, Satan chic and demonic rock groups, but he must be more enthusiastic about nuclear armament, gulags and exploitive imperialism (Lyons 1988, p.177).

McIver (1988, p.62) puts things into perspective as he says that the behaviour of many rock stars is abhorrent, but that 'it is the result of the words and behaviour of real people, not supernatural demons'.

Backmasking: the devil's latest weapon?

Some Christians allege that Satan is now using modern technology through backmasking - the insertion of backward messages into a track which allegedly enter the listener's mind without them being aware of it. This received much publicity in 1991 when Judas Priest were taken to court in America charged with contributing to a teenager's suicide by putting subliminal messages on to their *Stained Class* album(13). The case failed, as judges ruled that it could not be proved either that the messages got through or that, even if they did, they were the decisive matters in the death. But the case showed the spreading influence of fundamentalist critiques of rock.

The first book on backmasking to come to prominence was Aranza's *Backward Masking Unmasked*, published in 1983. Aranza argues that if a backwards message is placed on a record it is stored in the unconscious part of the brain, being on the surface nonsense. But if it is repeated several times it may later be decoded and accepted as fact. For example, "dog si natas" would be stored and, if repeated often enough, be confirmed as "satan is god" (Aranza 1983, p.2). Blanchard (1983, p.53) brings the theory to Britain and says that the worrying factor is that messages 'can be received, stored, unscrambled and impressed on the mind **without the knowledge of the listener**' (emphasis mine).

Alex Maloney is Britain's leading exponent of the backmasking thesis. He gathers information from many of the authors quoted here, including MacKenzie and Godwin. He sees rock as a religion and thinks bands such as Venom and King Diamond 'are building their own church' (20/20 February 1991). His critique of rock has two parts. First he objects to, and campaigns against, backmasking and secondly he objects to satanic imagery.

As the listener is unaware of what is going on, Maloney sees backmasking as an invasion of privacy and wants records containing it to be labelled, seeing this as 'informed choice', rather than a move towards censorship (ibid). He has claimed that the clauses in the 1990 Broadcasting Act which outlaw the use of subliminal techniques on commercial television and radio were included after his campaign with Tory MP Andrew Bowden (Maloney 1991). Although Maloney has appeared on television and in various national newspapers to publicize his claims, his overall influence is minimal. Nevertheless he has been credited with 'influencing changes in the law' (*Derby*

Evening News 17/12/91) and until backmasking on records becomes illegal Maloney's campaign seems set to continue.

Backmasking reversal techniques have particular relevance for fundamentalists. The British Satanist Aliester Crowley, who died in 1947, is a key figure here. His book *Magick* encourages the principle of reversal as a way of contacting the devil. Crowley tells his followers to walk, talk, think, read and play records backwards (Godwin 1985, p.69). Godwin (ibid) calls Crowley the 'patron saint of rock and roll' and warns that 'the single most important part of satanism is the principle of reversal' (ibid, p.255).

Crowley has undoubtedly interested rock musicians. Eric Clapton's *Layla* has connections with Crowley (M. M. Walker 1983, p.3) and Jimmy Page claims to have written *Stairway To Heaven* in Crowley's old house (ibid, p.4). Page owned the Equinox occult shop in Kensington and has claimed that 'Crowley was grossly misunderstood' (*NME* 7/12/74). Psychic TV's Genesis P. Orridge has written a preface to a collection of Crowley's writings and Ozzy Osbourne has a track called *Mr. Crowley*.

Within the literature on backmasking a number of examples recur including Prince's *Darling Nikki*, ELO's *Fire is High*(14) and The Rolling Stones' *Tops*. Two examples will be looked at here. The first is often used as an early example of the backmasking technique - Led Zeppelin's *Stairway To Heaven*. But there are various interpretations of what the song allegedly says when played backwards. Godwin (1985, p.77) lists the first message heard as 'I sing because I live with Satan', Blanchard (1983, p.54) has it as 'Oh, he is my prince satan', Anderson (1988, p.64) as 'Satan, Satan, my sweet Satan' and MacKenzie (1987, p.206) as 'Here's to my sweet Satan' which Maloney agrees with (Face The Music Ministries 1989, p.2), perhaps because they both use the analysis provided by the American evangelists Dan and Steve Peters (1984).

A similar confusion occurs in the next example. Queen's *Another One Bites The Dust* is often cited as encouraging drug usage: but how? According to Maloney (Face the Music Ministries 1989 p.2), Blanchard (1989, p.54) and Godwin (1985, p151) the backward message is '**start** to smoke marijuana', but for MacKenzie (1987, p.206) and Aranza (1983, p.7) the message is '**decide** to smoke marijuana'. Maloney (1991) has also claimed it as: '**It's fun** to smoke marijuana'. So the evidence is confused, even the number of syllables used is disputed. On the author's hearing the Zeppelin track is extremely difficult to decipher, the odd "Satan" perhaps: what else is anybody's guess. The Queen example seems to contain the word "marijuana", or something like it, but again what exactly remains unclear. In neither case have the bands admitted putting any messages on.

Some claims go further beyond belief. American evangelist Jim Brown claims that the theme tune to the television series *Mr. Ed*, the talking horse, played backwards says: 'Someone sung this song for satan' (Lyons 1988, p.169). Another bizarre claim, made by Godwin (1985, p.174) amongst others (for example Skynner nd.), is that the track *Kiss Kiss Kiss* on John Lennon's *Double Fantasy* album, which was released before his death, has the message "We shot John Lennon" on it, supposedly evidence of demons boasting in advance of what they would do to Lennon.

The evidence about backmasking is mixed. It **is** technically possible to put backward messages on to records. For example, Prince's *Darling Nikki* definitely contains an audible "message" at the end of it which only makes sense when played backwards. The debate thus hinges on whether this has any untoward effect on the unsuspecting listener. Certainly the fundamentalist critics would assert that it has and err on the side of caution and censorship.

Maloney maintains that backmasking is wrong, as 'with no warning of content with regards to backmasking you are totally unaware of what you are buying' (Face The Music Ministries 1989, p.3). But McIver (1988, p.56) notes that evidence in the backmasking debate is contradictory as:

> ... the scientific studies confirming subliminal influences so eagerly cited by the backmasking prophets are contradicted by other studies in which no influence is detected.

Nick Kabler, producer of Venom, a definite user of backmasking on their *In League With Satan* track, says that: 'To put backmasking on records is very easy to do' but he thinks that any "messages" are mere coincidences as any word spoken, or sung, backwards tends to sound like another. He doubts any effect as: 'If some form of subtle suggestion, like backmasking did work, the industry would have ... used it to sell more records' (*20/20* February 1991).

Overall the argument is edging away from those who see subliminals as harmful. Walker (1983, p.6) notes that backward speech is hard to decipher and in 1992 the British Psychological Society dismissed the postulated effects. Its report said that: 'There is no evidence that the effects of subliminal stimuli can be substantial enough to induce major changes in lifestyle' (British Psychological Society 1992, p.2) and that 'there is no evidence of harmful effects' (ibid, p.7). In the case of rock records it concluded that:

> ... even when backwards messages are present in a tape or record, **listeners are not effected by them,** whether or not these messages are subliminal, because the meaning cannot be perceived by the listener (ibid, pp.8/9. Emphasis mine)[15].

But the legal situation regarding records alleged to contain backmasking is still confused. McIver (1988, p.55) notes that 'broadcasting of subliminals was banned ... by Britain' in 1973 and, as noted earlier, the 1990 Broadcasting Act forbade the broadcasting of records containing backmasking over the commercial airwaves. Some want to go further, with Maloney writing of the need to 'stand by our convictions to **have the whole matter banned,** thereby making the use of back-masking illegal' (Face The Music Ministries 1989, p.3. Emphasis mine). Should this occur then tracks such as *Stairway To Heaven*, The Beatles' *Revolution No. 9* and Prince's *Darling Nikki* would be banned. Maloney has already enlisted the help of one Conservative MP in his campaign, but this campaign is only one amongst many and it is necessary to examine the fundamentalists' general tactics in order to see the full censorial implications of their critique.

The tactics of the religious censors - walking God's path?

Aesthetic critiques often underpin the fundamentalists' tactical approach. So Maloney's Face The Music Ministries says of heavy metal 'played forwards it's just bad music' (Face The Music Ministries *Rock Music The Truth Behind It* leaflet) and Godwin (1985, p.238) describes Mick Jagger's dancing as like a 'department store dummy'. Pyle (1985, p.14) writes of a generation whose 'musical taste buds have been destroyed with rock noise'. The message is clear - pop has no artistic worth so it is pointless to defend it and Sullivan (1987) and Flashman (1992, p.14) have documented the fact that many fundamentalist anti-rock campaigners are originally driven by aesthetic dislike.

Censorial moves are also influenced by the Church's perception of itself as protector of children who are again portrayed as becoming totally obsessed by pop. Larson (1988, p.86) writes that: 'As a parent you could overlook the depravity of some rock if it were your child's occasional interest. It isn't. He listens to it constantly'. Bevan, who claims to have taught over 400,000 school children about the dangers of rock, also paints a picture of obsession with pop (Kings Church *Are you dancing with the devil?* video) which, as noted earlier, is rarely the case.

Nevertheless some see children in danger and argue that if protecting them means a somewhat censorial role, then so be it. Godwin (1985, p.288) asks 'what's wrong with being a censor where ... children are concerned?'. MacKenzie (1987, p.36) says that:

> What we should ask ourselves is why we are allowing young children of today to be subjected to such lyrics as "Relax don't do it, relax when you want to come".

For these writers censorship is hardly an issue.

The fundamentalists have two main practical tactics, first the search to provide alternatives and, secondly, overtly censorial action against the problem. The most extreme case of the latter route comes from America. In Freedom Village, Lakemont, New York, Pastor A. Fletcher Brothers offers a rock "de-programming" service. Music is banned and students attend lectures on the evils of rock lyrics (Denselow 1989, p.264). The PMRC has used information supplied by Brothers and he bussed children in to the Senate "porn rock" hearings in September 1985 (Lyons 1988, p.164). A similar service is offered by two Californians, Darlyne Petlinicchis and Gregg Bodenhamer, whose Back In Control Center offers to "de-metal" teenagers and gives information to law enforcement agencies (ibid, p.172). Larson (1988, p.63) is amongst those who reports the Center favourably .

Larson (ibid, p.86) also tries the first route and says that rock's beat 'must be replaced with something better suited to healthy moral and musical development'. Pyle (1985, p.56) also offers a list of wholesome musical alternatives to rock, thus carrying on an old tradition of co-opting via the provision of superior culture.

Britain has yet to witness the record burning phenomenon that occurs periodically in America, but it is another possible tactic. Blanchard (1983, p.58) voices his support for destroying rock's trappings and Jones (1988, p.158) explains that the significance of the burnings is that: 'The Bible says that the best way to get rid of satanic tools is to burn them'. Godwin (1988, p.147) agrees, saying that: 'The spiritual thing to do is to BURN these records' (emphasis in original).

Godwin (1985, p.32ff) urges involvement in anti-rock movements, gives readers tips on how to stop gigs in their towns (ibid, p.325) and on how to pressurize shops into dropping certain records (ibid, p.327). Meanwhile in Britain Whitehouse, Blanchard, Skynner and Maloney have used American fundamentalist literature for evidence. Here the fundamentalist influence has thus far been confined to this "knock-on" effect, but as the Republican party in America falls under more overt fundamentalist influence and American moralist groups, such as the anti-abortion Campaign America, come to Europe it can be assumed that the fundamentalists will bring their moral agenda with them. In Britain the fundamentalist critique of rock remains on the fringes, but that could change as the Church of England declines and non-mainstream sects grow both in number and size (*The Guardian* 28/1/93).

Overall fundamentalists rightly point out that there is a lot of immorality in rock and that some people within it do have bizarre, even dangerous, beliefs. But the same could be said of, for example, politics, banking and the church. The fundamentalists present a highly selective picture of pop which would seem bizarre to most of its fans. Moreover, by ignoring the material causes of social problems and concentrating almost exclusively on perceived cultural ones fundamentalists expose themselves to easy attack - an attack made all the easier when they also get their facts wrong.

On the wrong track - factual inaccuracies in fundamentalist accounts of rock

Many of the fundamentalists' conclusions about rock are easy to take issue with. In particular, the attribution of causal qualities to rock without scientific evidence and the failure to see any humour and parody in rock are glaringly apparent. Ironically the fundamentalists believe that it is they who are telling the truth about rock for the first time. Indeed, they wish to monopolize the word. The Peters brothers' newsletter is called *Truth About Rock Report*, Godwin subtitles one book *The Truth About Rock*, Skynner's church is called "The Truth Temple" and one of Maloney's leaflets is called *Rock Music: The Truth Behind It*.

But inaccuracies, if not untruths, litter their accounts. Anderson (1988, p.61) calls Stevie Nicks of Fleetwood Mac Stevie Nix and is the only person the author has ever seen refer to Jimmy Page as "Jim Page" (ibid, p.62). He gets the lyrics to the forwards version of The Eagles' *Hotel California* wrong (ibid, p.64), so casting doubt on any allegations he makes about the song backwards. Aranza (1983, p.15) refers to The Rolling Stones as having songs called, *Satanic Majesties Request* and *Black N' Blue* (ibid, p.105) - but both are misquotes of album titles and no such songs exist. He also refers to a Led Zeppelin album called *Stairway To Heaven* (ibid, p.60): the album from which this song comes is in fact untitled and is generally known as Led Zeppelin 4.

Blanchard continues the catalogue of errors. He quotes a line of The Rolling Stones' *Sweet Virginia* which does not exist (1983, p.30) and misquotes their track *Sister Morphine* as "Sweet Sister Morphine" (ibid, p.61). He bizarrely refers to American blues/jazz star Dr. John as being 'of the group Tangerine Dream' (ibid, p.45). Aranza (1983, p.108) claims that Dr. John is a 'licensed witch', but neglects to give the licensing authority.

Godwin (1985, p.244) claims that 'punks sleep all day' and wrongly refers to the Sex Pistols' *Seventeen* by its refrain of "I'm A Lazy Sod" (ibid, p.250). He refers to Britain's "huge" National Front being 'flocked to by thousands of English "skinhead" punks' (ibid, p.265), calls Irishman Bob Geldof "English" (1988, p.203) and gives Timothy Leary's 1960s slogan "Turn On, Tune In, Drop Out" as "Drop out, Tune in, and Turn on" (ibid, p.201).

Hart (1981, p.85) mentions that at Elvis Presley concerts 'Theatres were demolished in London' and Mackenzie (1987, p.5) repeats this - but Elvis never played Britain. MacKenzie also misquotes the lyrics of Lennon's *Imagine* (ibid, p.145) and gives the date of The Rolling Stones' ill-fated Altamont gig as 6 December 1986, some seventeen years too late. Pyle (1985, p.7) makes the unsubstantiated claim that many pop videos 'are so violent that they have been banned in England and Australia' and says that Elvis 'managed to live to be forty-two, unusually long for rock musicians' (ibid, p.8).

This list could be multiplied. It stands simply as evidence of how potential censors can get their facts wrong and certainly undermines the plausibility of their research.

Conclusion

Much of the literature summarized here is of American origin and very much on the fringes of both mainstream religion and mainstream censorial agencies in Britain. It is included because it is a reference source for British censors like Maloney, Whitehouse and the Victory Chapel and so any account of British pop censorship would be incomplete without it. The fundamentalist critique has gained ground in America via the PMRC and labelling has become a common practice there, as has the harassment of artists such as the Dead Kennedys, 2 Live Crew and Ice T. This has already had knock on effects in Britain with the attempt to prosecute NWA, the removal of Ice T's *Cop Killer* track and the labelling of record sleeves.

It would be naive to say that what happens in America is bound to happen here, but it might be equally so to pretend that it will have no effect. Certainly the pressure from certain quarters will be kept up. In 1992 a new book, *Painted Black*, by Carl A. Raschke, was published in Britain to join the anti-rock literature and Maloney is also planning a book. Meanwhile American evangelist Morris Cerullo held a series of "healings" at Earls Court in July 1992 and is already claiming success in recruiting in Britain (*The Independent* 28/6/92). The beginning of 1993 saw Article 19 warn of fundamentalism spurring more censorship (*The Guardian* 2/1/93) and the rise of Medved talking, as Lennon (1993) put it, 'the language of fundamentalism'. With the expansion of cable television in Britain it may not be long before America's television evangelists bring their anti-rock message to Britain. The aim of this chapter has been to examine some of their arguments and to expose the fallacies within them. The devil is not abroad in rock and roll, but this does not mean that the such claims will go away.

Notes

1. The term "fundamentalist" here covers a number of Protestant sects whose common link is a belief in the literal truth of the Bible.

2. See for example Whitehouse 1977, p.38 for her reliance on the work of David Noebel.

3. Godbolt 1984, p.29 quotes the rector of Exeter College, Oxford, telling his students to avoid the "nigger music" of jazz.

4. See Meltzer 1970, pp. 100-101. Jehovah's Witnesses continue to oppose rock. See, for example, *Awake!* 22/3/93, pp.13-15.

5. See Walser 1993, p.143 for more on the use of the word "may".

6. See *NME* 19/9/87 for a review of this meeting. See also *NME* of 22/8/87 for Maloney challenging heavy metal label Music For Nations to attend. An Elim church leaflet called *The Top Ten* makes the common mistake of portraying children as obsessed with pop.

7. This video was shown in Watford in 1993, *Vox* February 1993. For a review of it see *NME* 4/1/92.

8. Attali 1977, p.12 notes that Islam forbade true believers from sitting at the same table as musicians. In Britain some Muslims opposed the inclusion of music in the National Curriculum, *The Guardian* 16/10/92.

9. For other "beatists" see comments by Slater of the CSA on drum beats above. See also Vermorel 1978, p.211 and above for Marcus Lipton MP comparing punk to jungle drums.

10. See M. Sullivan 1987, p.321 for the PMRC as "golden agers".

11. For PMRC links with fundamentalists see ibid and Wells, 1990a.

12. Larson calling one of his books *The Day The Music Died* marks him out as a "golden ager". Notably Medved is also a "golden ager". See him 1990d, p.25.

13. This case finally resolved in 1993. See *NME* 12/6/93 and Walser 1993, pp.145-7.

14. ELO's satanic links saw them banned from playing Antrim by Democratic Unionist Party councillors in 1993, *NME* 27/3/93.

15. See M. M. Walker 1983, p.9ff for more on this.

13   Pressed into censorship?

The press' role in the censorship of pop is twofold. First it can create scares around the latest pop outrage (often raising the spectre of exploitation of the young) and secondly it provides aesthetic critiques with which to stoke the censorial flames. These two roles can overlap. The term "the press" encompasses a wide range of publications, but here I am mainly concerned with the role of the national daily and Sunday newspapers, which have all contributed to censoring pop. A broad difference may be that the broadsheets often provide the aesthetic critique, whilst the tabloids are quicker to highlight calls for bans.

Evidence of the impact of the press upon popular music is widespread. For example, in 1967 the *NOTW*'s five week series on pop and drugs (29/1/67-19/2/67) instituted something of a moral panic. The paper was also alleged to have "set-up" the drugs prosecution of Mick Jagger and Keith Richards around this time (Wyman 1991, pp.520, 529 and 532) and, as noted above, a report it carried on an "orgy" at the UFO club in London led to it having to move from its original site and, subsequently, close (*M M* 28/10/67).

The press' role as labeller and moral entrepreneur has often been commented upon (for example see Frith 1984, p.30) and has long been apparent in the realm of popular entertainments. In 1879 the *Daily Mirror* brought out the *Boy's Own Paper* to combat the influence of the "penny dreadful" comics (Barker 1989, p.34). In 1898 *The Times* asked 'how far a Music Hall programme may be held to encourage lawlessness' (Pearson 1983, p.63)(1) and in 1927 the *Daily Mail* blamed dance halls for youth crime and commented that: 'Victims of the dancing craze multiply with the frequency of adapted jazz "melodies"' (Vermorel 1989, p.10). Note the mixture of moral and aesthetic critiques here.

By the time rock 'n' roll arrived the press had this long tradition to draw upon. *The Sunday Pictorial* depicted Johnny Ray fans as victims and asked if he was a mass hypnotist (ibid, pp.26-27), but the *Daily Mail* was the most fiercely anti-rock. In September 1956 it reported that:

> Tin Pan Alley has unleashed a new monster, a sort of nightmare in rhythm ... Rock 'n' Roll, often known now as rock, roll and riot is sexy music. It has something of the African tomtom and voodoo dance

and that:

> It is deplorable. It is tribal. And it is from America. It follows rag time, blues, dixie, jazz, hot cha cha and boogie woogie, which surely originated in the jungle. We sometimes wonder whether this is the negroes revenge (Pearson 1983, p.24).

Elsewhere in the 1950s, it was the *Daily Sketch* picking up an *NME* comment that caused Cliff Richard to tone down his act (Whitcomb 1982).

By 1967 press calls for anti-pop action grew, as was reflected in the *NOTW*'s series on drugs. This made it clear that the paper felt that the music itself was helping to spread the drugs menace. It blamed Donovan for many of the links between pop and drugs (*NOTW* 29/1/67). Noting that his *Sunshine Superman* contained drugs references and had appeared on both television networks, the paper warned ominously that: 'the line must be drawn somewhere' (ibid). Its censorial agenda was shown by comments on The Game's *The Addicted Man* single. Despite it being an anti-drugs record the paper called it a 'particular horror' and lamented that: 'Despite the BBC ban, the record is on sale to the public' (ibid) - so implying that it should not be.

The *NOTW* raised the spectre of hapless kids being exploited when it referred to the use of LSD of some stars by saying that:

> The effect which this **may** have on kids who rush to buy each new release and regard the pop stars as gods, is incalculable and **could** be damaging (ibid. Emphasis mine).

The series concluded with a selection of readers' letters headlined: 'Drugs: The Great Debate.' One letter contained the comment that: 'Pop stars should be subjected to a series of tests - like horses and greyhounds - before they go on stage' (*NOTW* 26/2/67).

Press coverage also contributed to pop festivals' problems. Hall et al (1978, p.250) say that at the 1968 Isle of Wight one:

> ... the media constructed an image of the event which contained just-about every permissive demon that had ever haunted the imagination of the morally indignant.

The 1973 Stevenson Committee report on festivals said that the press 'have behaved with great irresponsibility and **have to a certain extent created the problems surrounding pop festivals**' (Advisory Committee on Pop Festivals 1983 pp.8-9. Emphasis mine).

That the music itself was not the focal point of the press' attention does not make its actions any less censorious. The spectre of drugs and violence dominated festivals that it painted was undoubtedly at the backs of the minds of many festival opponents. The press contributed to a situation where the announcement of a festival was tantamount to the declaration of war in some areas.

It also played a role as aesthetic critic. In August 1975 the *Daily Telegraph* carried this quote from former war correspondent L. Marsland Gander:

> The wealthy pop idols are the most grievous example of the wrong kind of heroes. Their main achievements are to cause premature deafness by battering young eardrums and to provoke hysterical riots among weeny boppers. Luckily only limited sections of the community are affected ... (*NME* 30/8/75).

But, as we have already seen, the press was at its most assertive and censorious during punk, especially after Grundy. The following day's reports are amongst the most vitriolic ever seen in British press coverage of pop. The *Daily Mail* (2/12/76) had: 'Four letter group in TV storm' and reported on 'the Bizarre Face of Punk Rock'. The following day it reported that Grundy's programme 'goes out early in the evening, **a time when many children are watching**' (emphasis mine) - thus portraying the Pistols as corrupters of the young.

It also presented the now familiar, if barely credible, scenario of hapless youngsters being duped by unscrupulous businessmen. Its television critic, Shaun Usher, wrote an article entitled "The Mercenary Manipulation of Pop - Never Mind The Morals or Standards ... The Only Notes That Matter Come In Wads." The following quotes give its tone:

> The ultimate peddlers of the pop industry - slick, agile of brain, fast of mouth, trained to sniff out the greasy tang of available banknotes, know that the same three chord product can be sold over and over again as long as the package changes ...

These "peddlers" apparently didn't care that such packages 'were getting nastier, less responsible, more decadent.'

Overall, said Usher: 'If pop is the modern opium of the masses, and of course it is - then Punk Rock is now heroin' (Usher 1976).

Noticeably the same day that the *Daily Mail* was promoting this moral and intellectual high ground its "Femail" page featured an article on how to "Tempt him with silk" at Christmas.

The various levels of Usher's attack are noteworthy. The analogy of pop and drugs is familiar, as is the audience as victim argument. The aesthetic critique was also present, as Usher wrote that:

> Even the promoters of punk rock hesitate to claim the music has merit ... Unlike The Beatles, good enough to take root in the hearts and minds of every generation, Punk Rock is poor, ungainly, derivative and quite simply no good (ibid).

The *Daily Mirror* (2/12/76) headlined with 'The Punk Horror Show' which occurred 'at peak children's viewing time'. It also told of a viewer who had kicked in his television in disgust. It informed readers that: 'The essence of punk is anarchy and outrage' and evoked images of the destruction of childhood innocence by including the story of 14 year old Dee Generate and his punk band Eater, whose average age was 15(2). On 4 December a minor incident at a London Bill Haley gig was enough to get *Mirror* and *Telegraph* headlines - again showing links between the censorial climate and contemporary events.

The Sun was slower off the punk mark. It ran a two page punk special in October 1976, which used the damning term "cult" to describe it (*The Sun* 15/10/76), but did not headline with the Pistols after Grundy. But it soon ran a 'Were The Pistols Loaded?' story about how much the band had drunk before the interview and employed the aesthetic critique by commenting on 'the so-called "artists" paid to entertain us' (*The Sun* 3/12/76).

The *Daily Express* (2/12/76) linked the Pistols and Quirke cases and dismissed the movement as another music business hype in an article called: "Punk? Call it filthy lucre" (Pearce and Clancy 1976). Columnist George Gale attacked EMI for releasing *Anarchy In The UK* and the commercial stations for playing it. He saw the BBC as even worse, as they played it without being paid (*Daily Express* 6/12/76). Gale called for new BBC governors and for

> ... new legislation to protect our children from the panderers of the record companies, whose desire for easy money without sufficient thought for their responsibilities is the very ground on which punk rock is contrived to flourish (ibid).

This was particular nonsense as at this stage only three punk bands, the Pistols, The Vibrators and The Stranglers had been signed.

The *Daily Telegraph* (8/12/76) pressurized EMI by writing of the various warnings it was said to have given the band. A story about Labour MP Tom Swan threatening to punch Norman Tebbit whilst in the Commons got the headline: 'Punk politics at peak debating time' (ibid). The Tory bogey of rate payers' money being wasted on punk was raised with a claim that the Sex Pistols' fee for a cancelled gig at the University of East Anglia would come 'from public rates funds' (*Daily Telegraph* 18/12/76).

The *Times* used veteran moral campaigner Ronald Butt to attack punk: his comments on "exploitation" were noted earlier. Aesthetics surfaced in the term this 'kind of rubbish' (Butt 1976). Butt proposed that EMI drop the band, but did not see this as censorship as: 'It is not being a censor for a company not to promote, for a publisher not to publish, for a bookshop not to sell' (ibid).

The *Guardian* printed a piece by Christian rock critic Steve Turner blaming porn magazines such as *Forum* for punk. They, in turn, complained about this allegation (*The Guardian* 3 and 4/12/76). The paper also headlined: 'Punk concert brings trouble' (9/12/76), when the concert concerned had taken place two months earlier. Not all of the press called for censorship, but the net effect of their coverage was censorial. As seen above, the planned tour all but collapsed as venue after venue pulled out in the wake of it.

At a press conference the day after the Grundy interview the press demanded to know how signing such a band could be justified (Savage 1991, p.264). Pressure was continually applied to EMI and evidence suggests that it was such pressure that made EMI sack the band (ibid, p.286)(3). Although EMI would not defend the interview, they were apparently prepared to keep the Pistols until the *Evening News* report, on 4 January 1977, of the alleged incident at Heathrow airport. Robert Adley, MP for Christchurch and Lymington, wrote to EMI asking what they were doing 'financing a bunch of ill-mannered louts' (ibid, p.287). Soon the band were dismissed. Whilst a number of factors underlay the band's dismissal, the press had played a vital role in pressurizing EMI for over a month. Savage (ibid) portrays the sacking as a victory for the press.

The press pursued punk throughout the summer of 1977. The *Sunday People* (12/6/77) investigated the "Bizarre Cult that's sweeping Britain". Its conclusion was that: 'It is sick. It is dangerous. It is sinister' (ibid). The following week (19/6/77) it raised the spectre of audience exploitation by claiming that this 'freaky music craze' was being exploited by 'the raucous bands themselves, their promoters, record companies, magazine publishers and pop boutique owners'(4). *The People* covered a Heavy Metal Kids concert with phrases such as 'Worse was to come' and a tone similar to that used by American fundamentalists. The fact that the band concerned was actually a heavy metal band and **not** a punk one escaped the *People*. It also got a quote supporting its exploitation thesis from an official of the National Association of Boys Clubs who said that:

> ... the flames of this are being fanned by commercial interests, particularly the record companies, who are exploiting teenagers weaknesses for their own profit (ibid).

When The Sex Pistols released *God Save The Queen* to coincide with the Jubilee celebrations the press again reacted angrily. The single was released on 27 May 1977, just days before the *People's* punk expose began. The record's subtleties escaped the press. The *Sunday Mirror* (12/6/77) wrongly claimed that it called the Queen "a moron" and when the Jubilee was underway it headlined with: 'Punish The Punks' (ibid). Some took this advice to heart and a series of assaults on the Pistols and their friends followed (Savage 1991, pp.365-366).

The Pistols again antagonized the press in November with the release of their *Never Mind The Bollocks* album. *The Sun* took a particular interest in this release and the subsequent attempt to prosecute Virgin for displaying its cover. It headlined with: 'Sex Pistols in a new "four letter" storm' on its release (ibid, p.415) and called the decision to acquit the album 'astonishing' as it 'gives Johnny Rotten and his foul mouthed Sex Pistols the chance to put up two fingers to the world' (ibid, p.425). But moves against punk generally waned after the Jubilee.

Subsequently *The Sun* was active, along with London's *Evening News*, in getting Kevin Coyne's *Babble* show cancelled in 1979 by drawing attention to parts which dealt with the Moors Murderers. Possible press reaction was also cited when the Au Pairs *Come Again* was cut from the BBC2 youth programme *Look Hear* when producer Roger Casstles said that: 'The popular media just aren't ready for those kind of lyrics yet' (*NME* 2/2/80).

The press was also prominent in the censoring of Oi. Oi was heavily promoted by Gary Bushell and the *Sounds* magazine during 1981. The *Daily Mail* attacked it after Southall's Hamborough Tavern was burnt down during clashes between local Asian youths and right wingers at an Oi gig. It headlined with 'Terror in Southall' (4/7/81), but paid little attention to the music, just the 'skinhead venue'. The *Mail* (9/7/81) accused those promoting the music of 'fanning the flames of Southall'. To its supposed horror it found that this was being done by *Sounds*, then owned by the Trafalgar House group and wrote of 'the skinhead Bible of hate from an establishment stable' (ibid). However it neglected to tell its readers that this 'establishment stable' was owned by its main rival, the *Daily Express*.

The *Mail* noted ominously that *Sounds* was 'directed at the young' (ibid), attacked Bushell's sleeve notes for the *Strength Through Oi* album, which *Sounds* had promoted, and reported that the skinhead featured on the album's cover was a British Movement member then serving a sentence for causing an affray. It happily reported that Decca had now withdrawn the album. Decca appeared to have accepted the causal argument which the *Mail* was promoting and commented that: 'It is obvious that there is an association between some of the music and the violence and this is extremely undesirable' (*Daily Mail* 10/7/81). So the album was censored. But perhaps this was a sign of the times, as even the more liberal *Observer* editorialized in 1981 that amongst: 'The causus belli of a youth war ... (was) the violence of youth culture, of **some rock music**' (*The Observer* 19/4/81. Emphasis mine).

Individual journalists also took on censorial roles. It was the *Mirror*'s pop columnist, Robin Eggar, who, in 1981, alerted his brother, and Tory MP, Tim to the existence of Crass' *How Does It Feel* single and thus sparked off the unsuccessful attempt to censor it (*NME* 6/11/82. See below for more).

In May 1986 the *Daily Express*' George Gale warned readers that:

> Minds indeed become mindless when stuffed with the trash poured out by the pop industry everyday, without restraint, without control, without decency, without discipline (Street 1986, p.14).

This quote combines aesthetics - pop is "trash" and therefore artistically indefensible - and the causal allegation that 'minds indeed become mindless' when 'stuffed' with it. The word "industry" evokes images of unscrupulous businessmen duping their hapless audiences. Then comes the note that it is 'without restraint'. This is both factually incorrect and also sets up a censorial agenda. If the "trash" is being poured out with no regard for its effects, then someone should take steps to remedy this appalling situation.

In 1987 rap became the focus of media attention via the Beastie Boys, who were subject to a "shock horror" expose in the *Daily Mirror* (14/5/87) after some members allegedly told British children suffering from leukaemia to: 'Go away you fucking cripples' at a pop festival in Montreaux. The *Mirror* headlined with: 'Pop Idols Sneer At Dying Kids' (ibid). The band vehemently denied the story, but the *Mirror* stuck to it and carried news of MP Peter Brunivels' campaign to keep the band out of the country and of Capital DJ John Sachs smashing their records on air (*Daily Mirror* 14 and 15/5/87). The *Mirror* editorialized that:

> The CBS record company ought to have nothing more to do with them, even though they are top sellers.
> It should have put decency before profit long ago. The least it can do now to save its reputation is to cancel the tour at once and stop putting out the group's records.

To do less would be for CBS to climb down further into the filth with the Beastie Boys (*Daily Mirror* 15/5/87).

The next day the *Mirror* lamented that Home Secretary Douglas Hurd had 'refused to bar the loutish American pop group', apparently feeling that immigration rules did not cover barring them on the basis of unsubstantiated newspaper stories.

But the *Mirror* **did** harm the band in other ways. *NME* reported that they received death threats following the story. The tour itself, as support to Run DMC, reached an ugly climax in Liverpool when the band had to leave the stage after 10 minutes when the crowd showered them with missiles. Band member Adam Horowitz was later found guilty of assault for throwing a can at a fan[5]. One impression given was that parts of the crowd had decided to "get" the band (*NME* 6/6/87)[6]. The *Mirror's* role in contributing to the Beasties' image allied it to those who chanted: "We're the Scouse army and we've beaten the Beastie Boys" (ibid).

Some other points about the *Mirror's* coverage of the band need noting. Words like "loutish" and "filth" gave potential censors ammunition and the *Mirror* also exhibited the censorial impulse of xenophobia by referring to the band's 'middle class American homes' (15/5/87), and to the 'loutish American' band (16/5/87) who were 'foul mouthed Yanks' (29/5/87), including Adam Yaunch, a 'jumped up jerk from New York' (ibid). It also raised the spectre of the "cult" (14/5/87) and of business manipulation by saying that the band 'stand to make a fortune' from their tour (16/5/87).

1987 was also the year when one broadsheet returned to aesthetic critiques of rock. *The Times'* Bernard Levin (1987) invoked the "beatist" critique, attacking pop for its 'violent rhythm' and likening it to drug taking as 'both thrills are the thrills of malpractice' and 'immediate gratification'. He also claimed that pop's fans had no appreciation of 'real art or real love or real wisdom'[7]. After quoting the 25 year old and disbanded Beatles he claimed that there was 'nothing to remember' in pop.

Another part of Rupert Murdoch's press empire aided the clampdown on raves in the late 1980s. The *Sun* initially tried to promote acid and sold various accessories. But after the death of 21 year old Janet Mayes at a Surrey disco, it turned against the movement and headlined a story with "Shoot these evil acid bastards" (*The Sun* 1/11/88). It also quickly employed aesthetics. Its pop writer, Jonathan King, labelled acid 'sheeit' and asked 'how dare they call it music?'. It was 'a repetitive bore' which turns 'the kids already empty minds into jelly' and was, King concluded, 'Music for pinheads by brain death victims' (*The Sun* 25/10/88).

The context in which these remarks were made underlines their importance. They formed part of a *Sun* led media backlash against acid. By this time Mecca in Birmingham had stopped acid nights after scare stories in the local press (*NME* 17/9/88) and leading rave DJ Paul Oakenfield claimed around this time that: 'Acid will die, because of the media' (*NME* 19/11/88). Radio 1 DJ Pete Tong said that:

> ... it's really sad that that organisations such as the BBC, who have banned the word ("acid"), take notice of the tabloids and are dictated to by them (ibid).

Soon came allegations that the number of raids upon raves, and therefore the effective censorship of them, was determined by the amount of tabloid pressure exerted. Wells (1988b) speculated as to whether the police were at the beck and call of the Murdoch organization. He continued:

> Not so, says a Met spokesman. It is apparently a mere coincidence that three separate and independent forces decided to concentrate vast manpower on smashing up Acid parties all on the same weekend. Total coincidence, there was no co-ordination - even if a Scotland Yard "support unit" was used at Sevenoaks, Kent. The Met don't pander to idle whims and fancies of the tabloid press. Of course not.

Wells' cynicism was shared by others. In January 1989 *Q* noted that more raids on raves followed the *Sun's* campaign against it than had previously occurred (Sutcliffe 1989), an accusation that also surfaced in *Select* in August 1990. One does not have to be a conspiracy theorist to believe this. It is hard for the police **not** to act once the press has highlighted something and enlisted the support of MPs and other establishment figures in a campaign against it.

The press also has a history of calling on people from the pop world to denounce its latest outrage. The *Mirror* (23/5/64) headlined a story on mods and rockers with: 'They're just louts says Dreamer

Freddie'. Bill Haley was used by the *Evening Standard* to attack punk as 'going too far' (Vermorel 1978, p.48) and during raves DJ Peter Powell and Bros' Matt Goss were used to pour scorn upon it(8). Thus the deviant must be made to appear so not only by the standards of "normal" society, but also by those of the "abnormal" pop world itself.

Pop has constantly to be wary of the press which uses pop to sell copies, but which can also take on the role of unelected moral guardian to the nation. The press has often played an important role in attempts to censor pop. With the press on their side censors have a much better chance of achieving their aims.

For example, the *Daily Mail* was active in the early stages of the campaign to prosecute NWA's *Efil4zaggin* (Marot 1991b) and the *Sun* had previously been involved in creating a scare around a proposed gig by the band in Birmingham (*NME* 9/6/90). 1991 also saw the press ensure that one record never reached the market, as it was a *Star* story calling it 'a sick record about drugs' (*NME* 24/8/91) that led to the cancellation of Skin Up's *Blockbusters* single.

There are various other examples of press interference with pop. They were implicated in attempts to ban the Stones' *High Wire* in 1991 (*Sunday Times* 15/2/91), attempts to prevent GWAR gigs in 1990 (*NME* 26/5/90) and the *Daily Telegraph* was prominent in the attempt to get The Shamen's *Ebeneezer Goode* banned by Radio 1 (*NME* 26/9/92), whilst sensationalist press reports had previously led to the brewers McEwans dropping the band from a proposed advertising campaign (*NME* 6/4/91).

Overall the mainstream press has yet to act as responsibly towards pop as it would often have pop itself behave. Even when it tries to be objective about pop it has veered toward the sensationalist. In December 1989 an *Independent* review of a gig at London's Marquee carried the following comments:

> The huge volume of the music, the mechanical hammerings of its rhythms, its sheer physical impact and total lack of nuance left an audience to trail out at the end in a state of complete mental stupor, drugged and impervious to feeling (*The Independent* 28/12/89).

When pop is reviewed in this manner, using language akin to that of its fundamentalist critics, it is little surprise that it is subject to calls for censorship.

Little appears to have changed. In 1967 *M M* (7/1/67) complained that: 'Newspapers and magazines are continually hammering pop music and its exponents'. In 1993 the *Sun* attacked 1 for devoting a programme to the influence of gays on pop (*Vo x* March 1993, p.8) and the *Sunday Times* promoted Medved, who had pop amongst his targets.

This chapter has shown that newspapers have a history of attacking pop both aesthetically and censorially. The press is hardly anti-pop - the broadsheets review it and the tabloids use its stars to sell copies - but its role as unofficial moral guardian has led it into censorial campaigns. It retains important censorial influence, which the industry cannot afford to ignore. A BSC report of 1992 noted that when the tabloids scream MPs listen (Redmond 1991).

Notes

1. But *The Times* also helped make the Music Halls respectable, Russell 1987 p.85.

2. In comparison see the kid glove treatment given to The Goodies by the same paper on 18/12/76, when the BBC banned their *Blowin' Off* single.

3. EMI specifically mentioned the press' role when they sacked the band, see Wood, 1988 and Vermorel 1978, p.63.

4. See Laing 1985, p.101 for the idea of manipulation in punk and p.100 for the press and punk.

5. For more on this gig and the subsequent trial see *NME* 6/6/87 and McCready, 1987.

6. The *Daily Mirror* of 1/6/87 carried a picture of the girl who had been hit by the can and noted that the Royal Court venue had now banned the band.

7. Moelwyn Merchant's critique is similar to this (see above).

8. See *The Sun* 1/11/88 for celebrities condemning raves.

14   Rockin' the house? The role of MPs in censoring rock

MPs generally become involved in moves to censor popular music in three main ways. The first is via changing laws which can have censorial implications for pop. The second, and most frequent, is to be called upon by the press to make suitably indignant comments about the latest pop "outrage", which **may** then lead to personal campaigns against it. The third is leading opposition to festivals in their constituencies. The latter having already been covered, this chapter concentrates on the first two areas, dividing the main part of the chapter, for reasons of convenience, into sections on the parliamentary parts of the Conservative and Labour parties. (Liberal and Liberal Democrat MPs appear to have taken less interest in censoring pop).

MPs, pop and the law

The most obvious way MPs affect popular music is by framing the legal system within which it operates. For example, in 1935 the Ministry of Labour banned American musicians from performing in Britain, thus denying it non-British jazz for 17 years (Godbolt 1984, p.120). The years dealt with here saw such legislation as the 1967 Marine Broadcasting & Co and the 1990 Broadcasting Acts, which both had censorial implications for pop broadcasting.

In the years around 1967 MPs' primary censorial activity against pop was in opposing proposed festivals in their constituencies (Clarke 1982, pp.383, 389, 395 and 396), one result of which was the Night Assemblies Bill, mentioned earlier. In 1973 came the

Cinematograph and Indecent Displays Bill which attempted to tighten anti-pornography legislation. It aimed to counter "objectionable displays" and, whilst aimed primarily at the cinema, it covered anything with which the public might come into contact. The main implication of the Bill for rock was that album covers could have fallen within its definition of an "indecent display". The NCCL, which formed a committee to fight the Bill, said that under its proposals:

> ... the police would only have to go into a record shop and seize the record sleeves of, say, an Alice Cooper album and the shop could be prosecuted (*M M* 8/12/73).

At the Bill's second reading Philip Whitehead, Labour MP for Derby North, noted that *Je T' Aime* would fall foul of the Act (*Hansard* 13/11/73).

It also had implications for gigs. Clause 8 outlawed the amplified reproduction of "indecent sounds" and allowed private prosecutions by those offended. No defence of artistic merit was permissible. The NCCL believed that:

> Mick could well be prosecuted for a live concert because definition is so broadly based on the whim of a magistrate ... (*M M* 22/8/73).

The Bill fell in February 1974 when the Conservative Government called a General Election. By this time it was considering amending the clause covering "indecent sounds" so that it covered only "artificially reproduced" sounds, rather than including human sounds. An Environment Bill which could have affected sound levels in clubs and gigs also fell at this time (*M M* 16/2/74).

All campaigns to "clean up" the media have implications for pop. Tory MPs Winston Churchill, in 1986, and Gerald Howarth, in 1987, both failed with attempts to tighten up the laws on pornography, which could have cramped rock's style . Sir Michael Neubert called for new laws after the NWA case and Tory MP Michael Stephens campaigned for tighter obscenity laws in 1992 (*Hansard* 9/7/92). Only one of these was directly aimed at pop, but all would have made the climate within which pop works more censorial.

Truly blue? - Conservative MPs and pop censorship

The most common way in which MPs get involved in pop censorship is when the press reports "outraged" Tory MPs calling for the banning of the latest "obscenity" emanating from the pop world. Often the mere expression of outrage was enough, but recent years have seen increasing attempts to silence the perpetrators of the offence.

Concern on Conservative benches about the pernicious nature of pop music has a long history. Street (1986, p.71) notes that in 1949 Tory MP Sir Waldron Smithers:

> ... told the Beveridge Committee on Broadcasting that crooning ... should be forbidden as it was part of a Communist conspiracy to demoralize people.

In 1956 Robert Boothby MP said of the *Rock Around the Clock* film that: 'As soon as this film is banned altogether the better' (*NME* 19/2/77). In 1965 W. R. Davies MP told the party conference that the '"hairy idols" of the entertaining world' were leading their fans into 'anti-social, anti-moral' values (*National Union of Conservative and Unionist Associations* 1965, p.119).

Such concern has remained. The main campaigner against the Isle of Wight festivals was its Tory MP, Mark Woodnutt and in 1971 Conservative MPs put down a House of Commons motion praising the RAH for banning Frank Zappa's *200 Motels* show (*M M* 23/7/71). In February 1973 Harold Soref, MP and Monday Club member, complained to the BBC about them playing The Strawbs' *Part of The Union* and said that:

> The lyrics are obviously a serenade to the trouble makers. This song is typical of the subversive propaganda put out by the BBC ... It misrepresents the unions and its tone could only lead to industrial troubles (*M M* 17/2/73).

Apart from his casual causal claim, the ironic thing about Soref's protests is that they are entirely misdirected. The song is actually **anti** trade union and Richard Hudson, co-writer of the song, admitted that 'we're Conservatives actually, true blue' (*M M* 23/7/71).

The next incident marked the start of attempts by Tory MPs to **prevent** pop's latest outrage. In October 1976, as punk rose, the bands Throbbing Gristle and Chelsea played the POUM multi-media event at London's ICA. Items displayed here included tampons and pornographic pictures. Tory MP Nicholas Fairbairn condemned the show as "sickening" and "obscene". He declared that: 'The Arts Council (who partly funded the show) must be scrapped after this' and demanded to know why the ICA had been allowed to put on such a show (*NME* 30/10/76 and *Daily Mail* 19/10/76).

After Grundy The Sex Pistols were continually pressurized by Tory MPs two of whom, Robert Adley and Geoffrey Howe, were involved in the sacking of the band (Savage 1991, pp.286/7). In addition Ray Mawby, Tory MP for Totnes, wrote to Lady Plowden, head of the IBA, protesting about their Grundy appearance (*Daily Mail* 14/12/76) and Tory MP Neville Trotter helped Labour MP Marcus Lipton's campaign to get shops to boycott the band's *God Save The Queen* single (*NME* 18/6/77).

When a twenty second snippet of *God Save The Queen* was played in a Radio 4 documentary entitled *Listen to The Banned* in December 1978 Tory MP Dr. Rhodes Boyson complained about this 'affront to the public' and commented that: 'The BBC is a public service and if it can't keep up moral standards then why should we have the BBC?' (*NME* 6/1/79). ITV also caused problems. Tory MP Jill Knight took part in a successful campaign to prevent Revolver broadcasting the Sex Pistols/Ronnie Biggs *No One Is Innocent* video in 1978 (*NME* 19/8/78).

Returning to a case mentioned in the previous chapter, we find that Tim Eggar, MP for Enfield North, tried to bring a prosecution under the Obscene Publications Act against Crass' anti-Falklands War/anti Margaret Thatcher single, *How Does It Feel? (To Be The Mother of A Thousand Dead)*, but was told that this was not possible. Eggar complained about the record's "bad language" (in fact this occurred on another track called *Don't Tell Me You Care*) and said that he believed in free speech but that the record was an insult both to Thatcher (which Crass accepted) and to families of those who had died (which they denied). Eggar said:

It was purely the way they expressed themselves that I objected to. Authority has to draw the line somewhere ... I used to enjoy and still do, many of the anti-Vietnam (war) songs that were made, but they carried their message in a sophisticated way, without resorting to foul language (*NME* 6/11/82).

Crass believed that it was the war rather than their record that was obscene.

Eggar is here both a "golden ager" and misinformed - Country Joe MacDonald's popular anti-Vietnam war song *Feel Like I'm Fixing To Die Rag* starts with the "Fish chant" of "F-U-C-K". Apparently senior members of the Conservative Party told Eggar not to pursue his case and to ignore provocation by the band (Crass 1991). Around six Labour MPs sent letters of support to Crass (ibid). Crass were also investigated by a Commons Select Committee for possible breach of parliamentary privilege by using radio broadcasts from Parliament on their *Sheep Farming In The Falklands* single (Street 1986, p.17).

November 1982 saw Tory MP John Carlisle protest to Channel 4 over the antics of The Virgin Prunes on their *Whatever You Want* programme. He also attacked the BBC's broadcast of the 1988 Wembley Stadium concert celebrating Nelson Mandela's 70th birthday, claiming that during it the BBC was 'hi-jacked by left wing extremists' (*NME* 18/6/88). The right wing Freedom Association tried to prevent the BBC from showing a 1990 concert celebrating Mandela's release, unless it gave an assurance to retain political impartiality. But the BBC went ahead with the broadcast on the grounds that the concert was a major public event (*IOC* Vol.19 No.6 June/July 1990).

In 1983 former Lindisfarne singer Alan Hull's *Malvinas Melody* single, which criticized the loss of life in the Falklands War, was condemned by Tory MPs as 'sick and cynical' (*NME* 1/10/83) and in 1985 Tory MP Piers Merchant attacked Bruce Springsteen's donation to Durham Miners Women's Support Group (*NME* 22/6/85). But the most active Tory pop censor at this time was the MP for Leicester East and member of the Church of England's General Synod, Peter Brunivels.

Brunivels first came to pop prominence in January 1986 when he described a French single by Renauld Sechan, *Miss Maggie*, which was anti-Thatcher, as 'in the worst possible taste' (*NME* 10/1/86). But it was the Beastie Boys who really enraged him. After the *Daily Mirror*'s reports of the band insulting disabled children, Brunivels tried to prevent them performing in Britain via the 1824 Vagrancy Act which forbids 'wilfully exposing to view, in any street road, highway, or public place, any obscene print, picture or other indecent exhibition'. Brunivels said the band were 'obscene and violent, they undermine family values and they encourage anti-social activities like glue sniffing' (*NME* 23/5/87). In a causal remark he said the band 'shouldn't be allowed to corrupt the nation's youth' (*Daily Mirror* 14/5/87) and exhibited the censorial trait of xenophobia by saying 'why do we need the American filth, we have got plenty of British bands' (*NME* 23/5/87).

Brunivels tried to to ban the broadcasting of Beasties' records and some DJs did ban them. He asked Secretary of State for the Home Department, David Mellor, 'if he will introduce legislation to provide for a mandatory system for licensing of new audio and audio visual recordings for broadcasting or public performance' and 'what representations he has received on the playing of obscene, indecent or violent records' (*Hansard* 30/4/87).

Mellor replied that the relevant broadcasting companies had responsibility and that existing legislation was sufficient (ibid). So ended this attempt by an MP to seriously curtail the activities of a pop group.

In 1986 the *Sun* asked Tory MP Teddy Taylor what he thought of the title of The Smiths' *The Queen Is Dead* album and ran a story saying that he had called for the the album to be banned, which Taylor denied. But he said that:

> I don't believe that publicity should be gained in this fashion and, therefore, I had hoped the broadcasting networks wouldn't play the record (*NME* 5/7/86).

In 1990 Taylor was amongst a number of Tory MPs who called on Home Secretary David Waddington to prevent a tour by American band Revolting Cocks, after it was alleged that lead singer Al Jourgensen simulated sex with a mechanical horse on stage. Taylor said: 'Present laws can prevent people like this from performing in this country. The real tragedy is that so little is done to stop them' (*NME* 15/9/90). The band responded by threatening to decapitate models of the Queen Mother on stage and, when the tour subsequently went ahead, they invited Taylor to join them (*NME* 21/1/91).

As acid house rose Tory MPs again called for censorship. John

Hebble, a mid-Staffordshire MP, failed in a legal attempt to prevent Children Of The Night's *It's A Trip* reaching the shops because of its references to acid and ecstasy, but Tory MPs' complaints resulted in the IBA cancelling the broadcast of the song on ITV's late night *The Hitman and Her* programme (*NME* 12/11/88 and 3/12/88).

The 1991 Gulf War saw much media censorship and some Tory MPs wanted this extended to pop. Several called for The Rolling Stones' aforementioned anti-arms trade *High Wire* single to be banned. Sir John Stokes MP called it: 'Appalling in the time of war ... why can't they do something with a bit of jingoism in it' (*NME* 23/2/91).

These examples, along with the attack on Radio 1's gay programme by Tory MP Geoffrey Dickens (*Vox* March 1991 p.8), help show that Tory moves against rock have got more overtly censorial over years. I found little direct intervention in pop by Tory MPs in the years around 1967 but much more in later years. Meanwhile the parliamentary Labour Party also has a history of attempting to censor pop.

Labouring under misconceptions? The Labour Party, the left and pop censorship

In the early 1960s Labour tried to court The Beatles with Mary Wilson assuring voters in 1964 that 'Harold and I are both tremendous fans of The Beatles' (Carr and Tyler 1975, p.32). Wilson awarded them with MBEs in 1965 - officially for 'services to export', but unofficially as a crude attempt to court the youth vote. But, as noted above, Wilson was less keen on The Move and sued them for using a picture of him in bed with a secretary to advertise their 1967 *Flowers In The Rain* single. The band's manager later had his home raided by Special Branch (Denselow 1989, p.100)(1). It was also Wilson's government which took the censorial action of closing down the pirate radio stations.

Individual Labour MPs began censorial campaigns during the late 1960s. Gwilym Roberts, MP for South Bedfordshire, made *M M* headlines in January 1969 when he tabled parliamentary questions about the noise level at some concerts. This followed reports he had read of 'teenagers in Bournemouth suffering certain types of epileptic fits after being subjected to loud pop for a long time' (*M M* 198/1/69). If there was any danger to health, said Roberts, 'there should ... be some sort of legislation' (ibid). Roberts was unsuccessful in his attempts to control volume level, but his concern was also voiced elsewhere and led to censorial action in the 1970s (see above).

In May 1973 Alice Cooper's plan to tour Britain did not impress Labour MP Leo Abse. He tried to get the Home Secretary to ban Cooper from Britain, accusing him of 'peddling the culture of the concentration camp' and of 'evil attempts to teach our children to find their identity in hate and not in love' (*MM* 26/5/73). In a xenophobic tone Abse noted that Cooper was 'an American import which I am sure our parents, teachers and welfare offices can well do without' (ibid). Cooper's subsequent British gigs went ahead.

During punk another case showed how the censorial atmosphere is often shaped by contemporary events. The mid-1970s saw a moral panic over glue sniffing, with 20 children held to have died from its effects in Scotland between 1974 and 1975 (Savage 1991, p.260). Against this backdrop The Ramones released their eponymous debut album, containing the track, *Now I Wanna Sniff Some Glue*. Jack Dempsey, MP for Coatbridge, Lanarkshire, was then preparing a Bill to make it illegal for children under 16 to buy solvents and he set out to get the album banned (*NME* 11/9/76). Dempsey did not succeed, but, as noted earlier, his campaign **did** have a censorial effect later, when the track *Carbona Not Glue* was kept off the band's *Leave Home* album after The Ramones' British label, Phonogram, received correspondence from the Home Office regarding glue sniffing (*NME* 5 and 12/3/77).

The Sex Pistols were the next target of a Labour MP. When *God Save The Queen* was released Lambeth Central MP Marcus Lipton commented that: 'If pop music is going to be used to destroy our established institutions it ought to be destroyed first' (*NME* 18/6/77) and so tied his colours firmly to the censorial mast. He raised the spectre of faceless businessmen exploiting pop's audience, saying that: 'It's a pure deliberate commercial exploitation by ... managers' (Vermorel 1978, p.211) and used the racist beatist critique by saying that punk bands:

> ... work up the kids into a state of frenzied excitement, just like witch doctors in Central Africa ... you keep on **banging** the drums and that sort of thing, and they start foaming at the mouth (ibid. Emphasis in original).

Lipton tried to get shops to boycott the record, which several did. He later objected to the band's next single, *Pretty Vacant* as the "B" side contained swearing (*NME* 16/7/77) and to the track *Belsen Was A Gas* (*NME* 1/2/86). Lipton's censorial efforts were only partially successful as, whilst the band had many of their records banned from the airwaves and some shops, they continued to sell well. Outbursts from Labour MPs about pop died down after punk as Rock Against Racism, Live Aid and Red Wedge made pop respectable in some Labour quarters. However, this did not involve endorsing all popular music.

In 1989 MP Joan Richardson objected to a T-shirt of a withdrawn cover for Guns 'n' Roses' *Appetite For Destruction* album, which featured a robot raping a woman. She wanted a consumer boycott of the shirt (a tactic popular with American censors) and commented that:

> This shirt displays a complete lack of sensitivity towards rape victims, it's disgusting that someone should exploit such a harrowing experience just to sell pop music (*NME* 16/9/89).

Labour expressed disapproval of NWA's *Just Don't Bite It* in 1990 (*NME* 20/10/90) and in December 1991 EMF's *Schubert Dip* album, was criticized by Labour MP for South Glamorgan, John P. Smith, for containing the word "fuck", but no warning sticker. He called for 'guidance stickers to be placed on the band's album sleeves clearly stating that some of the material is unsuitable for children' (*NME* 14/12/91). The band's label, EMI, regretted the offence but said that 'we think that stickering can have a detrimental effect, encouraging the kids to buy the records' (ibid). So it remained unstickered.

Aside from some Labour MPs there are other examples of left wing attacks on pop in Britain. Thus far most of the censors I have looked have tended to be reactionary, if not actually right wing(2). But the left has also censored pop.

First it needs to be acknowledged that some on the left have always been suspicious of pop. Many socialists opposed the Music Halls (Russell 1987, p.111) and Adorno (1990) saw pop as catering for a false need. Hoggart implicitly attacked Radio Luxembourg in his comments on 'lowbrow gang-spirit of some gramophone-record features' in *The Uses of Literacy* (quoted by Bennett 1986, p.10) and A. L. Lloyd praised youth for returning to folk after indulging in the "depravity" of the Rolling Stones (Chambers 1986, p.146).

But it was not until punk that the British left really got into its censorial stride. Partly this concerned the reaction of trade unions to it. The Sex Pistols' *Anarchy in The UK* and *God Save The Queen* were both subject to attempted industrial action; at the EMI's Hayes plant (*The Sun* 4/12/76) and CBS' pressing plant (Savage 1991, p.347) respectively. In 1978 union intervention led Ivor Biggin and the Red Nose Burglars to rename their *Wankers Song* the *Winkers Song* (Radio 1, 1993a).

In the live arena strike action by University staff led to the cancellation of a punk gig in Southampton in May 1977 (Laing 1985 p.136), whilst the public sector union NUPE got the cancellation of a Siouxsie and The Banshees gig at Liverpool University because of concerns about security (*Sounds* and *NME* 18/11/78). The SU has also been involved in censorial activity over the years, most farcically in banning the anti-apartheid activist Johnny Clegg from playing Britain because he had played gigs in his South Africa home (*NME* 2 and 16/7/89).

The Labour run GLC's attempt to ban artists who had played South Africa from its halls also marks an example of this form of censorship on the basis of "political correctness". This has lain behind many censorial actions coming from the left in recent years. Feminists have often objected to pop's imagery and took action against Torri B's *This Bitch Raps* single in 1990 (*NME* 8/12/90), Fabulous' *Fucked By Fabulous* T-shirts (*NME* 15/2/92) and Spinal Tap's *Bitch School* in 1992 (*NME* 14/3/92). Homophobic attitudes have also drawn attack[3] and after Shabba Ranks supported Buju Banton's homophobic *Boom By By* single and then appeared on *TOTP* the gay rights pressure group Outrage! flooded the BBC with protest calls (*Vox* June 1993 p.7).

"Political correctness" also illustrates that the left has its own censorial agenda and again disproves Wells' (1990a, p.19) allegations that all of pop's censors are conservative. Ironically leftist critiques of racism and sexism have now been appropriated by organizations like the PMRC and NVALA[4].

Conclusion

MPs' actions against pop generally continue to be isolated outbursts rather than concerted campaigns against the music, but this trend is slowly changing. As the mass media expands and ever more theories are postulated about its effects, MPs have moved from criticizing pop to trying to stop certain aspects of it. Street (1986, p.17) is incorrect to say that MPs have 'continued to show little interest in the music industry', rather what has occurred is a slow, uneven, growth in intervention from MPs. Occasionally this has had, as in The Ramones case, a direct censorial effect. Most of the cases uncovered by the author came after punk and the subsequent onset of Thatcherism. With ever more government concern over regulation and control of the media, and the possibility of further EC intervention, it may only be a matter of time before pop in Britain gets much closer attention from MPs.

Notes

1. Denselow also notes that an advert for the Edgar Broughton Band's *Trust* featuring a Ralph Steadman cartoon of Wilson and Edward Heath as buttocks was banned by London Transport.

2. See Durham 1991, pp.161-78 for the problems of labelling NVALA etc. as right wing.

3. See, for example, SU moves against First Offence above.

4. For examples see Durham 1991, p.97 and Wells 1986, p.17.

Conclusion

Early on in this history I said that I hoped not only to show that censorship of popular music **has** occurred in Britain, but also to give insights into the **type** of censorship it has been. As I conclude it is perhaps better to say that I have given insights into the type**s** of censorship and illustrated recurring characteristics. British pop censorship emerges as a somewhat disjointed phenomenon. No set pattern is apparent and the overall picture is one of periodic intervention rather than sustained attack. Nevertheless, a number of characteristics can be discerned. These include the ebb and flow of censorship (rather than continual liberalization or suppression), the link between censorship and contemporary events (partly because pop often **is** a contemporary event), the market as a censorial agent and a perennial concern for the welfare of children. It is to be expected that these features will continue in the future, varying only in their prominence and relevance to particular cases. I have merely told part of a continuing story.

Pop historians now have a place from which to draw cases of censorship and in future such historians should concern themselves with a number of issues. First, this work essentially concerns the **outcomes** of censorial decisions, thus pointing the way towards more work on the **processes** of censorship. Negus' *Producing Pop* is a valuable guide to industry's decision making process, but too little is known about the specific processes of decision making at Radio 1, within local government (for example, the records of council leisure committees in 1977 should make fascinating reading), within venues, of artists themselves and by retailers. More knowledge about who the "member of the public" who instigates legal cases would confirm or deny my suspicions about the pressure groups discussed here.

Where the industry is concerned access will remain a problem (Negus' book is filled with unnamed sources) and artists themselves can be difficult to gain access to. But these stories also need to be told. In order to see the effects of the market as a censorial agent more needs to be known about the way artists shape their work with reference to it.

In broadcasting the BBC must become more open to the public which finances it. There seems no good reason why I could not be given information about the decision making process behind, for example, the bans on *Je T'Aime* or *Give Ireland Back To The Irish*. The secrecy with which the BBC surrounds itself gives rise to the suspicion that it is much more censorious than it actually is.

Censorship of popular music also needs to be thought of in much broader terms than is usually done. Too often it is seen merely in terms of banned records on Radio 1. I have shown that the issue is more complicated than that and goes beyond pop in its recorded form.

Censorship of British pop is rarely a matter of sinister figures putting blue pencil lines through texts, but more often an amalgam of processes, from market led decisions over which acts to sign, through broadcasting marginalization, to the control of live music, all under the auspices of an occasionally interventionist law. These processes combine to limit musical free speech without needing conspiracies.

I have endeavoured to broaden the way censorship is thought of and to show that the dividing line between censorship and regulation is very hard to draw. In places I am not even sure that it **can** be drawn. A label not signing an act or 1 not playing a record are, at one level, simply commercial or editorial decisions, but their net effect can be censorial.

The debate around pop censorship takes the censorship debate as a whole into unchartered waters, especially in the live arena. Here the right of free expression meets the need for social control. The needs of residents can clash with those of fans. There is no simple resolution to this conflict and attempts to control live pop again have censorial overtones. Live performance is a vital part of pop's "speech" and its silencing needs explanation. If one person's "regulation" is another's "censorship" then the processes behind such regulation need the fullest exposure.

I have also shown that it is dangerous to make assertions about censorship. Wells (1990, p.19) was wrong to say that rock's opponents 'are all conservatives' as the left has its own censorial agenda. Street (1986, p.115) was wrong to say that the censorship of pop was 'ineffective', as what emerges is uneven effects, rather than any lack of effect. Smith (1991, p.53) was wrong to say that censors have realized that their activity 'almost always backfires', as increasingly British censors have gained the upper hand, as video legislation and bans on broadcasts by "terrorists" have shown. But the increasingly international nature of censorship also needs further consideration. The *Cop Killer* case showed how a censorship decision taken in one country effects Britain and such cases have continued(1).

As to the future, a number of possibilities emerge. Within the industry several factors are of importance, not the least of which is the George Michael legal case, which is on its way to appeal as I write. But it seems that the industry rather than the artist is likely to retain control over product. Meanwhile, the issue of sampling again shows how control and censorship can blur. It is still a moot philosophical point as to whether free speech involves the right to use the recorded speech, or instrumentation, of others or to significantly alter that "speech".

Retailers seem to be nervous about the present law and willing to comply with stickering in order to keep sales. Their hand may yet be forced by the Government. The Conservative Party conference of 1993 saw more calls for new obscenity legislation and John Major's speech mentioned moves against pornography (*The Guardian* 9/10/93). The Government has agreed that 'the law could be usefully tightened' (Michael Jack, Home Office Minister, *Hansard* 9/7/92). It remains to be seen whether new legislation is forthcoming, but a swing to the right in Tory ranks is apparent and any new legislation on pornography would inevitably have effects on pop. For example NWA's *Efil4zaggin* may not have passed a tighter law.

The immediate future of broadcasting seems to lie with the market. Radio 1's changes came in October 1993 and seem only to have hastened its decline. It has responded by asking for listeners' opinions, but the lack of listener representation and of explanation of editorial policy look likely to remain. On the rare occasions that 1 bans records it should declare them. It has nothing to lose from debate. Meanwhile commercial radio has yet to prove that it can do more to prevent the marginalization of genres than 1 has.

In television *TOTP* seems set to continue and BBC2 continues initiatives such as *D Energy*. The fact that independent stations periodically have to bid for their licences means that a long running pop show remains unlikely there(2). Meanwhile as satellite TV, including MTV, builds its audience exclusion via profitability seems likely to increase. The slow growth of the EC superstate also has a censorial potential, especially if pan-European broadcasting policy is adopted.

The lack of purpose built venues for pop and the lack of a permanent festival site are blots on the British cultural landscape constituting indirect forms of censorship, another form of which comes via government restrictions on funding. Local authorities now have less to spend on the arts and thus pop suffers at the crucial local level(3). The important college circuit is also threatened by lack of funding.

Ironically as the world gets more technological, the problem of travellers - those committed to a nomadic, almost pre-capitalist lifestyle - linked to raves is causing problems. The free festival spirit lives on here, but may be extinguished by the Criminal Justice Act, which was passed in 1994. Its provisions restrict raves and could thus censor pop by limiting its space for growth. Reports on safety at gigs are also awaited and may yet yield censorial proposals(4).

The censors I outlined in part five will continue their activities. The only change I anticipate here is in their relative power. NVALA gained publicity in early 1993 (Peters 1993) and in 1994 Whitehouse published her biography which again contained inaccuracies when reporting pop (Whitehouse 1994, p.117 and 139). They will be lobbying strongly for changes in the obscenity law and gained support from "back to basics" calls from a government preaching the virtues of pre-1960s, notions of "commonsense" and "responsibility". The international links I noted in the chapter on pressure groups means that censorial campaigns, like pop itself, may yet go global. The global village enables censors to take their messages throughout it and form networks within it.

Religious censors seem set to carry on combating "the devil's music" and may claim the odd local victory, but their main role seems destined to be that of providing the censorial bullets for organizations like NVALA and the PMRC to fire. However the rise of Islam may yet yield a more censorial climate and the rise of Christian fundamentalists in America means that there is likely to be more battles ahead.

The press can be expected to continue their censorial role via periodic outbursts such as ones linking heavy metal to murder (see *The Sun* and *Daily Star* 30/3/94) and via the popularizing of critics like Medved. MPs' censorial role will also remain of vital importance. They can change laws and may do so to the detriment of pop. Elements within both major parties have their own censorial agendas[5] and growing intolerance is the hallmark of both camps. Victorian morality is paralleled by political correctness. Contrarily MPs may find their powers increasingly restricted by Europe.

The censorship debate itself seems likely to remain dominated by the twin axes of offence (now underpinned by notions of political correctness) and causality (similarly underpinned by notions of "commonsense" and shifted in places to notions of "encouragement"). But changes in technology may change the parameters of the debate. Already there is a shift from concern about the effects of television and pop upon children to the effects of computer video games[6]. Concern about computer porn and the illicit use of virtual reality technology seems set to expand the debate and to raise more technological problems for would be censors. Whether this adds anything new to the debate remains to be seen.

Thus far virtually all resistance to British pop censorship has been led by artists themselves[7], but if artists face a struggle and inevitable compromises in order to get heard, British fans have hardly begun to struggle. Although ravers organized against Bright, much of this was done by those whose main concern was profits (Saunders 1993, pp.216-22). Otherwise fans, with rare exceptions such as the free festivals and campaigns to change 1's output, have put up with cancelled gigs, stickered albums, radio bans, record prosecutions and so on with hardly a whimper.

The lack of a "consumer" body for pop fans is a noticeable one. This is particularly so when, unlike the followers of literature, art or classical music, they cannot depend on spontaneous support in the media or politics - far from it. Indeed the commonplace denigration of pop on aesthetic grounds means that the growing strength of censorial movements may continue to go largely unrecorded by heavyweight commentators. As the pop audience matures it is to be hoped that some organized force emerges to defend the rights of consumers of Britain's most vibrant cultural medium.

I have documented numerous cases of pop censorship here, but I noted in the introduction the need to keep a sense of perspective. It was never my intention to portray a pattern of authoritarian state intervention in pop or to suggest that pop in Britain has been subjected to indiscriminate censorship. It is undeniable, however, that censorship has taken up a growing amount of the music press and that in Britain in recent years a creeping process of censorship via increased state pressure has occurred. Historically, pop has suffered more from the insidious forms of marginalization[8] and denial of cultural value (highlighting the importance of aesthetic critiques) than it has from overt censorship. But as economic adversity and uncertainty take on the status of something immovable in British society so more and more attempts are likely to be made to blame that society's ills not on its material depravations, but its ill mannered popular culture. Such attempts should be resisted. Vigilance remains the watchword of liberty.

I would like to end by emphasizing why it is important to defend pop. Morrison's 1992 survey noted that pop was 'the music of the people' (p.24) and it is this that needs defending. Pop music is popular, in the sense of being enjoyed by the vast majority of the population. It is therefore defensible on democratic grounds. I also believe it is worthy of aesthetic defence. Popular music remains a vital part of British cultural life and, at a minimum, deserves as strong a presumption against censorship as any other cultural form. Rock and roll is rightly here to stay. The nature of its residence, however, seems likely to remain a battleground.

Notes

1. See for example *NME* 6/11/93 for Warners' more cautious attitude to the material it releases after the *Cop Killer* case. It is also interesting to note that pop may be unique in the way it can be effected by censorship in other countries, as most censorship tends to be domestic.

2. ITV's Chart Show seems to have carved itself a niche and may be an exception here.

3. For the importance of the local see Sara Cohen 1991 and Street 1993.

4. For safety as censorship see Saunders 1993, pp.216-22.

5. In March 1994 Michael Alison, Tory MP for Selby, unsuccessfully tried to prosecute Jackie Leven's *So My Soul Can Sing* from the album *Songs From The Argyll Circle* for blasphemy, *Yorkshire Evening Press* 29/3/94.

6. See, for example, *The Guardian* 13/4/93 Part Two pp.8-9; *The Guardian* and *The Independent* 18/5/93; and *The Independent* 15/10/93.

7. A notable exception here were the No More Censorship gigs organized in Britain to help the Dead Kennedys defence against censorship charges in America. See *NME* 26/9/87. America has several fan based anti-censorship organisations, such as Music In Action, the National Coalition Against Censorship, SLAM, Rock Out Censorship and the Free Music Coalition. The best source for information about such group's is the LA based *Rock and Roll Confidential*.

8. For the marginalization of pop see Morrison 1992, p.4.

Bibliography

Abraham, G. "Censoring music" (1983), *Index on Censorship,* Vol. 12, No. 1, February 1983, pp.3-4.

Advisory Committee on Pop Festivals (1973), *Report and Code of Practice,* HMSO.

Adorno, T. (1990), "On popular music" in Frith, S. and Goodwin, A. (eds.) *On Record,* Pantheon, pp.301-314.

Anderson, P. (1988), *Satan's Snare,* Evangelical Press.

Aranza, J. (1983), *Backward Masking Unmasked,* Huntingdon House.

Aries, P. (1973), *Centuries of Childhood,* Penguin.

Arnold, F. (1971), "Pop go the festivals" *New Statesman,* 2/7/71, p.11.

Attali, J. (1977), *Noise,* (translated by Brian Mussami), Manchester University Press.

Baddeley, G. (1992), "Sympathy for the devil", *Rockpower,* February 1992, pp.16-18.

Bagehot, R. (1992), "When copyright runs out", *Music and Copyright,* Vol. 1, No. 1, 12/9/92, p.11.

Bailey, P. (1978), *Leisure and Class in Victorian England,* Routledge and Kegan Paul.

Bangs, L. (1977), "We are all obscene (and we want our freedom)", *NME*, 5/3/77, p.16.

Barker, M. (1984a), *A Haunt of Fears*, Pluto.

Barker, M. (ed.) (1984b), *The Video Nasties: Freedom and Censorship in the Media*, Pluto.

Barker, M. (1989), *Comics, Ideology, Power and the Critics*, Manchester University Press.

Barnard, S. (1989), *On The Radio*, Open University Press.

Beadle, J. J. (1993), *Will Pop Eat Itself?*, Faber and Faber.

Becker, H. (1963), *Outsiders*, Collins-MacMillan.

Bell, E. (1993), "Singles reach the vinyl frontier", *The Observer*, 14/3/93, p.29.

Benedictus, D. (1979), "Cleaning Up", *New Statesman*, 21-28/12/79, pp.996-998.

Bennett, T. (1986), "The politics of "the popular" and popular culture" in Bennett, T., Mercer, C. and Wollacott, J. (eds.), *Popular Culture and Social Relations*, Open University Press, pp.10-20.

Berry, D. (1984), "The nasties of yesteryear", *The Observer Magazine*, 11/3/84, pp.42-44.

Blackhurst, C. (1993), "Backing up Boots", *Independent on Sunday*, business section, 2/5/93, pp.14-16.

Blanchard, J. (1983), *Pop Goes The Gospel*, Evangelical Press.

Blom, E. (1943), *Music in England*, Penguin.

Bloom, A. (1987), *The Closing of The American Mind*, Simon and

Schuster.

Bogle, J. (1986), *The Seductive Sell*, The Responsible Society.

Bradley, D. (1992), *Understanding Rock 'n' Roll*, Open University.

Briggs, A. (1979), *The History of Broadcasting in the United Kingdom*, Vol. 4: Sound and Vision, Oxford University Press.

Briggs, A. (1985), *The BBC: The First 50 Years*, Oxford University Press.

British Broadcasting Corporation (1974), *Children as Viewers and Listeners*, BBC.

British Broadcasting Corporation (1992), *Extending Choice*, BBC.

British Psychological Society (1992), *Subliminal Messages*, British Psychological Society.

Broadcasting Standards Council (1989), *Code of Practice*, BSC.

Broadcasting Standards Council (Andrea Milward Hargreave ed.), (1991), *A Matter of Manners: The Limits of Broadcasting Language*, (Annual Review 1991), John Libby.

Broadcasting Standards Council (1992), (Andrea Milward Hargreave ed.), *Sex and Sexuality in Broadcasting* (Annual Review 1992), Jonathan Libby.

Bromberg, C. (1989), *The Wicked Ways of Malcolm McLaren*, Harper and Row.

Brownmiller, S. (1976), *Against Our Will*, Penguin

Burchill, J. (1977), "New wave neat say Nazis", *NME* 23/7/77, p.11.

Butt, R. (1976), "The grubby face of punk promotion", *The Times*, 9/12/76, p.14.

Calder, J. "The return of the censor", *IOC*, Vol. 13, No. 5, October 1984, p.2.

Carr, R. and Tyler, T. (1975), *The Beatles: An Illustrated Record*, New Copplestone English Library.

Caulfield, M. (1975), *Mary Whitehouse*, Mowbays.

Chambers, I. (1985), *Urban Rhythms: Pop Music and Popular Culture*, Macmillan.

Chambers, I. (1986), *Popular Culture: The Metropolitan Experience*, Methuen.

Chapman, R. (1992), *Selling The Sixties*, Routledge.

Chapple, S. and Garofolo, R. (1977), *Rock 'n' Roll Is Here To Pay*, Nelson Hall.

Cheshire, D. F. (1974), *Music Hall in Britain*, David and Charles.

Chester, G. and Dickey, J. (eds.) (1988), *Feminism and Censorship: The Current Debate*, Prism Press.

Chevigny, P. (1991), *Gigs*, Routledge.

Clare, A. (1989), "Divine Purpose", *The Listener*, 10/8/89, pp.10-11.

Clarke, J. and Critcher, C. (1980), *The Devil Makes Work: Leisure in Capitalist Britain*, Croom Helm.

Clarke, M. (1982), *The Politics of Pop Festivals*, Junction Books.

Cliff, D. (1979), "Religion, morality and the middle class" in King, R. and Nugent, N., *Respectable Rebels*, Hodder and Stoughton, pp.127-152.

Cline, V. B. (1974), *Where Do You Draw The Line?*, Brigham Young University Press.

Cohen, Sara (1991), *Rock Culture in Liverpool*, Clarendon Press.

Cohen, Stanley (1973), *Folk Devils and Moral Panics*, McGibbon and Kee.

Committee on Obscenity and Film Censorship (1979) Report, HMSO Cmmnd. 7772 (The Williams Report).

Coon, C. (1982), *1988: The New Wave Punk Rock Explosion*, Omnibus.

Cooper, M. (1986), "The blasphemy of stardom", *The Guardian* 21/7/86, p.11.

Coren, M. (1981), "Steps to stop the right rocking", *New Statesman*, 11/9/81, p.4.

Cosgrove, S. (1985), "Revenge of the X Cert parents", *NME*, 14/9/85 p.2.

Cosgrove, S. (1986), "The righteous sisters", *NME*, 4/10/86, pp.12-13.

Cosgrove, S. (1988a), "Death of the single", *New Statesman and Society*, 4/11/88, p.39.

Cosgrove, S. (1988b), "Forbidden Fruit", *New Statesman*, 3/9/88, p.44.

Cosgrove, S. (1989) "Acid Enterprise", *New Statesman*, 13/10/89, p.39.

Coward, R. (1990), "Family of man", *New Statesman and Society*, 20/7/90, p.10.

Curran, J., Guervitch, M. and Wollacott, J. (eds.), (1977), *Mass Communication and Society*, Edward Arnold.

Davies, C. (1975), *Permissive Britain: Social Change in the Sixties and Seventies*, Pitman.

Davis, S. (1985), *Hammer of The Gods*, Sidgwick and Jackson.

Davis, T. (1991), "The moral sense of the majorities: indecency and vigilance in late Victorian Music Hall", *Popular Music,* Vol. 10, No. 1, January 1991, pp.39-52.

de Jongh, N. (1991a), "A glimpse of something shocking", *The Guardian,* 21/3/91, p.25.

de Jongh, N. (1991b), "In those crazy old days of Oz", *The Guardian,* 9/11/91, p.27.

Denisoff, R. S. and Peterson, R. (eds.) (1972), *The Sounds of Social Change,* McNally.

Denselow, R. (1989), *When The Music's Over,* Faber and Faber.

Dunaway, D. K. (1987), "Music as political communication in the United States" in Lull, J. (ed.), *Popular Music and Communication,* Sage, pp.37-51.

Durham, M. (1991), *Sex and Politics: The Family and Morality in The Thatcher Years,* Macmillan.

Dworkin, A. (1981), *Pornography: Men Possessing Women,* The Women's Press.

Eccleshall, R. (1986), *British Liberalism,* Longman.

Eliot, Marc (1987), *Rockonomics,* Omnibus Press.

Fabbri, F. (1982), "What kind of music?", *Popular Music 2,* pp.131-143.

Face The Music Ministries (1989), *Backmasking* - presentation to Broadcasting Bill Committee.

Farren, M. (1975), "God is alive and well and living off rock and roll", *NME,* 22/3/75, pp.24-25.

Feinberg, J. (1985), *Offence To Others,* Oxford University Press.

Flashman, S. (1992), *Rock Music: An Informed View*, Soapbox.

Fowler, P. (1972), "Skins rule" in Gillett, C. (ed.), *Rockfile*, New English Library, pp.10-26.

Frith, S. (1983), *Sound Effects*, Constable.

Frith, S. (1984), *The Sociology of Youth*, Causeway Press.

Frith, S. (1988), "Copyright and the music business", *Popular Music* 7,1 January 1988, pp.57-74.

Frith, S. and Goodwin, A. (eds.) (1990), *On Record*, Pantheon Books.

Garofolo, R. (1987), "How autonomous is relative?: popular music, the social formation and cultural struggle", *Popular Music 6*, 1 January 1987, pp.77-91.

Garfield, S. (1992), "The machine that ate George Michael", *The Independent*, 21/11/92, p.29.

Gillett, C. (1983), *The Sound of The City*, Souvenir Press.

Gipps, R. (1975a), "A personal credo", *The Musician Spring 1975*, pp.12-13.

Gipps, R. (1975b), "What's wrong with pop", *The Advertiser*, 10/10/75.

Godbolt, J. (1984), *A History of Jazz in Britain 1919-1950*, Quartet Books.

Godwin, J. (1985), *The Devil's Disciples*, Chick.

Godwin, J. (1988), *Dancing With Demons*, Chick.

Goffe, L. (1989,) "An attitude problem in LA", *The Guardian*, 19/10/89, p.27.

Goodwin, A. (1988), "33 revolutions a minute", *The Listener*, 29/9/88, pp.43-44.

Goodwin, A. (1990a), "Sample and hold: Pop music in the age of digital reproduction" in Frith, S. and Goodwin, A. (1990), *On Record*, pp.258-273.

Goodwin, A (1990b) "Sharpening the blue pencil", *New Statesman and Society*, 8/5/90, p.46.

Graef, R. (1991), "Taking Liberties", in *BSC* 1991, pp.72-79.

Gray, L. (1987), "Fairlight robbery", *NME*, 11/7/87, pp.28-29 and 37.

Greer, H. (1981), "Double Standards", *IOC*, Vol. 11, No. 5, October 1981, pp.31-32.

Grossberg, L. (1987), "Rock and roll in search of an audience", in Lull, J. 1987, *Popular Music and Communication*, pp.176-196

Grossberg, L. (1992), *We Gotta Get Out of This Place*, Routledge.

Gummer, J. S. (1971), *The Permissive Society*, Cassell.

Halassa, M. (1990a), "Banned in the USA", *New Statesman and Society*, 10/8/90, pp.27-28.

Halassa, M. (1990b), "Biting off more than they can chew", *The Guardian*, 22/11/90, p.30.

Hall, S., Critcher, C., Clarke, J. and Roberts, B. (1978), *Policing The Crisis*, Macmillan.

Harding, S. (1988), "The decline of permissiveness", *New Statesman*, 4/11/88, pp.25-26.

Harker, D. (1980), *One For The Money*, Hutchinson.

Harrigan, B. (1975), "Pirates of the air", *MM*, 15/3/75.

Harrigan, B. (1977), "Local censors out in force to ban punk rock groups", *M M*, 4/6/77, p.3.

Hart, A. (1991), *Understanding The Media*, Routledge.

Hart, L. (1981), *Satan's Music Exposed*, AGM Publishers.

Hawkins, G. and Zimring, F. E. (1988), *Pornography In A Free Society*, Cambridge University Press.

Hebdige, D. (1979), *Subculture: The Meaning of Style*, Methuen.

Hebdige, D. (1987), *Cut 'n' Mix*, Comedia.

Heller, Z. (1992), "Teenage monsters", *The Independent*, 6/9/92, pp.2-4.

Heslam, D. (1990), *The NME Rock 'n' Roll Years*, Hamlyn.

Hewison, R. (1986), *Too Much: Art and Society in The Sixties*, Methuen.

Hewitt, P. (1986), "Slaves to the rhythm", *NME*, 14/6/86, pp.25-27 and 49.

Hillman, B. C. (1968), "When the king banned pop songs", *The Times*, 3/8/68, p.15.

Hilton, T. (1993), "Art kisses", *The Independent*, 14/2/93.

Hind, J. and Mosco, S. (1985), *Rebel Radio*, Pluto Press.

Hinton, B. (1990), *Nights in Wight Satin*, Isle of Wight County Council.

Hoffman, F. (1989), *Intellectual Freedom and Censorship: An Annotated Bibliography*, The Scarecrow Press.

Hoggart, R. (1971), *The Uses of Literacy*, Chatto and Windus.

Holden, D. (1993), "Pop go the censors", *IOC* Vol. 22, No.5/6 May/June 1993, pp.11-15.

Hughes, G. (1991), *Swearing*, Blackwell.

Humphries, S., Mack, J. and Perks, R. (1988), *A Century of Childhood*, Sidgwick and Johnson.

Hunter, N. (1989), "UK sets videoclip content standards", *Billboard*, 5/8/89, p.56.

Hustwitt, M. (1983), "Caught in a whirlpool of arching sound: the production of dance music in Britain in the 1920s", *Popular Music 3:1* pp.7-32.

International Congress for The Family (1990) Conference brochure.

Itzin, C. (1992), *Pornography: Women, Violence and Civil Liberties*, Oxford University Press.

Jansen, S. C. (1988), *Censorship*, Oxford University Press.

Jasper, T. (1986), *Rock Solid*, Word UK.

Jassell, S. (1967), "The pop world and its freakish laws", *The Times*, 11/9/67, p8.

Johnson, P. (1964), "The menace of Beatlism", *New Statesman*, 28/2/64, pp.326-327.

Jones, R. (1988), *Stairway To Hell*, Chick.

Jones, S. (1991), "Banned in the USA: Popular music and censorship", *Journal of Communications*, Vol. 15, No. 1, Winter 1991, pp.71-87.

Keating, M. (1991), "The electronic generation", in *International Congress for The Family: Families For Tomorrow*, Fowler Wright, pp.139-144.

Kershaw, L. (1992), "Pop go the big-wigs", *The Guardian*, 29/3/92.

King, S. (1987), "Bring on the banned", *Sounds*, 19 and 26/12/87.

Knight, F. (1977), "The food of love", *Community Care*, 24 August 1977, p.16.

Laing, D. (1985), *One Chord Wonders*, Open University Press.

Larson, B. (1988), *Larson's Book of Rock*, Tyndale House.

Laurie, P. (1965), *Teenage Revolution*, Anthony Bland.

Lemon, D. (1992), "The love that dared to speak its name", *Gay Times*, July 1992, pp.30-32.

Lennon, P. (1991), "Relative values in a time of war", *The Guardian*, 21/2/91, p.23.

Lennon, P. (1993), "Who's throwing the book at Hollywood", *The Guardian*, 15/3/93, Part Two pp.2-3.

Leonard, N. (1964), *Jazz and The White Americans*, The Jazz Book Club.

Levin, B. (1985a), "Don't let censors call the tune", *The Times*, 12/9/85, p.14.

Levin, B. (1985b), "Livingstone bans for the greater evil", *The Times*, 11/12/85, p1.4.

Levin, B. (1987), "Popping up all over", *The Times*, 21/9/87, p.12.

Longrigg, C. (1991), "Singled out for abuse", *The Independent*, 8/8/91, p.17.

Lull, J. (1982), "Resistance to new wave", *Journal of Communications*, Vol. 32, Winter 1982, pp.121-131.

Lull, J. (ed.) (1987), *Popular Music and Communication*, Sage.

Lyons, A. (1988), *Satan Wants You: The Cult of Devil Worship in America*, The Mysterious Press.

McAliskey, B. (1992), "Silenced", *The Guardian*, 5/9/92, p.14.

McCready, J. (1987), "The Beastie Bit", *NME*, 21/11/87, p.4.

McDonald, J. (1988) "Censoring rock lyrics: An historical analysis of the debate", *Youth and Society*, Vol. 19, No. 3, March 1988, pp.294-313.

McFarlane, G. (1989), *A Practical Introduction To Copyright*, Waterlow.

McIver, T. (1988), "Backward masking and other backward thoughts", *The Skeptical Enquirer*, Vol. 13, No. 1, Fall 1988, pp.50-63.

MacKenzie, R. (1987), *Bands, Boppers and Believers*, Campaign For Cleaner Rock.

McQuail, D. (1977), "The influence and effects of the mass media" in Curran, J., Guervitch, M. and Wollacott, J. 1977, *Mass Communication and Society*, pp.70-94.

McSmith, A. (1983), "Anti-war song silenced", *New Statesman*, 30/9/83, p.6.

Mann, B. (1987), "Porn to be wild", *Sounds*, 10/1/87, pp.8-9.

Mann, W. (1963), "What songs The Beatles sang", *The Times*, 27/12/63 (as anon).

Marot, M. (1991a), "Censorship rant", *Vox*, November 1991, p.65.

Marsh, D. (1977), "Dole Queue Rock", *New Society*, 20/1/77, pp.112-114.

Marshal, G. (1991), *Spirit of '69: A Skinhead Bible*, S. T. Publishing.

Martin, G. (1993), "Knee jerk city", *NME*, 27/3/93, p.21.

Martin, L. and Segrave, K. (1988), *Anti-Rock: The Opposition To Rock and Roll*, Archon Books.

Medved, M. (1992), *Hollywood vs America*, Harper Perenial (Extracts published in *Sunday Times* as (1993a) "Hollywood vs Civilisation" 7/2/93, (1993b) "Hollywood's addiction to violence" 14/2/93, (1993c) "Hollywood's hostility to heroes" 21/2/93 and (1994d) "The corruption of rock" 28/2/93.

Melechi, A. and Redhead, S. (1988), "The fall of acid reign", *New Statesman*, 23 and 30/12/88, pp.21-23.

Meltzer, R. (1970), *The Aesthetics of Rock*, Something Else Press.

Merck, M. (1988), "Television and Censorship: Some notes for feminists", in Chester and Dickey 1988, *Feminism and Censorship*, pp.185-196.

Mill, J. S. (1974), *On Liberty*, Penguin.

Mitchell, J. (1985), "Disturbing the equilibrium", *NME*, 22/6/85, p.23.

Morley, P. (1977), "BOFS close punk venue", *NME*, 27/8/77, p.13.

Morrison, D. (1992), *The Role of Radio One in People's Lives*, University of Leeds.

Morrison, D. and Tracey, M. (1979), "American theory and British practice: the case of Mary Whitehouse and the National Viewers and Listeners Association", in Dhavan, R. and Davies, C., *Censorship and Obscenity*, Martin Robertson, pp.37-53.

Morrison, L. (1978), "Freedom and the family", in K. W. Watkins, *In Defence of Freedom*, Cassell, pp.73-83.

Mullen, P. (1986), "Dirty rock", *The Times Educational Supplement*, 30/5/86, p.17.

Music Master (1990), *Music Master Heavy Metal Catalogue*, John Humphries.

National Heritage Department (1992), *The Future of The BBC*, HMSO.

National Society (1992), *All God's Children*, Church House Publishing.

National Union of Conservative and Unionists Associations (1965), 83rd Annual Conference Report.

National Viewers and Listeners Association (1990), *Obscene Publications Act - The Need For A New Law*, NVALA.

Negus, K. (1993), "Plugging and programming: Pop radio and record promotion in Britain and the United States", *Popular Music*, Vol. 12 No. 1, pp.57-68.

Negus, K. (1992), *Producing Pop*, Edward Arnold.

Negus, K. and du Gay, P. (1994), "The changing sites of sound: music retailing and the composition of consumers", *Media, Culture and Society*, Vol. 16, pp.395-413.

Neville, R. (1971), *Playpower*, Palladin.

Newburn, T. (1992), *Permission and Regulation: Law and Morals in Postwar Britain*, Routledge.

New Statesman, (1991), Banned Supplement 5/4/91.

O'Brien, L. (1992), "Everybody's gone drop of the pops", *The Guardian*, 14/11/92, p.32.

Obscenity Report (1971), Olympia.

O'Hagan, S. (1991), "Turning Down The Ghetto Blasters", *The Times*, 27/7/91, Saturday Review p.12.

O'Higgins, P. (1972), *Censorship in Britain*, Thomas Nelson and Sons.

O'Sullivan, J. (1992), "Muslims all shook up over pop group", *Independent on Sunday*, 28/6/92, p.2.

Palmer, T. (1976), *All You Need Is Love*, Futura.

Palmer, T. (1971), *The Trials of Oz*, Blond and Briggs.

Parents Music Resource Center (PMRC) (1990), *Let's Talk About Rock Music*, PMRC

Parents Music Resource Center (nd.) *The Influence of The Media on Adolescents*, PMRC.

Parsons, T. (1977), "Punk", *NME*, 29/10/77, p.23.

Pattison, R. (1987), *The Triumph of Vulgarity*, Oxford University Press.

Pearce, G. and Clancy, P. (1976), "Punk? Call it filthy lucre", *Daily Express*, 3/12/76, p1.

Pearsall, R. (1973), *Victorian Popular Music*, David and Charles.

Pearson, G. (1983), *Hooligan: A History of Respectable Fears*, Macmillan.

Peters, D. and Peters, S. (1984), *Why Knock Rock?*, Bethany House.

Peters, P. (1993), "Why didn't they listen?", *Evening Standard*, 6/3/93, p.11.

Peterson, R. (1972), "Market and moralist censors of a black art form: Jazz", in Denisoff, R. S., and Peterson, R., *The Sounds of Social Change*, 1972, pp.236-260.

Petley, J. (1991a), "Taking Flak", in *New Statesman*, 1991, pp.31-32.

Petley, J. (1992b), "The Lord Chamberlain" ibid, p.19.

Pyle, H. (1985), *The Truth About Rock Music*, Sword of The Lord Publishers.

Redhead, S. (1990), *The End of The Century Party*, Manchester University Press.

Redhead, S. (1991) "Rave Off", *Social Science Review*, Vol. 6, No.3, pp.92-94.

Redmond, P. (1991), "Class, decency and hypocrisy", in *BSC*, 1991, pp.45-52.

Rich, B. R. (1983), "Anti-porn: Soft issue, hard world", *Feminist Review 13*, Spring 1983, pp.56-68.

Richard, C. (1981), *Cliff In His Own Words*, W. H. Allen.

Rimmer, D. (1985), *Like Punk Never Happened*, Faber and Faber.

Roberts, K. (1983), *Youth and Leisure*, George Allen Unwin.

Robertson, G. (1974), "Badly burned books", *New Statesman*, 23/8/74, pp.242-243.

Robertson, G. (1991), *Freedom, The Individual and The Law*, Penguin.

Robertson, G. and Nicol, A. (1984), *Media Law*, Sage.

Robson, E. (1977), "A night out with the punks", *The Listener*, 4/8/77, p.145.

Rogers, D. (1982), *Rock 'n' Roll*, Routledge and Kegan Paul.

Rowan, D. (1992), "Larger than life sexist fun rules monster metal bash", *The Guardian*, 22/8/92, p7.

Russell, D. (1987), *Popular Music in England 1840-1914*, Manchester University Press.

Ryle, T. (1976), "Not in Front of MY Children", *Daily Express*, 3/12/76, p10.

Saunders, N. (1993), *E For Ecstasy*, Nicholas Saunders.

Savage, J. (1990), "And the banned played on", *Observer*, 11/11/90, p.26.

Savage, J. (1991), *England's Dreaming*, Faber and Faber.

Schauer, F. (1982), *Free Speech: A Philosophical Enquiry*, Cambridge University Press.

Segal, L. (1991), *Is The Future Female?*, Virago.

Simpson, A. W. B. (1982), "Obscenity and The Law", *Law and Philosophy*, Vol. 1, No.2 August 1982, pp.240-259.

Simpson, J. (1991), "Free men clamouring for chains", *IOC*, Vol. 20, Nos. 4/5, April/May 1991, p.3.

Skynner, R. (The Truth Temple) (nd.), *The Truth About Rock*, Apolisitc Ministries.

Smart, B. (1982), "Offensiveness in The Williams Report", *Philosophy*, No. 57, pp.237-243.

Smith, A. (1972), "Mrs Whitehouse's Innocents", *New Statesman*, 3/11/72, pp.628-629.

Smith, R. (1991), "Pop, sex and censorship", *Gay Times*, November 1991, pp.5-7.

Spence, P. (1988), "Harmony in my headache", *NME*, 16/7/88, pp.12-14.

Stallings, P. (1984), *Rock 'n' Roll Confidential*, Vermillion.

Starmer, K. (1990), *Acid House Parties: Civil Liberties Implications*, Liberty.

Steward, S. and Garratt, S. (1984), *Signed, Sealed and Delivered*, Pluto.

St. John-Stevas, N. (1965), *Obscenity and The Law*, Secker and Warburg.

Stratton, J. (1983), "What is popular music", *Sociological Review*, Vol. 13, pp.293-309.

Street, J, (1986), *Rebel Rock*, Blackwell.

Street, J. (1987), "Playing for a change", *Social Studies Review*, November 1987, pp.70-74.

Street, J. (1993), "Local differences? Popular music and the local state", *Popular Music 12:1*, pp.43-55.

Sullivan, C. (1991), "Plain Unfair", *The Guardian*, 7/5/91.

Sullivan, M. (1987), "More popular than Jesus: The Beatles and the religious far right", *Popular Music 6:3*, pp.313-326.

Sutcliffe, P. (1989), "The selling of smiley culture", *Q*, January 1989, pp.8-12.

Sutherland, J. (1982), *Offensive Literature: Decensorship in Britain 1960-1982*, Junction Books.

Syal, R. and Davidson, N. (1992). "Once giant leap for dance kind", *Sunday Times*, 14/6/92, p4.

Toop, D. (1991a), "America's most wanted", *Sunday Times*, 24/11/91, pp.68-87.

Toop, D. (1991b), "Taking the rap for their rhymes", *The Times*, 17/12/91, p.12.

Tracey, M. and Morrison, D. (1979), *Whitehouse*, Macmillan.

Traitor, R. (1988), "Not in front of the parents", *Sounds*, 10/9/88, p.12.

Turner, S. (1974), "Is God just another hangover?", *NME*, 2/11/74, p.40-42.

Turner, S. (1976), "The anarchic rock of the young and doleful", *The Guardian*, 3/12/76, p.13.

Tynan, K. (1988), *The Life of Kenneth Tynan*, Methuen.

Usher, S. (1976), "The mercenary manipulation of pop - Never mind the morals or standards ... The only notes that matter come in wads", *Daily Mail*, 3/12/76, p.6.

Vermorel, F. and Vermorel, J. (1978), *The Sex Pistols*, Universal.

Vermorel, F. and Vermorel, J. (1989), *Fandemonium*, Omnibus.

Wale, M. (1972), *Vox Pop: The Pop Process*, Harrap.

Walker, A. (1984), "The latest intruders on official morality", *The Listener*, 1/3/84, pp.5-6 and 12.

Walker, M. (1993), "Pressed down in the wicked kingdom", *The Guardian*, 29/3/93.

Walker, M. M. (1983), "Backward messages in commercially available recordings", *Popular Music and Society*, 10 (1), pp.2-13.

Walser, R. (1993), *Running With The Devil: Power, Gender and Madness in Heavy Metal Music*, Wesleyan University Press.

Welch, B. (1990), *Rock 'n' Roll I Gave You The Best Years of My Life*, Penguin.

Welch, C. (1967), "Stop picking on pop", *MM*, 21/10/67, p.13.

Wells, S. (1985), "The decline of western civilisation (Part 45)" (interview with Mary Whitehouse), *NME*, 17/8/85, p.22.

Wells, S. (1986), "Bound and gagged", *NME*, 9/8/86, p.3.

Wells, S. (1987a), "Leave it F***ing out!", *NME*, 19-26/12/87, p.39.

Wells, Steven (1987b), "The chill factor", *NME*, 29/8/87, p.16.

Wells, S. (1988a), "Paranoid, Me?" (interview with Jello Biafra), *NME*, 5/3/88, pp.20-21.

Wells, S. (1988b), "Get right off one chummy", *NME*, 15/11/88, pp.24-25.

Wells, S. (1989a), "Full metal racket", *The Listener*, 4/4/89, p.12-13.

Wells, S. (1989b), "Where Britain goes, so goes America", *No More Censorship*, No. 3, Summer 1989, p6.

Wells, S. (1990a), "Censors working overtime", *NME*, 11/8/90, pp.18-19.

Wells, S. (1990b) "Friend or phobic", *NME*, 17/3/90, p.7.

Wells, S. (1991a), "In the realm of the censors", *NME*, 13/4/91, p.11.

Wells, S. (1991b), "Review of Dave Marsh's 50 Ways To Fight Censorship", *NME*, 10/8/91, p47.

Wells, S. and Stewart, J. (1986), "Revenge of the parents", *NME*, 20/27/12/86, pp.16-17.

Whitcomb, I. (1982), *Whole Lotta Shakin'*, Arrow.

White, D. (1972), "End of Scene", *New Society*, 2/3/72, pp.432-433.

Whitehouse, M. (1967), *Cleaning Up TV: From Protest To Participation*, Blandford Press.

Whitehouse, M. (1971), *Who Does She Think She Is?*, New English Library.

Whitehouse, M. (1974), "Inverted censorship that turned morality on its head", *The Times*, 4/2/74, p.12.

Whitehouse, M. (1977), *Whatever Happened To Sex?*, Wayland.

Whitehouse, M. (1982), *A Most Dangerous Woman?*, Lion.

Whitehouse, M. (1985), *Mightier Than The Sword*, Kingsway.

Whitehouse, M. (1994), *Quite Contrary*, Sidgwick and Jackson.

Wicke, P. (1990), *Rock Music: Culture, Aesthetics and Sociology*, (Translated by Rachel Fagan), Cambridge University Press.

Willis, P. (1990), *Common Culture*, Open University Press.

Willis, P. (1978), *Profane Culture*, Routledge and Kegan Paul.

Wistrich, E. (1978), "I Don't Mind The Sex It's The Violence", Marion Bayers.

Wood, L. (1988), *The Sex Pistols Day By Day*, Omnibus.

Working Group on Pop Festivals (1976), *Free Festivals*, HMSO.

Working Group on Pop Festivals (1978), *Pop Festivals and Their Problems*, HMSO.

Wyman, B. (1991), *Stone Alone*, Penguin.

Young, T. (1993), "To bleep or not to bleep", *The Guardian*, 5/1/93.

Zappa, F. (1989), *The Real Frank Zappa Book*, Picador.

Correspondence

Beyer, John, General Secretary, NVALA, 26 March 1991 and 18 March 1992.

Boots, 9 December 1991.

British Broadcasting Corporation Written Archives Centre, 19 December 1991.

Foskett, Marr, Gadsby and Head, Solicitors, (to Crass), 10 October 1984 and personal letter, 4 November 1991.

Gregory, Steve, owner Fierce Records, 3 October 1991.

HMV, 10 June 1991.

Home Office (to NCROPA), 11 July 1991.

Independent Television Commission, 15 October 1991.

Metropolitan Police (To NCROPA), 18 July 1991.

National Campaign For The Reform of The Obscene Publications Acts: (to Sir Peter Impert, Chief Commissioner of The Metropolitan Police), 17 June 1991.

Neubert, Sir Michael, MP, 6 February 1992.

Our Price, 20 November, 1992.

Riches, Valerie, Director of Family and Youth Concern, 22 March 1991 and 15 October 1992.

W. H. Smith, 25 August, 1992.

Woolworths, 8 January 1991.

Interviews

Birkett, Derek, member of Flux, 19 April 1991.

Carcass, 10 June 1991.

Crass, 30 December 1991.

Dig, owner, Earache Records, 21 May 1991.

Gilliam, Bill, head of Alternative Records UK, 4 June 1991.

Grundy, Stuart, Radio 1 producer, 31 May 1991.

Maloney, Alex, 4 March 1991.

Marot, Marc, MD Island Records, UK, 15 November 1991 (1991b).

Price, Martin, part owner of Eastern Bloc, 22 January 1991.

Robinson, Paul, Chair of Radio One playlist committee, 14 November 1991.

Silver, Jeremy, BPI spokesman, 13 November 1991.

Slater, Ruth, Merseyside CSA, 15 October 1991.

Wells, Steven, 18 February 1991 (1991b).

Lecture

Robert Chapman: University of Liverpool 15/2/93.

Radio programme

Radio 1 (1993) : *Listen to the banned*. Series of 3 programmes 15(a), 22(b), and 29/5/93(c).

Videos

International Films: *Hells Bells: The Dangers of Rock 'n' Roll.*

King's Church: *Are You Dancing With The Devil?.*

Index

317

RAVE OFF

POLITICS AND DEVIANCE IN CONTEMPORARY YOUTH CULTURE

Edited by **STEVE REDHEAD**

POPULAR CULTURAL STUDIES: 1

"...recommended as student reading." Youth and Policy

"...stimulating and provocative opening contribution to the Popular Cultural Studies series. Courses on youth culture will look a little incomplete if they do not now include them as set reading ...central texts for any up-to-date specialist course." Leisure Studies Association Newsletter

Steve Redhead and a team of authors associated with the Manchester Institute for Popular Culture at Manchester Metropolitan University have written a unique account of deviant youth culture at the end of the century, concentrating on the much-hyped 'rave' scene and its connections to recreational drug use - for instance Ecstasy - contemporary pop and dance music, youth tourism, football hooliganism and the 'enterprise culture'.

The book attempts to provide answers to such questions as: What is 'rave culture'? What had 'Madchester' got to do with it? Has the rave (formerly acid house) scene merely parodied an earlier moment in pop history (60s psychedelia, 70s punk or Northern Soul)? Is illegal 'party drug' use a passing fad or here to stay? What political and legal implications are there of this new 'hedonism in hard times'? Has 90s youth culture embraced or rejected the values of the market, individualism and enterprise?

1993   208 pages   Hbk   1 85628 463 8   £29.50
                 Pbk   1 85628 465 4   £12.95

Price subject to change without notification

arena

THE MARGINS OF THE CITY

GAY MEN'S URBAN LIVES

Edited by **STEPHEN WHITTLE**

POPULAR CULTURAL STUDIES: 6

Within cities, gay life has always been marginalised. Despite the fact that their significant places are often centrally placed geographically within cities, gay communities are not centrally placed in the political, social and cultural lives of cities. These international accounts draw on first hand ethnographic research and reflect the responses of gay men in particular to the changes that have taken place during the last 25 years in urban settings. They look at the physical and spatial development of gay places, at the same time as viewing the social placing of the communities that use those places.

The cross-disciplinary studies within this book look at the tensions that arise between gay communities and their cities, the political and economic implications to city planners of the "pink pound" and the legal and social implications for gay men as they attempt to reconcile being both the outsiders and insiders of city life.

Stephen Whittle is Lecturer in Law at Manchester Metropolitan University.

1994   184 pages   Hbk   1 85742 201 5   £29.95
Pbk   1 85742 202 3   £12.95

Price subject to change without notification

THE GULF WAR DID NOT HAPPEN

POLITICS, CULTURE, AND WARFARE POST-VIETNAM

Edited by JEFFREY WALSH

POPULAR CULTURAL STUDIES: 7

This interdisciplinary collection of essays breaks new ground in studying the complex relationships between the historical Gulf war of 1990–91, and those myths, narratives and extended images commonly drawn upon to explain it. Such a distinctive mode of enquiry reveals the ideological symmetry between the political debate and popular culture, or between foreign policy and artistic production. A linking theme running through the volume is the shadow of Vietnam, how the Gulf war was perhaps the culminating event in what has come to be known as "the Vietnam syndrome".

As well as focusing upon the central role of mass media the contributors address issues and events that are not usually treated in the same political and historical context, for example, popular music, comic books, war memorials, anti-war expression, literature, and the effects of war upon language. These essays will be of great interest for students of history, politics, war studies, American studies, cultural studies, oriental and Middle Eastern studies, the social sciences, media studies, literature and art history.

Jeffrey Walsh is Principal Lecturer in English at Manchester Metropolitan University.

1995   224 pages   Hbk   1 85742 292 9   £35.00
Pbk   1 85742 286 4   £12.95

Price subject to change without notification

arena